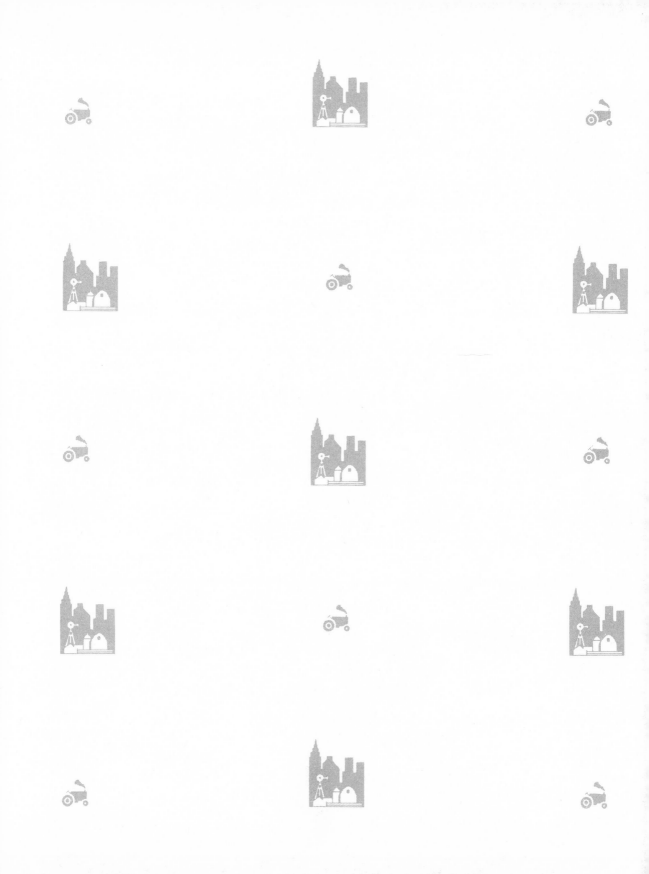

T H E
F A R M
M A R K E T
C O O K B O O K

Conversations, Recipes, Cooking Tips, Growing Hints, Mail Order

Sources, a Geographical Guide, and Everything Else You Should

Know About American Farmers' Markets

Also by Judith Olney:

Summer Food
Comforting Food
Judith Olney's Entertainments
The Joy of Chocolate
Judith Olney on Bread

THE

FARM MARKET

COOKBOOK

Text and Photographs by Judith Olney

DOUBLEDAY
New York London Toronto Sydney Auckland

PUBLISHED BY DOUBLEDAY
a division of Bantam Doubleday Dell Publishing Group, Inc.
666 Fifth Avenue, New York, New York 10103

DOUBLEDAY and the portrayal of an anchor with a dolphin
are trademarks of Doubleday,
a division of Bantam Doubleday Dell Publishing Group, Inc.

Library of Congress Cataloging-in-Publication Data
Olney, Judith.
The Farm market cookbook: conversations, recipes, cooking tips,
growing hints, mail order sources, a geographical guide, and
everything else you should know about American farmers'
markets/ Judith Olney; photos by Judith Olney.—1st ed.
p. cm.
1. Farmers' markets—United States. I. Title.
HF5472.U6046 1991
381′.41′0973—dc20 90-45592
CIP
ISBN 0-385-41096-4

BOOK DESIGN AND ORNAMENTATION BY CAROL MALCOLM

To America's Small Farmers

# ACKNOWLEDGMENTS

TO THE MANY PEOPLE WHO HAVE HELPED ALONG THE journey, from dedicated market managers Lynn Bagley, Barry Benepe, Laura Da Venazio, Laura Dingle, Bob Geigle, Ted Langford, Randii MacNear, David O'Neil, Chuck Pierce, Hill Rylander, Hilda Swartz, Nancy Torrence, and Doug Wiley, who have taken the time to show me around; to marketing specialists Hilary Baum, Pamela Boyar, Vance Corum, Paula De La Fuente, Steve Evans, Marilyn Magaro, and John Vlcek, I offer heartfelt thanks for sharing so generously your time and expertise.

To Naomi Spahr and George Pyne for research undertaken, and to my assistants, Katie Barwick, Barbara Bluestone, Beth and Gin Wiegand, for help and diligence in testing recipes, I'm most appreciative.

Sharon Scott was a great help with manuscript preparation. I am grateful also to my agent, Pam Bernstein; to Stephen Rubin and John Duff for their enthusiasm; and to Judy Kern for her ever-splendid editorial help.

The staff at Pike Place's Sur La Table and Rachel Jordan both helped with photo propping.

Matthew Klein provided valuable photographic advice. My son, Nathan, functioned frequently as photographic assistant, and I thank him and David Paletz both for undertaking part of the journey.

I especially thank Betty Wall for her ever-creative love and support.

ONTENTS

PRINGTIME

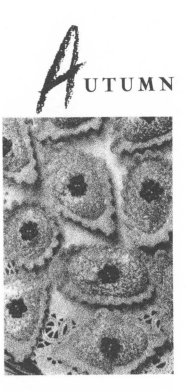

AUTUMN

*I*NTRODUCTION

 **T**HIS COOKBOOK IS A LOVE SONG TO FARMERS'
markets. It springs first from a cherished memory of childhood visits to the Lansing,
Michigan, market with my mother, but of late it has been regenerated by a deep and
longing need within my soul to reaffirm what matters in this new and evolving decade.
And there is overwhelming evidence that millions of Americans like me are searching for
new ways to better their lives, purify their environments, to make peace with the past, and
to build a healthier, better world for their children.

For the past few years I've spent most Saturday mornings in my local farmers' market.
It has become a kind of ritual, a changing drama that focuses the eyes unmistakably on
nature and its seasons in a time when the rest of life seems increasingly enclosed and
controlled—climate controlled, color coded, cocooned by the plastic surfaces of modern
secularity.

In the market is life, vitality, health, abundance, grit, prime produce, color. In markets
lie the thick of things, sociability, the throb of human community. They provide links with
the past, and all indications suggest that farmers'-market networks will create far-reaching
and revolutionary changes in the ways we shop and eat—alterations that will affect the
face of agriculture's future.

That I am not alone in my need for honest food, for a sense of community and
change, became startlingly clear when I began work on this book. In my travels, food

editors told me of new markets started in their cities. An Iowa government worker reported that every town in the state with a population of over five thousand seemed to have generated a market in the past three years. Bellwether California was booming—5 markets ten years ago, 120 markets in 1989. All across America, behind city halls, in parking lots of malls, in refurbished deserted warehouses, farm markets were springing up like a bountiful nationwide crop of wild edible mushrooms. The collective conscience had to be at work.

And even deeper in the dense social fabric of city centers urban markets were thriving. Those wonderful institutions, many of them established by waves of immigrants who had mainstreamed into American society in the stalls of the markets, were coming back to life. Fragile some of them were, threatened by developers, freeways, proposed new convention centers, unstable economies, but concerned and caring citizens were forcing city bureaucracies to keep them alive. In cities on the brink of extinction, wise planners were learning that closing off Main Street, inviting in farmers, and cultivating public celebration was the way to generate urban renewal. The market in all its diversity counteracted the polarization of urban and suburban people and brought them and rural dwellers into one another's orbit.

And so life spins round. The booming markets of our agrarian past, those links to our foreign-born heritage that we rejected in the 1960s and 70s like brash teen-agers disowning embarassing parents, we have now embraced in our wiser maturity. And it's none too soon, for in markets we find pure sources of food harvested at its prime, and the growers who are committed to the sustainable agriculture and organic production necessary to our ecologically sound future. In frequenting farmers' markets, not only do we fortify our own health, but also we support those "stewards of the land" who take its ecology seriously.

I visited heartland markets in over a third of our nation's states while researching this book. It became a sort of obsession to collect markets and pin them like fine specimens into the cabinet of my mind. Now I set them out in display for you, and the collection, taken as a whole, is dazzling.

What I learned on the journey is that we no longer need to yearn nostalgically after the markets of Europe when we have a growing body of markets here to make us proud. You will tour markets and meet, as I did, a wealth of generous people—young farmers, old farmers, organic farmers, retired farmers, farm-market managers. You will visit farms and hear in overview about state-of-the-art *and* state-of-the-heart farming. The farmers shared their lives and expertise with me, and now I share them and the bountiful display of foods they produce with you.

The recipes in this book, a full range of soups, salads, appetizers, main courses, and wonderful desserts, have all been inspired by markets. The best markets offer foods intrinsic to them that you can purchase and eat while you shop. There are homemade, home-preserved foods, local and regional specialties, unique fast foods. A few of these recipes were given to me by farmers, but most I developed after tasting or being inspired by food or produce I saw along the journey, then tested upon my return home. Some were given to me by the new breed of chefs who frequent the markets, form symbiotic relationships with growers, and become fortifying links in the growth-harvest-consumption chain.

There is a wonderful linear quality to the recipes in this book—the food is as straight and true and honest as the farmers who grew it, and to them I dedicate this book.

J.O.

— ⚬ —

I have often thought that if heaven had given me choice of my position and calling, it should have been on a rich spot of earth, well watered, and near a good market for the productions of the garden.

Thomas Jefferson

— ⚬ —

Support local "farmers' markets." Locally-grown produce is typically fresher, cheaper, and less laden with pesticide residues than produce shipped long distances.

From 50 *Simple Things You Can Do to Save the Earth,* Earthworks Press

THE
FARM
MARKET
COOKBOOK

SPRINGTIME

SMALL-TOWN MARKETS

Carrboro Market
North Carolina

AFTER MY WINTER'S WRITING OF THIS BOOK, THE small-town market in Carrboro, North Carolina, just next to Chapel Hill, has revived again for the season. Winter was mild this year and farmers took a chance and planted two weeks early. On March 30, even though it was a cold wet day, the market opened. Bakers were out in force, growers had mostly bedding plants, pure white spring onions, and small leaves of deep green spinach. You size the place up, always spotting at least one acquaintance, and so begins another season of the farm-market ramble. Walking in lag time we circle and circle. We wouldn't go down a supermarket row twice, but here it seems only proper to trace and retrace steps, like a promenade on the boardwalk in a nineteenth-century novel. Time slows in small-town markets. We affirm ourselves here. Yes, we all made it through the winter, look blanched like the onions perhaps, but we've sprouted again, the sun will soon color us up, and we'll be as healthy as the farmers.

What's new? Well there seem to be *two* goat-cheese sellers now, and a bright lady has rigged up a deep fryer. She's cooking fat brown fritters and rolling them in powdered sugar. The smells fills the air. It's the first "animation" in the market and she should do a whopping business. Everyone is walking around with powdered sugar on their mouths and greeting everyone else. There's Betsy Chandler with her grapevine wreaths; Maggie and Jane with Maggie's Muffins (stop and drink a cup of their coffee); Charlie Thompson of Whippoorwill Farm (blackberries, blueberries, llamas, and sheep); flamboyant Pat Sterling, who sets pink flamingo balloons among her bread offerings; Nat Burwell, ex-banker, maker of vinegars; Bill Dow in his beat up hat . . . howdy, howdy.

I'd like to make a flip book of the market. Take a panoramic picture each week then flick them fast past your eyes and you'd see all the living seasons:

—✣ First, dark green sproutings of the earth turn lighter and brighter—from spinach to asparagus to yellow green lettuces and peas.

—✣ Monochromatic greens give way to color—spots of marigold and bachelor button bedding plants.

—✣ Vegetables ruddy up—radishes, carrots, blushing young beets.

—✣ More and more flowers—pastels first, then nasturtium and zinnia brights.

—✣ Deep, vivid summer primaries, tomato reds, peaches, yellow squash, vegetables, and flowers vie with one another.

—✣ A sudden cooling in fall, and one day all secondary colors—purples, astors, pumpkin, green starts turning olive.

—✣ By mid-October all is drab, dried flowers, persimmon pudding.

—✣ In December, holiday greens markets are the exact same shade again as spring's first spinach.

It is good that markets tender us life's cycle.

At the best farm markets you can eat, walk around with your mouth stuffed if you want. One of my favorite breakfasts in Carrboro market is fried apple pies. These homey little pastries are a farm breakfast specialty in the mid-Atlantic states. Usually fried in lard, they are best when thin as thin can be.

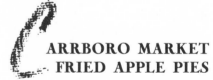

CARRBORO MARKET FRIED APPLE PIES

MAKES 10–12 PIES

For the Filling:

½ pound dried apple slices (preferably unsulfured)

1 teaspoon ground cinnamon

⅓ cup sugar

For the Crust:

1¾ cups all-purpose flour
½ teaspoons salt
1 teaspoon baking powder
1 teaspoon sugar
3 tablespoons butter or margarine, chilled

1 egg
½ cup milk

Peanut oil or a mix of lard and vegetable oil
    for frying

Place the dried apples in a lidded saucepan. Add ½ teaspoon of the cinnamon and the sugar. Just cover the apples with water, put the lid on the pan, and place over medium heat. Let the apples come to a boil, then turn down the heat and simmer until tender and saucelike, around 30 minutes. Continue cooking a bit if necessary to ensure that the apples are thick, jamlike, and not watery. Stir in the remaining ½ teaspoon of cinnamon.

To make the crust, combine the dry ingredients in a bowl. Cut the butter or margarine into pieces and work it into the flour with your fingertips until it has completely disappeared.

Stir the egg and milk together, then make a well in the middle of the dry ingredients, pour the liquid in, and stir the dough together. It should be of medium consistency and easy to work. Add a few drops of water if necessary to ensure a soft dough.

Flour a surface and roll out half of the dough until it is very thin (aim for transparency). Use a saucer as a form to cut out five 5½-inch circles. Place a heaping tablespoon of the apple mixture slightly off center in each circle. Wet your fingers with milk and moisten a ½-inch band around the edge of the dough. Fold the dough over to enclose the filling, and press the edges together with your fingertips to make a thin turnover. Continue cutting and filling pies. Heat a half inch of fat in a medium-sized frying pan with tall sides. The heat should be set to medium high. Test a small piece of dough, which should sizzle and turn brown within 30 seconds when the oil is hot enough.

Fry the apple pies 2 at a time. They brown quickly. When golden on the bottom, turn the pies over and brown the other side. Lift the pies out with a strainer onto absorbent toweling, and continue frying until all are cooked. Wrap them individually if you so desire. These may be warmed up over the course of 2 or 3 days for breakfast.

The pretty peach kuchen for sale in the Carrboro market was made by Pat Sterling. Here is my version, baked on a crisp, cinnamon-flavored cookie crust.

PEACH BREAKFAST KUCHEN

SERVES 8

Around 3½ cups thinly sliced peaches (save the stones)
Juice of 1 lemon
1¼ cups all-purpose flour
1¼ teaspoons baking powder
½ teaspoon ground cinnamon
Large pinch of salt

⅓ cup sugar
3 tablespoons butter, chilled, plus 2 tablespoons, melted
1 egg
⅓ cup milk
Additional sugar and cinnamon

Place the peaches in a bowl and sprinkle with the lemon juice.

Using a hammer, gently crack open each peach pit and extract the "almond" at the center. Bring a small pan of water to a boil and add the "almonds." Boil for 1 minute, then turn off the heat and let them sit. Preheat the oven to 350°F. Lightly grease a 10-inch baking or pizza pan (or the dough may be spread into a 10-inch round on a baking sheet).

To make the crust, combine the dry ingredients in a bowl. Cut the chilled butter into cubes then work it into the dry ingredients with your fingertips until it disappears into a uniformly flaky mixture.

Beat the egg and milk together, then stir the egg mixture into the flour mixture.

Place the dough into the prepared pan. Dampen your fingers with water and pat the dough out to a diameter of 10 inches . . . it will be quite thin.

Arrange the peach slices in a rosette pattern over the dough. Brush the slices with the melted butter. Sprinkle lightly with a small handful of sugar and a bit of cinnamon. Skin, then sliver the peach pit "almonds" and scatter them over the fruit.

Bake for 30 minutes. Cool for 10 minutes, then slide the pastry onto a rack so that the crust can cool and crisp.

— ⚬ —

A FARM MARKET SUCCESS STORY

In 1981, Maggie Middleton and her partner, Jane Hamborsky, left their jobs as musicians in New York to move to North Carolina. They intended to start a café where Maggie would cook, Jane's photography would be for sale on the walls, and they could hold chamber music concerts on the weekends. No sooner had they arrived than their backers pulled out and, to complicate life further, Maggie hurt her back. She decided that you could put everything you need to make muffins within easy reach, and to make money she baked 121 muffins on Friday to sell at the early Saturday Carrboro market. Of course, she sold out within the hour, then built up sales of one thousand within two hours by the end of her first market season. Soon commercial accounts started coming, and this past year Maggie and Jane made enough money to back their original dream. Maggie's Muffins Café is open and thriving, but the girls still bring coffee and a few sentimental dozens of muffins to Carrboro each Saturday just to keep in touch.

MAGGIE'S SPINACH-NUTMEG MUFFINS

MAKES 12 QUICHELIKE MUFFINS

2 cups all-purpose flour

1½ teaspoons baking powder

½ teaspoon baking soda

¼ teaspoon grated nutmeg

1 tablespoon sugar

½ teaspoon salt

10 ounces fresh spinach, washed, stemmed,
   steamed, squeezed dry

1 cup buttermilk

2 tablespoons butter, melted

¼ cup grated Swiss cheese

¼ cup grated Parmesan cheese

1 egg

Preheat the oven to 400°F. Generously grease a 12-cup muffin tin.

Sift the dry ingredients into a bowl.

Chop the spinach. In another bowl, combine the spinach, buttermilk, butter, half of each cheese, and the egg.

Make a well in the middle of the dry ingredients and add the liquid.

Stir briefly—never mind if everything is not perfectly mixed. Spoon the batter into the greased muffin tins, sprinkle with the remaining cheeses, and place in the oven as soon as possible.

Bake for 25 minutes. Let the muffins cool in the tin for 5 minutes before turning them out.

Every Saturday at Carrboro market I see Ben Barker, the chef and owner of Durham's Magnolia Grill, filling his van with fresh produce. He is the market's largest buyer of produce, preferably organic, and local growers know that if watercress blossoms in their streams in January, or spring greens make an early show, they've only to carry the harvest to Ben and he'll buy.

In the best restaurants all over the country, chefs realize that you don't just order from the wholesaler and let him deliver cases of trucked-in produce picked long ago and far away. Instead, they set up complex networks of small farmers who supply them with the morning's crop, and that freshness transfers itself to their finished food. You can see the look in the dishes. There's a brilliance of color, a crisper texture; salads taste of sun, fresh air, substance sprung from earth.

Small producers profit immensely from this "subscription farming" that guarantees them repeat sales to a known customer. In turn, restaurant chefs influence the crops and lives of the growers, and health- and ecology-conscious diners can only profit from this tightening farmer-cook-consumer link.

BEN BARKER'S MAGNOLIA GRILL ZUCCHINI "LATKES" WITH RED PEPPER CREAM

SERVES 6–8

¾ pound tender zucchini, stems trimmed
Salt
2 heaping tablespoons grated onion
1 very large red bell pepper, roasted, skinned, seeded, and diced
1 egg, beaten
¼ cup grated Parmesan cheese
¼ cup milk

2 teaspoons minced fresh herbs (rosemary in winter, basil in summer)
¼ teaspoon Tabasco sauce
Freshly ground pepper
½ cup all-purpose flour
1 teaspoon baking powder
Olive oil for frying
⅓ cup sour cream

Grate the zucchini through a medium-fine blade. Place it in a bowl and salt lightly. Let it sit for 1 hour, then drain and press to rid it of all water. Squeeze out by handfuls.

Mix the zucchini, onion, and 2 tablespoons *only* of diced red pepper (reserve the rest for the sauce) in a bowl.

In another bowl, stir together the egg, cheese, milk, herbs, ½ teaspoon of salt, and other seasonings. Sift the flour and baking powder together. Stir the vegetables into the egg mixture, then gently sift on the flour and stir until everything is mixed.

Heat 3 to 4 tablespoons of oil in a frying pan over medium heat. When hot, spoon 4 small ladles of zucchini into the pan and press into thin 3-inch rounds. Fry on both sides until lightly brown. Wipe and re-oil the pan as necessary and continue frying.

Puree the remaining diced red pepper with the sour cream.

Serve the "latkes" as a first course or side dish and place a spoon of the pepper cream atop each serving.

This salad is delicious served with fresh bread and a slice of terrine or pâté on a summer's day.

WILTED ZUCCHINI SALAD WITH MUSTARD SEED DRESSING

SERVES 4–6

5–6 small crisp zucchini, washed, and
  stemmed

2 teaspoons salt

4 tablespoons olive oil

1 small sweet red onion, sliced thin

2 teaspoons Pommery or other seeded
  mustard

2 tablespoons red wine vinegar

2 tablespoons minced fresh parsley

Freshly ground pepper

Slice the zucchini paper-thin (either by hand or machine). Sprinkle with the salt, refrigerate, and leave to drain in a bowl for 30 minutes.

Heat 2 tablespoons of the olive oil in a frying pan and sauté the onion until it is just tender/limp. Leave to cool.

In a bowl, whisk together the mustard, vinegar, parsley, the remaining 2 tablespoons of oil, and ground pepper to taste. Stir in the onion.

Gather up the zucchini in handfuls and press and squeeze as hard as possible (work over a sieve or colander), until the vegetable slices are limp and dry.

Combine the zucchini and onion and serve the salad just slightly chilled. This holds nicely for a day or two.

Bateau Landing
Lynchburg, Virginia

The small town of Lynchburg has had a market since 1783. In the early eighties it appeared to be collapsing. Farmers dwindled, attendance dropped, but the city fathers were wise. They spent good money revitalizing, hiring market manager Nancy Torrence, and letting her organize all the special events necessary to draw people back downtown. How often around the country do markets serve as focal points for community spirit, symbols of vitality and rebirth in dying towns and cities.

Called Bateau Landing, the market now flourishes and it's one of those fine, friendly places where you can find three generations of family all selling at different stands. You can get a good breakfast too.

Inside the market building, Dencia Hunter makes wonderful biscuits from scratch right there in front of you. She runs a stand called Ma's Kettle (a sign on the stove reads HAPPINESS IS HOMEMADE) and has a long pigtail, granny glasses, and desert boots. She is very pregnant with her ninth child. She pours flour, sugar, lots of cinnamon and raisins into a bowl, claps her hands to shake off the flour, then unwraps a stick of margarine. Nothing gets measured.

"I use margarine because it mixes in faster. I use evaporated milk, sugar, water, walnuts, raisins, cinnamon, about 5 cups of apples I think, but the real trick to a good biscuit is not to over liquid. Don't add as much as you think necessary. Make the dough very tender, don't knead, just fold it over easy as pie, then pat it out and cut out your biscuits."

She uses a Styrofoam cup to press out the dough, makes twenty-four large biscuits, then puts them to cook in a tabletop oven. While they bake, she stirs potatoes and onions put to a long slow stew in a black iron skillet.

"You try some of this too," she says, spooning me out a breakfast of home fries, country sausage, milk gravy with sausage specklings, "I tried doing this low-cal but they like good ole home cooking here, nice and fattening.

"That's my husband over there and my two boys selling vegetables. We don't need a lot—I like living sparse. We lived in Seattle, Los Angeles, came out of the hippie movement, but we had it with cities and wanted something better for our children. I'm pregnant now, so I just thought I'd start this little stand and take it easy here. I'm so used to cooking in quantity after all, what's an extra hundred biscuits."

DENCIA HUNTER'S APPLE AND CREAM BISCUITS

MAKES TWELVE 3-INCH BISCUITS

For the Biscuits:

4 cups fresh self-rising flour (Martha White or Gold Medal recommended. See measuring instructions.)

½ cup sugar

1 stick margarine

1 cup raisins

1 cup walnuts or pecans, broken into pieces

2 big red Delicious apples, peeled, cored, diced

1 14-ounce can sweetened condensed milk

2½ tablespoons ground cinnamon mixed with 2 tablespoons sugar

For the Cream Cheese Frosting:

2 tablespoons butter

3 ounces cream cheese

½ teaspoon vanilla extract

2 cups sifted confectioners' sugar

Preheat the oven to 425°F. Lightly grease a baking pan.

Here is how to measure the flour: Pour 4 rough cups of flour into a large bowl. Stir the flour to aerate it. Scoop it into a dry measuring cup and scrape the flour level with the blade of a knife. Measure your 4 cups this way.

Stir the sugar into the flour. Cut the margarine into slices and add it to the flour. Work the margarine into the flour with your fingertips or a pastry cutter until it disappears.

Add the raisins, nuts, and apples and toss lightly in the flour.

From now on, work very gently and never knead. Sprinkle the condensed milk over the dough ingredients and turn them briefly with a spoon or your fingers—never mind if not everything gets wet. As you are gently turning the dough, sprinkle the cinnamon in swirls.

Pat the dough together. Cut the biscuits with a 3-inch cutter.

Place the biscuits on the baking pan and bake for 12 minutes. Remove and cool briefly.

When just warm, prepare the frosting: Melt the butter and cream cheese over low heat. Stir in the vanilla and then the sifted confectioners' sugar. Add a few drops of water if necessary to make a thick, drizzling frosting.

Drip the frosting over the biscuits. Serve while still warm.

— ⚬ —

You find a lot of Dencia Hunters in small-town markets, and perhaps one of the reasons we are so fascinated by markets is that we can catch glimpses of what we would have been had we been true to the ideals of the sixties and given up cities, relinquished the adrenaline charge, deliberately slowed life down to the basics.

I like, also, that small-town markets give you a chance to know older people. They are lively in the market, talkative, the pace of the place suits them. "Well," they say, "I'd rather be doing this every year than sitting around in Florida." Markets keep them young.

MRS. O. T. SMITH ON EGGS

"In 1954, my husband and I started selling just after Hurricane Hazel hit. Had a load of melons threatened to go bad with too much water, so we tried selling them here in Lynchburg and people picked them right off. Then we started with our white eggs, but this is a brown egg market—people here like what their parents used. You take an old Rhode Island Red and a Barred Rock and mix 'um and you have a bird called Sal-Sexlink. We have fourteen hundred chickens at any time and we sell three hundred dozen eggs a week now. My husband is gone, but that's my daughter and grandson across the aisle with vegetables. We got up at three this morning, left the house at four together from Prospect, that's twenty miles below Appomattox, just a little speck in the road.

"I'm so glad that I've got a clear head. I'm seventy-six. I've got arthritis right bad and I don't hardly dust the house much any more. My son looks after the chickens. I used to, but I've got age now and my children baby me some, but I did get out and pick four bushels of beans yesterday. I like butter beans. I put up a hundred packages last year.

"We buy fertile eggs from Pennsylvania, they're hatched at Blackstone, then the chicks are grown in Charlotte Center. I get them when they're twenty weeks old and ready to lay. Some people say hens cackle when they lay, but I think they're singing. They scratch, they sing, you can hear them sing clear down to the house. They almost talk to you. A hen's happy when she lays an egg, she thinks she's done something proud. We don't keep roosters . . . not a rooster in the place. Fertile eggs don't keep as well, though those organic people, that's all they'll eat. I don't think those hens are any happier with a rooster in there. I been widowed for years now and you can get along just fine without a man. Here's customers now."

"Good mornin' . . . just fine, Skip, how you?"

"You doin' all right, Ms. Smith?"

"Doin' fine and good. (That one has a dairy farm. He's lonesome, I think. He'll sit and talk till market closes if you let him.)"

"Sizes? Large, extra large, jumbo large, thank you."

"I don't see anything wrong with these eggs but I don't want any with cracks," says a fragile elderly lady who examines each egg as if it was family heirloom lace.

The two ladies peer at the eggs, bring them up close to their glasses.

"Those are both good," says Mrs. Smith. "Five cents each."

"I'll take those two then. I have to limit myself for cholesterol. Praise the Lord I eat eggs at all."

"Well, you could try living by faith alone," snaps Mrs. Smith as the lady leaves. "She's a Blankenship . . . a little related to us. Why would she think I'd bring cracked eggs to market? Next time people ask if she's my cousin I'm going to say 'no kin.'

"I expect I'm the oldest one in the market now. There's lots of nice people here, even ones who I don't know their names they know mine. I think sometimes you have influence when you're here every day, every week, every year. Some boy grew up and they wrote in the paper about him. Asked him about adults who influenced him as a child. He said Mrs. O. T. Smith in the market did. Lordy, I don't even remember who he was, so there you are, wouldn't think selling eggs could mean that much would you."

MRS. O. T. SMITH'S PAN SCRAMBLED EGGS

"**I** just take some hot sausage, crumble it up, and brown it good in a pan. Spoon off a little of the juice then add in some beaten eggs and give it a good quick scramble. You can have high-flying recipes but sometimes down to earth is best."

— ⚮ —

SOME HIGH-FLYING SPRING RECIPES

I don't know whether to call this a soup or a stew. At any rate, it is wonderfully comforting. If you have a spaetzle maker, now is the time to use it for the drop noodles. Failing that: 1) place the noodle batter in a pastry bag and cut off small snippets as it comes out of the nozzle; 2) place the mixture in a colander and press it through the holes with a flexible spatula; or 3) place the batter in a large square cut from a heavy plastic trash bag, twist it tight, and punch out a few holes from which the batter can be pressed.

SPRING VEGETABLES WITH BUTTER-MILK EGG NOODLES

SERVES 4–6

For the Noodles:

1 egg
1 cup buttermilk

2 cups chicken stock
1½ cups milk
Large pinch of sugar
1½ teaspoons salt
3 tablespoons butter, melted

½ teaspoon salt
1¾ cups all-purpose flour

1½ cups asparagus, sliced ⅓ inch thick
1½ cups peas
½ cup buttermilk
Generous grindings of fresh black pepper
4 scallions, including tender white and green parts, sliced thin

To make the noodles, whisk together the egg, buttermilk, and salt. Place the flour in a bowl, make a well in the center, and, using a fork, slowly stir the liquid into the flour. Transfer the batter to the noodlemaker of your choice.

Place the chicken stock, milk, sugar, and salt in a large saucepan. Cover and bring to a simmer. Press half the noodle mixture over the surface of the liquid. The batter should fall in small lima bean–sized droplets. Use scissors to clip them off. Cover the pan and let the noodles cook for slightly under 2 minutes.

Place the melted butter in a bowl. When the noodles are tender, strain them out of the liquid, place in the butter, and coat them gently. Cook the other half of the noodles, strain them out, then keep the noodles covered while you continue with the recipe.

Add the asparagus and peas to the remaining broth. Cover and simmer until the asparagus is tender-crisp, 3 to 4 minutes. Stir in the buttermilk and the cooked noodles. Add several grindings of pepper and scatter the scallions over the top.

Serve in soup plates with a lump of butter in the middle of each portion.

17

Here is asparagus in a different form than you usually find it. It is ground to make a wonderful thick, green essence, then a few eggs are beaten in to give it body—a sort of reverse scrambled eggs with asparagus if you will, and delicious for brunch or lunch.

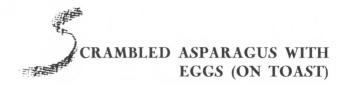

SCRAMBLED ASPARAGUS WITH EGGS (ON TOAST)

SERVES 4

1½ pounds fresh asparagus
4 tablespoons (½ stick) butter
3 large shallots, peeled and sliced thin, or
   1 small onion, minced
¼ cup cream
Around 1 cup chicken stock
4 eggs, lightly beaten

½ teaspoon salt
Freshly ground pepper

4 slices heavily buttered hot toast (white
   bread is best)
Minced fresh parsley

Cut the tender purple tips off the asparagus and reserve them. Break the stalks at their tender point, discard the woody bottoms, and slice the stalks into 2 or 3 pieces. Put the sliced stalks in a food processor and process until you have an oatmeal-consistency mash.

Melt the butter in a large frying pan. Add the shallots and cook over low heat until they are tender. Turn up the heat to medium, add the pureed asparagus, cream, and enough stock to make a thick but loose "gravy." Stir with a whisk until the brew starts to make thick bubbles, then add in the eggs and whisk rapidly just until the eggs are coagulated (add a bit more stock or cream if necessary to keep things liquid). Add the salt and pepper to taste.

Ladle the asparagus and eggs over the toast and garnish with the crunchy tips and minced parsley.

Here is a pretty use for the first bunches of tender asparagus you find in the farm market. You can use this sauce on poached or sautéed fish fillets, on grilled chicken breasts, or, to gild the lily, on perfectly cooked asparagus.

ASPARAGUS SAUCE

SERVES 4

1 large bunch asparagus
3 tablespoons butter
4 scallions, including tender green and white
    parts, chopped

2 tablespoons minced fresh parsley
1/3 cup cream
1/2 teaspoon salt
Freshly ground pepper to taste

Break the asparagus at its tender point. (If the stalks are very large, peel them down with a vegetable peeler in the French manner so as not to waste the extra flesh). Chop the stalks coarsely.

Bring a small pot of salted water to a boil and cook the asparagus just until tender and still bright green—test them frequently with the point of a small knife.

Immediately drain the asparagus and rinse with cold water to set the color. Drain well.

Melt the butter in a saucepan. Add the scallions, parsley, cream, and asparagus and cook gently for 4 minutes. Stir frequently.

Puree the mixture in blender or rub it through a sieve to make an especially elegant sauce. Add the salt and season with pepper.

A lump of butter or a bit of extra cream can be added if you want a thinner sauce.

This intense "essence" takes a classic oriental combination, stir-fried asparagus with sesame seeds, and turns it into a soup. Whereas cream and egg yolks would more frequently thicken a soup like this, our version lets a puree of potatoes serve instead.

ASPARAGUS SESAME SOUP

SERVES 8–10

2 pounds asparagus

¼ cup peanut oil

2½ cup finely chopped onions (2 medium onions)

½ cup minced scallions (white and tender green parts)

2 large all-purpose potatoes, peeled and diced

1 quart chicken stock

¼ teaspoon sugar

⅓ cup toasted sesame seeds

3 tablespoons soy sauce

1–2 teaspoons sesame oil, to taste

Generous grinds of fresh pepper to taste

Break the asparagus at its tender point and discard the ends. Cut off 1 inch of the tips and reserve. Slice the rest of the stalks thin.

Heat the peanut oil in a saucepan large enough to hold all the soup ingredients. Add the onions and scallions and stir over medium heat until wilted and soft, around 5 minutes. Add the potatoes and sliced asparagus (except for the tips). Pour in the stock and a bit of extra water if needed to cover the vegetables. Add the sugar and half the toasted sesame seeds.

Bring to a simmer, cover the pot, and continue cooking for around 20 minutes, or until all the vegetables are just tender. Try to keep the asparagus as bright a green as possible.

Pour the soup into a food processor or blender and puree.

Add the reserved asparagus tips, the soy sauce, sesame oil, and pepper.

Serve hot or lightly chilled. Place the remaining toasted sesame seeds in a bowl and let everyone garnish their own soup by adding a spoonful.

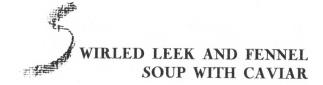

SWIRLED LEEK AND FENNEL SOUP WITH CAVIAR

SERVES 6–8

4 leeks
3 tablespoons butter
2 bulbs fennel
3 medium potatoes, peeled and diced
1 quart chicken stock

Handful of spinach leaves (optional)
Salt and freshly ground pepper to taste
Plain yogurt
1 2-ounce jar of lumpfish caviar

Trim the leek roots and cut off the green tops. Slice the white portions down the middle and wash the leaves thoroughly. Slice thin. Melt the butter in a large soup pot and start the leeks cooking over gentle heat.

Trim the roots and tough outer fennel leaves. Cut off the stalky tops but reserve the feathery fennel greens for garnish. Slice the fennel thin and add it to the leeks.

Add the potatoes, chicken stock, and optional spinach leaves (for color) and simmer for 30 minutes, until all the vegetables are tender. Puree. The soup should be quite thick but you may thin it with water or milk if you like. Taste for salt and pepper.

To serve, ladle the soup into plates. Whisk the yogurt to smooth and loosen it. Swirl a big spoonful of yogurt into each portion of soup so that it trails a feathering design against the green. Place a small spoonful of caviar in the center, add a sprig of fennel and perhaps some chopped fennel leaves, and serve. (The soup can be hot, lukewarm, or cool. It reheats nicely and perhaps is even tastier when made the day before it is needed.)

John Covington, the teen-aged grandson of Mrs. O. T. Smith, sells vegetables at the Lynchburg market. Straight A's his grandmother told me. He's an articulate kid with bright brown eyes, glasses, braces on his teeth. I didn't meet anyone else quite like him.

JOHN COVINGTON

"I was five years old when I started coming with my grandfather in 1978. We sold out by that curb there. People be hollering and telling you what they wanted and they wouldn't even get out of the automobile, so I'd run the produce to their cars. I liked to make change. I remember when I had to make six cents the first time. I started to get six pennies and my grandfather said get a nickel and a penny, that will make it easier. I was so excited to learn that. Now that grandfather's gone, I'm the one who helps my grandmother most. I work every day in the summer; in school times it's just Friday and Saturday. I pick vegetables and gather, grade, and size the eggs.

"After my grandmother passes I want to carry on the tradition. I'd like to buy my grandmother's house, I'd actually like to do that. Kids say why would you want to go and work so hard. I'd much rather be out on the farm working than lazing around. They say, but there's no money in it. They're looking at success and wealth and fame. I say it's better to be happy long as you're breaking even.

"It's getting harder and harder to make a living every day. The egg market is down, feed price is up—sometimes I wonder in ten to twenty years will there even be an egg market. Winter's hard. If we have to borrow in winter to cover the chicken-feed bill, we work harder to pay it back in the summer. Farming is seven days a week. Once the chicken house froze on Christmas day. My uncles and I had to keep toting water up the hill for the birds. Farming doesn't pay attention to holidays, hens don't take a day off of laying for Christmas. I try to go to church regular, but if the vegetables are going to perish, I'll make a sacrifice, though I don't know how to feel about that exactly.

"I have a garden now that I dabble in. Less than an acre but this summer I'll make seven hundred dollars or so selling here. Jumped the gun planting my beans this spring and they got frosted out. When I was little and started picking beans I sat on a five-gallon bucket. My grandmother said you're never going to get anywhere like that. I pick standing then I go sit on the tailgate for a while. I've got a dog who's some kind of cow dog. In the summer he'll lie in the shade between the bean vines. As you work along the rows, he'll creep along with you. I don't like to pick by myself, my mind wanders. I start calculating prices. Actually, I'm shocked by prices these days. Used to be three pounds a dollar for green beans, now its one pound a dollar. Shocks me, but you sure do learn first hand about inflation on the farm and in the market.

"As long as there's a community market here I'll come. It doesn't feel right on a Saturday not to be here. Had to take my SAT exam two weeks ago on Saturday and that upset me. A girl at school asked a friend of mine to find out if I'd take her to the homecoming prom. I said it's Friday night and won't get out till midnight. I have to get up at 4 A.M. to get to market, no way. My friends said the market's more important than homecoming? I said yes. People like to die when I didn't go to that prom, but I don't like to waste time. I listen to the radio for weather, TV for news. I could care less about David Letterman. People my age have a hard time getting it through their heads what's important sometimes."

—&—

TOP 10 REASONS TO SHOP AT FARM MARKETS

10. Pets rather than bags of stupid pet food

9. Aisles not so crowded

8. Check-out people knowledgeable

7. No Muzak

6. No children whining for Marshmallow Critter Puffs

5. No calcium proprionate to retard spoilage

4. No jammed wheels on carts

3. No squashed lettuce on linoleum floors

2. Good, wholesome pickup place

1. Produce makes car smell nice on way home

This is a delightful way to use fresh shelled beans. It makes a good luncheon dish, or the first course for an elegant meal. The polenta can be done the day before. Leftover untoasted polenta can be refrigerated for three or four days.

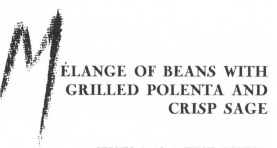

MÉLANGE OF BEANS WITH GRILLED POLENTA AND CRISP SAGE

SERVES 8 AS A FIRST COURSE;
4 AS A DINNER

For the Polenta:

1½ cups coarse yellow cornmeal (do not use
   self-rising)
1 teaspoon salt
Freshly ground pepper to taste
2 tablespoons minced fresh parsley or
   parsley-chive mix

4⅓ cups lukewarm water

Butter or oil for pan

Place all the polenta ingredients in a medium-sized heavy pan. Bring to a simmer over medium heat, then reduce heat to low and stir, slowly and continually, for a good 20 minutes. Grasp a heavy wooden spoon in the palm of your hand and go at the stuff. When the mixture becomes very thick at the end, stirring assures that it is not sticking. (This slow development of the corn's starch allows the grilled polenta to have a soft, creamy interior.) You can use 5-minute polenta mix if you must, but you won't get as tasty a result.) When the polenta is very thick and each turn of the spoon scrapes the whole mass almost into a sticky ball, remove it from the heat.

Butter or oil a large sheet of aluminum foil and put it on a cookie sheet. Scrape the polenta out onto the foil. Wet your hands and pat the meal into a rectangle ½ inch thick and approximately 8 x 12 inches. Square up the corners and edges as much as possible. Cover the polenta with foil and put to chill 30 minutes or until completely cold.

When ready to use, cut the polenta in quarters, then cut each quarter into 4 diagonals so that you have 16 triangular pieces. Place on an oiled grill, or toast under a broiler. Count on a long browning. The trick is to let it cook a good 5 or 6 minutes on each side so that the exterior turns a crisp spotted brown while the interior stays soft and creamy.

For the beans, allow 1½ cups of vegetables per person. Choose from:

Green peas
Tender green beans, cut to the size of peas
Small zucchini, sliced thin
Fresh limas, crowder peas, or butter beans
Fresh peeled fava beans
Defrosted frozen Fordhook limas popped
  from their skins
Perhaps a russet-colored dried bean (kidney,
  adzuki, fava) that has been cooked

1 stick unsalted butter
Large handful of sage leaves (around 30–35
  medium-sized)
Salt and pepper to taste

While the polenta is toasting, prepare the vegetables. Place them in a steamer or let them cook in a pan with just a bit of water, butter, and salt until al dente. Drain off all the water.

Place the butter and sage leaves in a frying pan and let the butter melt over medium heat. Watch carefully as the butter continues to cook and let it turn nut brown (use your nose as well as your eyes—you can always smell this). By the time the butter has browned, the sage will be wonderfully crisp. Pour the butter over the vegetables, season with salt and pepper, and give the pan a shake to coat everything with butter.

Serve 2 polenta wedges on each plate, with a portion of buttery vegetables in the middle and a few sage leaves on top as garnish.

This may sound like an odd combination, but it is wonderfully succulent. You can substitute elements within the dish, say sliced zucchini for the cabbage, peas for the asparagus, but the spring onions must stay constant.

GRATIN OF GREEN SPRING VEGETABLES

SERVES 6

1 large bunch asparagus
Freshly ground pepper to taste
1 cup thinly sliced spring onions (white and tender green parts)
2 packed cups finely shredded cabbage

1 teaspoon salt
1⅓ cups heavy cream
2 tablespoons grated Parmesan cheese
¼ cup fine dry bread crumbs
2 tablespoons butter, chilled

Preheat the oven to 350°F.

Lightly butter an 8-cup gratin or a 10-inch soufflé dish.

Break off the asparagus at its tender point and cut the tender stalks into thin slices. Lay the asparagus in the bottom of the prepared dish. Pepper to taste. Disperse the onions over the surface, then the shredded cabbage. Press the vegetables down as level as possible. Stir the salt into the cream and pour over the vegetables.

Mix the cheese and bread crumbs and scatter over the top. Use a vegetable peeler to scrape the butter into thin shards, then place them about the surface of the crumbs.

Bake for 30 minutes. Use as a luncheon dish, or as an accompaniment to a simple poach or sauté of fish fillets. (Not bad as a gently heated leftover, either.)

Here's a good reason to buy spring market bedding plants of Lemon or Tangerine marigolds or calendulas, even if you don't have a place to plant them.

MARIGOLD RICE

SERVES 4–6

2 cups water

½ teaspoon salt

¼ teaspoon saffron threads

4 tablespoons (½ stick) butter

¼ teaspoon ground turmeric

1 medium onion, stem end cored, cut into
   paper-thin slices

1 cup rice, preferably long-grain basmati

¼ teaspoon curry powder

¼ teaspoon ground cumin

2 tablespoons marigold or calendula petals

Put the water, salt, and saffron in a small pot and start it heating to a boil.

Melt 2 tablespoons of the butter in a saucepan. Add the turmeric and onion and cook over medium-high heat, stirring all the while. Let the onion fry quickly and hard until the tips turn brown. Add the rice and stir over heat for 1 minute while it turns translucent.

Pour the boiling saffron water over the rice, give a quick stir, then turn down the heat, cover the pot, and let the rice simmer for 20 minutes.

When the rice has cooked, melt the remaining 2 tablespoons of butter over high heat and add the curry powder and cumin. When the butter has browned, stir it and the flower petals into the rice and serve at once.

Tender freshly shelled beans become a whole new creation when prepared this way. Out of season, try the cakes with frozen baby limas.

OCK LIMA "COD" CAKES

SERVES 6–8

20 ounces (around 2½ cups) fresh baby
    limas or other shell beans
3 tablespoons butter
1 small onion, minced
1 large clove garlic, minced
1 small green bell pepper, minced
1 egg
1 teaspoon salt
Generous grinding of black pepper

1 teaspoon Old Bay Seasoning (or other
    seafood seasoning of choice)
Large pinch of cayenne
2 tablespoons minced fresh parsley
Around ⅔ cup sieved dry bread crumbs
Olive oil for frying
Tartar sauce
Lemon wedges

Steam the beans until just tender—do *not* overcook.

While the beans are steaming, melt the butter in a frying pan. Add the onion and garlic and sauté over medium heat until limp. Add the green pepper, turn up the heat, and cook, stirring, for 3 minutes.

When the beans are tender and still bright green, remove them from the steamer and run them under cold water to set their color. Drain well and cool.

Puree the beans and egg in a food processor. The mixture will look a bit dry. Scrape into a bowl and add the seasonings and parsley.

Stir in the onion.

Form the mixture into 16 flattened cakes about 2 inches round and ¾ inch thick. Press each cake into the bread crumbs. Refrigerate for at least 30 minutes.

Fry the cakes in olive oil over medium heat until the crumbs are golden brown.

Serve with a dab of tartar sauce. Squeeze on lots of lemon.

Dane County Market
Madison, Wisconsin

If I could take a visiting foreigner to only one representative small-town market in America, it would be Dane County's. The market extends in a giant square on the sidewalks surrounding the state capitol centered at the heart of town. One of the handsomest gold-domed capitol buildings in the country stretches its four wings to the corners of the square as if offering official beneficence to all who come to buy and sell. There is much vigor in this market, much sturdy midwestern hard work in evidence. The air is clean and clear, and just down from the market's hill are sparkling lakes. The Madison market is a well-supported community event and social gathering place. It has a slightly militant air about it that reminds me of the Davis market in California—the same sense of activist stirrings that academic towns cultivate in their public domains.

In 1968, the town's commercial center suffered when antiwar activity caused frightened merchants to board up their stores and leave the city center. In 1973, the market started up again. There were only five vendors in the first year, but slowly they began drawing people back downtown, and many cede the renaissance of Madison to that market date. After war, there could be no better healing potion than letting the cultivators of the earth restore a peaceable kingdom.

There are two hundred vendors now, which makes the Dane County market the largest open-air market in the Midwest. Early on, there were little "tiffs with the government." As one vendor put it, "Government claimed people were 'impacting on the grass' or walking into the capitol and using too much toilet paper. They said that paper costs, labor costs, dumpsters cost. One year they set up cameras and videotaped patrons. Well, let me tell you, when we thought they wanted to move us, we started a petition and got ten thousand signatures in one day to protect our market, and they haven't bothered us since." A wise decision.

On the long walk around the market you see nuts, vegetables, baked goods, lots of cheeses, and real wild rice. You can tell the rice is wild because it's long and a bit rougher looking than the cultivated paddy "wild" rice you tend to see more and more of these days.

Greg Isaaksen drives three hundred miles north to the lakes around Brule to harvest each summer.

"Used to be my wife and I. Now its the kids, thirteen and sixteen years old, and me. We've been going up the lakes for six years. You have to be a citizen of Wisconsin to harvest and it's even better if you're a Wisconsin Indian, because when the season opens every year they get a one-day jump on the rest of us and every day they get to harvest early in the morning. You can't rice before 10 A.M. if you're white. So you have two people in the canoe, one to paddle and one to knock. We use ash saplings, two rounded sticks not less than thirty-four inches. Indians have ricing sticks that pass down from father to son and bring luck they say.

"We scout in mid-July looking for a good crop area, then harvest in late August, early September. We spend five to six hours on the lake at a time, take soda pop and venison sausage sandwiches in the canoe with us. It's usually serene on the lake, loons glide around us in the shallows, the rice comes to canoe height and looks like oats standing out of the water. Some people go for a little rice, but we got real serious and now the rice we sell at the market is 50 percent of our annual income. We get five hundred to one thousand pounds a year, depending on our energy and the winds on the lake. I take the rice to a commercial processor and he charges fifty cents to husk every green pound. Rice is putting our children through college."

WILD RICE SOUP

SERVES 6–8

3 tablespoons butter
1 large carrot, scraped and sliced
1 large onion, coarsely chopped (around
   3 cups)
1 clove garlic, sliced
1 tablespoon flour
3–4 cups chicken broth
4 cups cooked wild rice (1½ cups raw)

1 bay leaf
1 cup cream
Freshly ground black pepper
Juice of ½ lemon
Generous ¼ teaspoon lemon zest
Salt to taste
Minced fresh parsley

Melt the butter in a heavy soup pot. Add the carrot, onion, and garlic and cook over medium heat until the onion is translucent and carrot just tender, around 12 minutes. Sprinkle the flour over the vegetables and stir for 1 minute to let it absorb the butter.

Add 3 cups of chicken broth, 3 cups of the cooked rice, and the bay leaf. Simmer for 15 minutes. Remove the bay leaf and puree the mixture, then add 1 cup of whole rice, the cream, pepper to taste, and lemon juice and zest. You may, if you wish, add more chicken broth or water to make the soup less thick. Taste for salt.

Ladle into bowls and garnish with the minced parsley.

Farm markets are ideal places for individual entrepreneurs to showcase their wares with the chance of mainstreaming products into public consciousness. Some of the people who prosper most from this are dairymen and cheesemakers. Every little micro-climate in France seems to furnish a specialty cheese. In our land of conglomerate processed cheese, how important it is that we support the small dairy endeavors we find only in farm markets. Certainly the best butter I've ever tasted in America is sold at the Madison market. Willi Lehner, a pink-faced thirty-five-year-old, lived six years in Switzerland and spent his summers there making cheese in a copper kettle over a wood fire. He also developed discriminating tastes in butter. When he returned to America, our butter tasted flat, salty, undistinguished, and he decided to make butter the right way. He found the richest, healthiest milk, let the butter age in a vat with a mother culture similar to the microbes used in cheese, then made forty-five pound churns of rich nutty butter and took them to the Dane County market.

About the same time Willi started with his butter, Judy Boree and Anne Topham bought a goat called Angie and her three-week-old kid. With a supply of fresh goat milk and the memory of delicate chèvre eaten in France as inspiration, they started making cheese, fresh chèvre plain and mixed with herbs or rolled in vegetable ash; small logs of chèvre Provençale submerged in olive oil; aged *boulets* with semisoft textures.

After market one Saturday in late summer, I visit their Fantome Farm in Ridgeway. They share equipment there with Willi, and he, in his rolled-up-sleeve T-shirt and paper dairyman's cap is mixing together a vat's worth of future butter:

4 ten-gallon cans of cream
5 gallons milk
5 gallons water

He fits a propellerlike blade into the cylinder and sets it churning away in a kettle jacketed with surrounding water. Heaters gradually raise the temperature of the liquid in the internal unit to 170°F. where it remains for thirty minutes until legally pasteurized, then he intensifies the heat to 183°F. to allow the butterfat to crystallize properly. Slowly the temperature will drop back down to 73°F. and he will add the mother culture, then leave the mixture overnight to develop flavor and acidity. He offers a peek inside the churn and I see a holey froth that looks like cottage cheese gone mad. The warm wood dairy room next to Anne and Judy's house smells like the milky spittings of a baby. Electric churns hum; Willi hand-stamps date codes on butter boxes; a dairy cat rubs and mutters against my leg; goats outside wanting to be milked, bleat impatiently.

An hour later Anne and Judy return from the market. They'd had a long, productive day and sold everything but two boulets, one of which they cut into now for us to eat, then it's out to the barns to feed and milk the goats.

"When we started, only two places were making goat cheese in the States. We read an article about Laura Chenel in California and one other farm in New York. We've been eight years in operation, six years now selling cheese once we got our license. When we first carried it to market, nobody knew what the stuff was. We started a sampling program right away and Judy badgered (that's a Wisconsin word) people into trying it. Once they tasted it, they'd buy, of course. Eating goat cheese is always sort of an adventure. It's always the same but different, depending upon what the goats have eaten. The cheese varies according to the season. It's higher in fat in spring and fall, but always the fat molecules in goat's milk are small and both cheese and milk are easier for people with stomach problems to digest.

"It's nice to come home to the goats after a day in the market. They like being milked. They are raised with individual attention and we know them all by name and the goats know their names. We've got litters named after:

Women Comedians	Women Writers	Grandmothers	Birds	Peppers
Lucy	Emily	Jenni	Falcon	Chili
Valerie	Jessamyn	Avie	Peregrine	Salsa
Gilda	Flannery	Meg	Robin	Haberera

Each year's set bonds to their own kidding group, hangs out with their own age mates, and likes to butt up together. Even though the goats are taken away at the instant of birth, they often behave like their mothers and have the same mannerisms. There's a strict herd hierarchy. Valerie there, the one they keep butting out of the feed trough, they are letting her know she's nobody because she's just joined the herd and has no kin here."

In the late afternoon light, the babies are fed grain then a handful of sweet hay. Soft susurrus fill the barn. Contentment. The mothers traipse daintily up the ramp into a side room and onto the raised ledges where they will be milked. There is order here, also. Clout and seniority give the pleasure of being milked first. The pink udders are washed in warm soapy liquid, the suction cups attached, the goats are rubbed and petted, scolded and coddled, depending on their personality and behavior. Chloe, usually a good goat, has to be pushed down the chute and out the door to make her leave after milking. Razzle won't stand still, gets a little spank, retaliates by mouthing up a strand of Anne's hair. Flo is clucked over. Seems she opened the gate, jumped the fence, got into the pen of the new buck, Luca, and spent last night in wanton pleasure. She is in disgrace though she's looking innocent now with wide "what me?" eyes and a strand of clover hanging from her mouth.

When the does are milked, we take old Claude, the veteran buck, his feed. He's a very masculine presence on this feminine farm. Tethered by a long rope to a stake, his Vandyke beard and shaggy eyebrows quivering, he stamps imperiously. I walk right up to him and he comes barreling at me, swings sideways, then butts me in the thigh.

"Don't let him touch you," yells Anne. "Oh, too late, he's gone and done it. Now your coat will smell like musk for a month. That was a very bucky thing to do, Claude, shame on you."

"She's not a goat, Claude. You should know the difference by now."

"Naughty old goat."

"Fie," says Judy. "Shame."

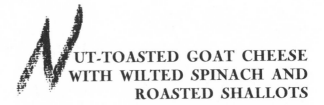

NUT-TOASTED GOAT CHEESE WITH WILTED SPINACH AND ROASTED SHALLOTS

SERVES 4 AS A FIRST COURSE
OR LUNCHEON DISH

½ pound shallots (choose small, evenly sized heads)
Olive oil
1 pound fresh spinach
Salt
4 small individual-size goat cheeses, soft and fresh

¼ cup fine dry bread crumbs
¼ cup ground toasted hazelnuts
4 slices peasant bread
4 tablespoons minced fresh herbs (parsley, chives, thyme, and tarragon mixed if possible)
Freshly ground pepper to taste

Place the shallots in their skins in a small baking pan and drizzle with olive oil until each one is coated and there is a light film on the bottom of the pan. Put to bake in a 375°F. oven for around 45 minutes, or until they are completely soft. Turn them in the pan once or twice during their bake.

While the shallots roast, wash and stem the spinach. Put it in a steamer, salt lightly, and allow it to steam just until wilted and still bright green, 2 to 3 minutes. Remove from the steamer, drain well, and place the spinach in 4 nests on 4 salad plates. Let cool to room temperature.

Brush the tops and sides of the goat cheeses with olive oil. Mix the bread crumbs and hazelnuts and roll the cheeses in the mixture until the tops and sides are heavily coated. Press on extra crumbs with your fingers. Place the cheeses on a small baking sheet and refrigerate for 10 minutes.

Heat the broiler. Brush the bread slices with olive oil and toast under the broiler until light golden brown.

Place the cheese briefly under the hot broiler until the tops are crusted brown. Cool, then use a spatula to transfer one cheese to the center of each spinach nest. Place a slice of toast on each plate.

Divide the shallots among the plates. Drizzle a bit of oil and scatter a tablespoon of herbs over each cheese. Season to taste. To eat, puncture the shallots and spread the warm pulp on the bread. Top with soft nutty cheese.

Any town, big or small, is lucky to have an Odessa Piper. She's the owner and guiding force behind L'Etoile, a restaurant on the second floor at 25 North Pinckney Street, one of the four streets on which the Dane County market is held. Wrapped in a shawl, her pale brown hair long about her shoulders, she is a passionate advocate of the symbiotic relationship between restaurants and growers. Running a good restaurant, after all, is like inviting cherished guests to dinner. You search out the freshest ingredients, organize a pleasing menu, bring to bear your best cooking talent—night after night.

ODESSA PIPER

"We have a farm menu all the way. We keep the menu small; focusing the food each night mirrors what is happening in the growing season. We're such a little bubble here in the membrane of Dane County, but a good small restaurant, like a small farm, helps keep down the topsoil and preserve the opportunity for land regeneration. A restaurant that supports those growers therefore does its part also.

"I started L'Etoile in 1976, three years after the market started up. To help support the restaurant, I began baking croissants. Wednesday nights I'd make butter sheets, Thursday nights I'd make dough and let it rest; Friday I'd roll the butter in before dinner service and let it relax in the cooler until 2 A.M. I'd hostess Friday evening, grab a couple hours' sleep, then come back at 2 A.M. and bake two thousand croissants. By the time market opened in the morning, I'd be running them across the street hot every half hour. I started putting savory ingredients in the croissants like Anne and Judy's chèvre. People didn't know if they liked goat cheese then. Then I'd grab cash from sales, race around the market square buying up vegetables, and come back to prep for dinner. Did that for eight years until the restaurant got popular.

"We have such loving growers now, such loving customers. We latched on to Fantome Farm cheese and tested the stuff out in our restaurant. Willi brings us his cultured butter. Once a year I have a dinner of thanksgiving and invite all the growers and the local foodies. It's important that they meet and know each other—that the growing process doesn't stop with production and that diners realize where their food comes from and who grows it.

"Last year's menu was:

Assorted Pesto-Stuffed Cherry Tomatoes

Cheddar and Cayenne Crisps

Sweet Corn Chowder with Bread and Willi's Butter

Sandwiched Eggplant and Chèvre,
with Roasted Red Pepper Butter

Rainbow Trout Baked in Parchment

Raspberry Vinegar Ice

Roast Lamb with Red Wine–Cassis Sauce

Seasonal Lettuce with Pancetta and Flowers

Forgotten Valley Aged Brick and
Fantom Farm Boulet with Butternut Toasts

Hickory Nut Sorghum Pie

"Here's the salad, the Sweet Corn Chowder, and Odessa's Hickory Nut Pie.

"Choose small tender butter heads, such as Bibb and Boston, for this salad as each serving should be one whole lettuce."

SEASONAL LETTUCE WITH PANCETTA AND FLOWERS

SERVES 4

4 heads spring lettuce, washed, dried, left
   intact
6 slices pancetta (if this is unavailable,
   substitute 3 ounces salt pork), chilled
⅔ cup fruity olive oil
⅓ cup balsamic vinegar

¼ teaspoon sugar
2 scallions, tender green and white parts,
   sliced thin
Violet, nasturtium, or other edible blossoms
   (optional)

Arrange each lettuce head prettily on a dinner plate with leaves spread open.

Slice the pancetta and chop until minced (this is more easily accomplished if it's chilled briefly in the freezer first).

Heat the olive oil in a frying pan and brown the pancetta. When all the particles look crunchy, add the vinegar, sugar, and scallions. Boil for 15 seconds, then immediately spoon out the dressing over the 4 lettuce portions and serve promptly.

If you can find them, a few fresh violet colored flowers are pretty scattered over each plate. This is a good salad to serve with homemade bread and a slice of terrine for a spring lunch.

The best place to get good practical gardening advice is at your local farmers' market. Last spring, Bunnies from Hell ate my newly planted lettuce to nubs.

LETTUCE PESTS

"**R**abbits? Well you could put up a chicken-wire fence, but then you'd go tripping on it. You could keep a dog out there, but maybe he's paying attention, maybe not. Best thing is to get spun polyester floating row covers. They're translucent to let in sunlight and rain. You stick them down with twenty penny nails and keep slack in the material so the lettuce can raise under it. You can start a crop two weeks early with that protection. Of course, you'll get an occasional hole where deer step through. I figure I lose a thousand dollars a year to deer eating lettuce and turtles gobbling tomatoes."

—Bill Dow, Carrboro market

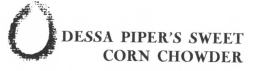

ODESSA PIPER'S SWEET CORN CHOWDER

SERVES 6

6 large ears sweet corn (yellow is prettiest though Silver Queen also works)

2 quarts water

Salt

Large pinch of sugar

3 tablespoons butter

1 small green bell pepper, seeded and diced

1 small red bell pepper, seeded and diced

1 jalapeño pepper, seeded and minced

2 stalks celery, diced

1 clove garlic, minced

1 medium onion, diced

½ cup white wine

¼ cup fresh lime juice

3 cups heavy cream

Freshly ground pepper

⅓ cup coarsely chopped cilantro

Shuck and string the corn. Place the water, 1 teaspoon salt, and sugar in a large pan. Cover and bring to a boil. Add the corn and cook just until the ears are tender, 3 to 4 minutes. Lift the corn out of the pan, but don't throw away the cooking liquid. Rinse the corn under cold water and cut the kernels from the cobs. Return the cobs to the liquid and simmer for 15 minutes to extract their flavor. This makes a tasty "stock."

Puree a good half of the corn.

Remove the cobs from the stock and discard them. Continue simmering the stock until it is reduced to half its volume (around 3½ to 4 cups).

While the liquid reduces, melt the butter in a large frying pan. Sauté the peppers, celery, garlic, and onion until tender. Add the wine and lime juice.

Add the sautéed vegetables to the stock. Stir in the reserved corn puree and kernels. Stir in the cream. Taste for salt and add pepper to taste.

At this point, the soup may be simmered and reduced a bit thicker if you so choose. Just before serving, stir in half the cilantro. Ladle the chowder into bowls and garnish with the remaining cilantro.

— ❧ —

CORN PESTS

"Well, there's worms in both silver and gold corn. I do dust some, but I go out to the chemical place and look around and there's enough chemicals to kill all the state. Those worms don't seem to heed chemicals anyway. They'll just hatch out twice as early or twice as late. I'd rather see a worm and clip off the ends of the ear. Then there's bigger varmits. So far I took one possum, two woodchucks, and seventeen coon out of my corn. Coon won't touch Silver Queen, but they like yellow corn. They tear it off, grip it, carry it down, get it in the mud and put teeth marks in it. Got a buck deer in my corn and he ate an acre of little ears. What you do to get rid of deer is have a beer party. Invite all of your men friends, give them plenty to drink, then let 'um piss all around the borders of your corn.

Deer don't like that smell and won't cross the line. Trouble is, you have to do it after every rain and that could get a tad expensive."

—Rolland Wehr, Lansing farmers' market

It would be a treat if you could find small sweet hickory nuts in a farm market, but even if you can't, do try this pie with pecans broken in half. Sorghum syrup is used for flavor. Lighter and nuttier than molasses, it almost has a licorice overtone.

ODESSA PIPER'S HICKORY NUT SORGHUM PIE

1 FAIRLY RICH PIE, SERVES 6–8

⅓ cup unsalted butter, at room temperature
1 cup sugar
4 eggs
½ cup sorghum

½ cup white corn syrup
2 cups whole hickory nuts
Pinch of salt
1 prebaked 9-inch piecrust

Preheat the oven to 425°F.

Cream the butter and sugar together until very soft. Beat in 1 egg at a time, then stir in the sorghum and white corn syrup. Add the hickory nuts and salt. Pour the mixture into the pie-crust and give it a shake on the counter to smooth and even the ingredients.

Set the pie in the oven and immediately turn the heat down to 400°F. Bake for 30 minutes, or until the pie appears set and a knife tip, when touched to the center, comes out clean.

Remove from the oven, place on a cooling rack, and cool completely before cutting. This is delicious garnished with a dollop of unsweetened whipped cream.

BIG-CITY MARKETS

SPRING MAY START WITH THE SAME PRODUCE
appearing in markets big and small, but that's about where it ends. If small-town markets are slow and sociable, gentle one-note turns, their fast, big-city cousins, mirroring as they do such striking urban diversity, are a cacophony of sights, sounds, symbol and meaning.

I take the F train out from Manhattan, rattling all the way to Parsons Boulevard for the opening day of the Jamaica, Queens, market. The market stretches down a raggedy block, graffiti-covered buildings at either end, an elevated railway track bordering the back side and noisy traffic at the large intersection. Little bedding plants for city window boxes. Lots of winter-crop apples, delicious cakes at Sweet Lou's stand. A spectrum of city folks of all colors, many elderly dressed up for market day. On a platform at one end of the street a bluegrass band starts fiddling and stomping. There's a sweet spring crop of small inner-city schoolchildren, their hands linked together, who've been let out for the day. One farmer has brought a goat for a petting zoo.

"Ooh eee, what that?"

"That's a cow."

"No it isn't, dumbhead, that's a sheep."

"How you know that?"

" 'Cause it's got horns."

"I wanna take it home."

"Your apartment's too small."

"We could cut him up and eat him."

"You don't eat sheep, you make clothes from him."

"It's a goat," says the farmer.

"Ooh eee," says a kid, "bacon!"

One of the things that often makes a big-city market so alluring is the juxtaposition of its vitality standing in marked contrast to the deterioration of the large city around it. When so much healthy, fresh vegetable reality plumps down in the midst of begrimed urbanity the frisson caused is electric. The market itself enlarges in scope and meaning to become a vital symbol of urban renewal and potential.

Probably no big-city market is as exciting as New York's set of Greenmarkets. The sheer willpower and man hours that were needed to launch the first tender market through the rough seas of city bureaucracy had to be astronomical, but Barry Benepe, the founding father of the markets, had a vision of greening the city and saving surrounding farmers from extinction, and he held to it with bulldog tenacity. In a small town you just set up in an accommodating lot. In New York you have to get permits or approvals from the departments of Real Estate, Transportation, Traffic, Highways, Consumer Affairs, City Planning, Police, and Economic Development. You have to placate community planning boards, local businesses, citizen action committees, cliques, factions, and downright ornery politicians. But once the first market got set up back in 1976 on East Fifty-ninth Street in Manhattan, the delight and patronage of customers guaranteed its success, and soon the City Planning Department suggested locations in downtown Brooklyn and at Union Square, which now houses the most famous of New York's Greenmarkets.

It's a hot day at the market. A tall, lithe Ford model in a silver trench coat and black leather mini-skirt is striding down the sidewalk past the apple stands, her arms laden with fresh flowers. Arthur Elgort, the fashion photographer, is doing a shoot for Vidal Sassoon shampoo—clean, healthy hair in a clean, healthy environment reads the story line, and what better place to shoot it than a farmers' market. At the other side of the square, Michael Romano, the chef at Union Square Café, is having his picture taken for an article on hot young chefs who cook healthy. Just regular doings for Bill Maxwell, the market's detective. He and I are trotting around the square looking for pickpockets (there's something you usually don't have to worry about in small towns). I like Bill. He's cool. Looks rather like Richard Pryor's younger brother and spouts a funny line.

"Now that dude over there, he's bagging. Moves too nervous, lots of hand movement. He'll try to dive into the crowds around the model and his hand will go in before he does. His eyes are darting all around, looking for the closest mark and the nearest getaway. I'll just jive along down there and if he's dirty, he'll look in my mean eye and split. If that doesn't work, I'll say 'Listen, you hump, it's three-thirty. How would you like your head to be in New Jersey and your heart in New York by four.'

"He'll say, 'I don't know what you talking about man.' I'll say, 'You put your hand in there one more time, I'll cut it off.' See I'd rather prevent it than catch it. Other than the pickpockets, it's pretty peaceful. There's some looney ones around who've been touched by the angels, but they're harmless. And the bums I move off the benches each Saturday morning so the farmers can set up are no trouble. Only real problem we had was when some kids tumbled drunk out of Club Underground a few months back and rumbled with John Gorzynski and a couple of other farmers who were trying to park their trucks. John got beat up pretty bad, had to have eleven stitches. All the farmers pitched in, and some gave their whole day's take to help with his medical bills. Now there's two patrol cars for full-time protection each Saturday morning, and me. I like the market. Like the people here. We used to get Andy Warhol sometimes. Beverly Sills shops here and Wendy O. Williams from the Plasmatics. You sure do see all kinds here."

That's the truth. Fashionable uptowners come downtown in their best Ralph Lauren Safari wear. Village types with green hair, knots and bows and rings in their nose and ears select their vegetables. There's every shade of skin, every language of man spoken here, and a good deal of the talk presses the farmers. I am reminded in Union Square market of the Santa Monica market in California. In both places the customers demand organic, ask about growing practices. I wonder if those cities' need and demand for wholesome product is in direct proportion to the state of environmental decay. At any rate, the amazing thing I found in big-city markets was that concerned urbanites seemed to be instrumental in changing farming practices, and I suppose that's only natural. The more you fear for your own inner pollution, the more you cry out for ways to stop the process.

Talk to Barry Benepe, the founder of the Greenmarket Coalition, and he'll tell you that farmers' markets are symptomatic of significant life-style changes in this new decade.

"Our ideology, the whole way we think about food and feed ourselves needs to change. Urban space has been too rigidly defined in the past. People are trying to 'green the commons' by planting community gardens, and areas all over the city are asking us to set up farmers' markets. Now, what we need is legislation that allows these markets to be permanent so the farmers feel secure knowing they have a future here. The problem is that as people leave the city, they go out to farmland and convert it to suburbs. Farmers have gold mines in their acreage and its tempting to sell for hundreds of thousands of dollars and walk away from farming and retire. Committed farmers can sign their land into the Farm Preservation Program and keep farming, but only if they have nearby selling outlets. We may look like we're sturdily in place, but the city makes us renegotiate fees each year. They're nibbling away at our edges. They say they could be making much more in revenues if they turned Union Square into a daily flea market. Everybody wants to use us, but not everybody supports us. The battle's not won yet."

Every operating market day, Michael Romano of nearby Union Square Café walks through the market buying up the tenderest produce and creating dishes in which vegetables act as stars and the meat, if any, is almost an accompaniment. Leeks are "frizzled"—julienned and fried in floured matchsticks; potatoes are turned into hot garlic potato chips; rutabagas are mashed and laden with crispy shallots; baby eggplant is roasted with shiitake mushrooms and covered with spicy sauce. One of New York's "hot" young chefs, Michael admits to being a "visual person." His jaunts through the stalls, where he sees unique combinations of foods, often inspire new dishes. Drawing from his Italian heritage, he created this fish "carpaccio," which might be garnished with fiddlehead ferns and morels in spring, or bright yellow squash in summer. "The market keeps me in touch with the seasons in a way a supermarket never could."

MICHAEL ROMANO'S "CARPACCIO" OF BLACK SEA BASS AL FORNO

SERVES 6

6 black sea bass or red snapper fillets
  (around 5 ounces each)
3 cups fish or clam broth
1 medium zucchini, trimmed
1 medium yellow squash, trimmed
3 large ripe tomatoes, peeled and cored

3 scallions, green and white parts
2 tablespoons white wine vinegar
2/3 cup extra-virgin olive oil
Salt and freshly ground pepper to taste
Minced fresh parsley

Thinly slice the fish fillets on the horizontal. (Fifteen minutes in the freezer before slicing and the fillets are easier to handle. Aim for as close to the thinness of smoked salmon as possible.) Arrange the slices on 6 ovenproof dinner plates; do not allow them to overlap (can be done ahead and refrigerated).

Reserve 2/3 cup of the fish broth. Place the remaining 2 1/3 cups of broth in a saucepan and reduce to 1/4 cup.

While the liquid is reducing, quarter the squashes lengthwise and cut long strips into paper-thin slices. Cut the tomatoes in half, squeeze out the juice, and chop small. Slice the scallions thin.

When the broth has reduced, pour the hot liquid and the vinegar into a blender. Turn on the blender and very slowly add in the olive oil, which will form a thick, creamy-looking emulsified sauce.

To prepare the servings, heat the broiler. Pour the reserved unreduced broth equally over each plate to keep the fish moist. Broil for 1 minute or until the fish loses its translucency.

Add the vegetables to the sauce, season, and heat without boiling. To assemble, pour the excess broth off each serving and wipe the border of the plate. Spoon the sauce and vegetables over the fish and sprinkle with parsley. Serve at once.

Louise Crenshaw has sold home-baked cookies, cakes, and pies in the Jamaica Farmers' market for four years now. The market allows her a second income, but her business, which she named Lovin' Spoonfuls, is one of those that threatens to spill over into full-time employment at any time. This cake has a delicious ripe banana taste. I added the brown sugar glaze, but a simple sprinkling of confectioners' sugar would also be appropriate

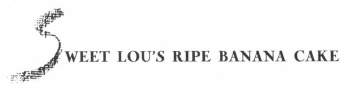

SWEET LOU'S RIPE BANANA CAKE

SERVES 10–12

2 sticks unsalted butter, at room temperature
1½ cups sugar
2 eggs
1 teaspoon vanilla extract
1 teaspoon banana extract
3 ripe bananas with brown spots, mashed

2¼ cups cake flour
½ teaspoon baking powder
¾ teaspoon baking soda
¼ teaspoon salt
¾ cup milk

Preheat the oven to 350°F. Oil or butter a 10-inch bundt or tube pan.

Cream the butter and sugar together. Add the eggs one at a time, beating well after each addition. Add the extracts and mashed bananas.

Put the flour, baking powder, baking soda, and salt in a bowl and give a quick stir. Alternately add the banana mixture and milk in 3 portions to the cake batter, beating well after each addition. Pour into the prepared pan and bake for 50 minutes or until a testing toothpick comes out clean.

Cool slightly before turning the cake out of the pan onto a cooling rack.

This is a dense, rich cake. When cool, you can sift confectioners' sugar over the top as a finishing touch, frost the cake with your favorite buttercream icing, or add some crunch with:

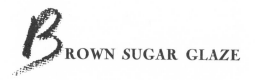

BROWN SUGAR GLAZE

2 tablespoons butter
¾ cup light brown sugar
¼ cup water

Pinch of salt
½ teaspoon banana extract
½ cup chopped pecans

Bring the butter, sugar, water, and salt to a boil over medium-high heat. Cook for 3 minutes. Off the heat, stir in the banana extract and pecans and immediately spoon the glaze over the top rim of the cake until a pretty crust builds up and drizzles down the sides. This version of the cake will keep moist for many days.

Reading Terminal Market
Philadelphia, Pennsylvania

Reading Terminal seems to me the grande dame of city markets. Close to one hundred years old and holding, the splendid old building next to the Reading Terminal Headhouse, where steam engines used to be garaged, has seen some rocky times. Like many city markets, its fortunes declined when Philadelphia's Center City went into a spin. In 1975, it was a gloomy place with many vermin and few merchants, and letters calling it a hazard and demanding it be closed started appearing regularly in the newspaper. In 1980, when the city council voted to revitalize Center City, Reading Company officials decided to give new life to the market. They hired David O'Neil, a young, forward-looking dreamer, as market manager and slowly the market quickened.

The Amish were invited back to sell, and they came from Lancaster County bringing prime produce. Reading had always had famous local food specialties—cheese steak sandwiches, hot pretzels, and Bassett's Ice Cream—which upped the butterfat to twenty-eight percent the day that Khrushchev came to visit. The new market encouraged a wealth of new ethnic food and grocery stands. There were festival days, hay rides around the market, and lots of used-book stalls that encouraged people to linger and browse. A new crop of gourmets drawn back to the market discovered Harry Ochs, the best butcher in Philadelphia, still at work and full of advice.

"The reason my lamb is so good is that I always buy female lambs, they don't run around as much. When you buy a leg of lamb, buy the left one. They scratch with their right and that makes it tougher meat. I came here when I was a kid in 1947 and worked full time with my father, Harry Ochs the second. I spent more time here than at home. We used to do London broils, larded fillets, then beef went out of style and people went on to veal. Now that's under fire so people buy white meat chicken and pork, though now beef is coming back again. We got lots of repeat buyers and gourmets, and they can be pretty picky at times. When they used to get snappy with my father, he'd say, 'Harry, my boy, we got to calm our nerves somewhat,' and we'd slip into the cooler where he'd take one swallow from a jug of Monk's Scotch whisky he kept hidden there. My father worked here until he was eighty-three and he ate a piece of red meat every day of his life. Over there's my son Harry the fourth."

One of the best indications that a market has stabilized is when a wonderful restaurant establishes itself in its heart. Reading is lucky to have Jack McDavid's Down Home Diner serving up Potlikker and Brunswick stews, Jambalaya, Corn Bread Pizza, and old-time shortbread, and Jack's lucky to have the farmers at the market. "I get beef, lamb, venison, duck, geese from them. My farmer goes out, sweeps the snow off the lettuce, and I have it fresh all winter long. Eggs are one hour out of the hen . . . eighty-five percent of what I use grows sixty miles from here. I couldn't ask for any better ingredients."

Seemingly all is well in the market now. Hoards of City Center workers take their lunch break here, no one is afraid anymore of its derelict depths, but other possible threats await, as David O'Neil suggests:

"Markets are such fragile places. This beautiful nineteenth-century building in all its neglected, falling down grandeur, was a living ruin. We opened up the sight lines and then let a hundred different ideas coming from a hundred different imaginations go to work. It mirrors the ethnic mix of the neighborhood and makes things so much more vivid than having a single architect's vision. In the old days, you'd have chickens and game with their feet tied hanging from those beams there, now we have to have sneeze guards in front of the meat, so it's not as romantic. Health departments do tend to desensitize the experience. You also have to avoid too much fast food, just keep it real as much as possible. Current threats? Well, the Reading Company has plans to expand the market into the adjoining engine house. There's a 150-space parking garage and a thirty-two story office tower planned over our heads and the proposed convention center next door wants to take some of our space, so I'm anxious over the future of the market. It would be a terrible waste to lose this precious place."

If you have never had real southern-style shortening bread, you are in for a treat. This recipe, from Jack McDavid's splendid Down Home Diner in Reading Terminal market, is baked in the shape of traditional shortbread, but contains much more "shortening" than that crisp hard cookie of Scottish origin. The interior will remain soft and chewy and have a butter-slick look, but the top and bottom will be crisp.

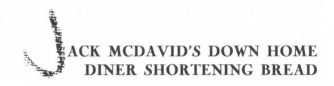

JACK MCDAVID'S DOWN HOME DINER SHORTENING BREAD

SERVES 8

2 cups all-purpose flour
1½ cups sugar
¼ teaspoon salt
¼ teaspoon grated nutmeg

2 sticks unsalted butter, chilled
1 cup coarsely chopped pecans
1½ teaspoons vanilla extract
1 egg

Preheat the oven to 350°F. Butter a 9- or 10-inch round cake pan.

In a large bowl, combine the dry ingredients. Cut the butter into cubes and work it into the dry ingredients until there are no discernible lumps. Work to a fine texture, much smaller than oatmeal.

Stir the pecans into the flour mixture.

Stir the vanilla and egg together. Gently drizzle it over the dry ingredients and give easy stirs (I use my hand here). Let the mixture just combine without compressing it into a firm, pasty dough.

Place the dough in the pan and press down gently to even the surface, but do not compact.

Bake for 20 minutes. Turn the heat up to 475°F. and bake for 10 minutes more to crisp the top and bottom.

Remove from the oven, place the pan on a cooling rack, and cool completely. The shortening bread will be very soft and seem unbaked at first, but it will crisp and harden as it cools. Cut it into wedges to serve. Delicious with unsweetened whipped cream.

Lexington Market
Baltimore, Maryland

*S*till on its original site, the Lexington market has been in existence for two hundred years. Washington, Jefferson, Daniel Webster, and Oliver Wendell Holmes all visited the market during their lifetimes, and in the mid 1800s, fifty thousand people went to market each Saturday to buy from over six hundred farmers. Housed in two block-large buildings, the now decidedly downscale market is plump with funky ethnic eateries, lottery stands, delis, bakery outlets, and meat stalls. I particularly like the east market that slants down toward Eutaw Street. Full of small, square, block stands, it looks like a child's toy town laid out before you. Breakfast grills border the left edge, and in the center stalls you can trace immigrant waves on the overhead signs. The city's wealth of German settlers left the bakeries—Berger's, Huber's, Muhly's; the Italians left the produce; today the oriental population is largely manning the old stalls and starting new ones. There are also black-owned bakeries with rich, heavy cakes and navy bean pies.

The seafood drawn from Chesapeake Bay is wonderful. From imperial crabcakes at John W. Fraidley's to the tempura fried soft-shells at the Japanese stands, and the swarms of fresh crabs scrabbling in their bushel baskets, the crab seems to dominate the market. I watched a sorter dressed in hip boots and a black rubber apron carefully grading crabs into five piles: males, small females, dead, too young (their translucent shells have a veined, unborn quality), and large females, most of whom are reared up on thin monster legs, their chelae locked in combat with their nearest sister.

If you like crab, you will particularly enjoy this witty, delicious play on a classic French preparation. Rillettes are traditionally made of pork that is gently cooked in lard over a period of time until the meat turns a rich brown. Then it is pounded in a mortar, placed in preserving jars, and topped with a thin layer of lard. These preserves are eaten with mustard and cornichons as a pâté might be.

"RILLETTES" OF CRAB

SERVES 10

1½ sticks unsalted butter
½ cup shredded scallions, white and tender green parts, cut into 1½-inch lengths
Juice of 1 lemon
Zest scraped delicately from 1 lemon
1 pretty, whole bay leaf
¼ teaspoon paprika
1 tablespoon mustard

Pinch of cayenne
1 clove garlic, pressed
½ teaspoon salt
Generous grindings of coarse black pepper
1 tablespoon red or white wine vinegar
1 pound crab meat
¼ cup minced fresh parsley
Whole black or green peppercorns

Have all the ingredients ready before you start cooking.

Melt 1 stick of butter in a large frying pan. Add the scallions, lemon juice and zest, the bay leaf, seasonings, and vinegar. Simmer for 2 minutes. Set aside and reserve the bay leaf.

Add the crab meat, turn up the heat, and, using a fork, cook and stir for 2 minutes. Shred the crab as you stir and turn. When finished, stir in the parsley, then pack the crab mixture into a small, attractive, rustic dish. Press the surface down flat.

Melt the remaining ½ stick of butter and pour it over the surface. Press in the reserved bay leaf and scatter a few peppercorns around the leaf at the center. Refrigerate when cool. This dish seems to taste even better a day or two after it is made. Good spread on crackers or toast points at a party or as a stand-and-nibble appetizer.

Any lover of pumpkin and sweet potato pie will like this Lexington market navy bean offering. People have a hard time guessing what the main ingredient is.

NAVY BEAN PIE

SERVES 8

For the Filling:

¾ cup dried navy beans
6 cups water
1 14-ounce can sweetened condensed milk
½ cup packed light brown sugar
¼ cup heavy cream
2 eggs
½ teaspoon ground cinnamon

½ teaspoon ground ginger
Large pinch of ground cloves (6 heads)
½ teaspoon salt

1 10-inch unbaked piecrust
Sweetened whipped cream

Rinse the beans and pick out any peculiarities. Place the beans in a saucepan and cover with the water and the lid of the pot. Bring to a boil, cook for 2 minutes, then turn off the heat and let the beans soften for 1 hour.

Return the beans to a simmer, cover, and cook for 15 minutes, or until puree-soft.

Preheat the oven to 350°F.

Drain the beans well and place them and all the remaining filling ingredients in the bowl of a food processor (or do this in 2 batches in a blender). Puree until smooth.

Pour the bean mixture into the piecrust and bake for 45 minutes. Check the pie about 35 minutes along, and if the top seems to be getting too brown, slip a sheet of aluminum foil over the surface for the last few minutes of baking.

Let the pie cool on a rack for 30 to 45 minutes before cutting. Serve topped with whipped cream.

Soulard Market
St. Louis, Missouri

Soulard Market comes the closest of any market in America to having the feeling of an old world "bazaar." Set plumb in the middle of St. Louis's near South Side, the market has been in existence since 1779 when the wealthy merchant Antoine Pierre Soulard, whose family escaped the French Revolution, started selling apples from his orchard on the spot. It survived the Civil War, a death-dealing tornado, and the Depression, and today it sells a variety of produce and peculiar objects. There is a distinct "foreign" cast to this market—odd stands of imported spices, tamarind, peculiar pods and nodes and rhizomes, scenting waters that remind me of West Africa. Rubber shoes and velvet slippers covered with bead work and sequins that would look at home in a middle-eastern souk, rub up against T-shirts with I LOVE MICHAEL JACKSON and ROLLS-ROYCE printed on them. There is an Avon Lady, a Watkins Lady, and two or three church fund-raiser stands. At the Last Days Pentecostal Church booth you will find lemon-fragrant cream cheese pound cakes made by the pastor's wife. At the St. Mary of Victories Hungarian Catholic Church stand, Margaret Rudy sells gooey cakes and middle-European baked goods. Seems Highway 55 got planted right through the middle of the old parish. Where the church used to have two hundred at mass, only thirty attend now, so the church custodian bakes to supplement the Sunday Collection and to keep the old church solvent.

Because the neighborhood is poor, the market functions as a community center. HUD and welfare services interview here; late in the day there's a flurry of price cutting, bargains to be had on less-than-perfect produce. There's hickory-smoked bacon, hocks, jowls, neck bones, chicken feet—inexpensive meat meant for frugal stews.

The German/Slavic neighborhood provides a wealth of old-style "characters" who vend with European flair and who can draw small crowds when they're on a roll. Uncle Ben "The Kiddies' Friend" Abkenmeir, purveyor of butter and cheese and a good German who looks like Zero Mostel's cousin, yells after the customers:

"Hey, you're rich, you got your health."

"Hey, you, buy some cheese. A sandwich without cheese is like a kiss without a squeeze."

"Hey, do you know what they call a cow that just gave birth? Decaffeinated."

There are soft pretzels, German bratwurst sandwiches, sticky chicken wings fried by Chinh Smith, newly arrived from Vietnam. And Soulard market is one of the few places in America where live animals are sold. Ducks and rabbits wait in cages for their largely foreign buyers. Pity that most old city markets can't have the hanging game and the live chickens they used to sell. How splendid to hear cocks crowing in the market.

On celebration days, a black-cloaked actress, a living reincarnation of Madam Soulard, old Antoine's widow, floats through the market, speaking only French, a gentle ghostly personification of the market's sweet long-standing heritage.

One of the lucky things to find in a farmers' market is someone newly immigrated from another culture, sharing a specialty from their homeland. In Soulard market, Chinh Smith fries chicken wings to a crisp, then lets them marinate in a hot spicy oil. The wings reminded me somewhat of Buffalo chicken wings. If we substitute vegetables with an oriental bent for celery, and Peanut Satay Sauce for the blue cheese dressing, we have:

BUFFALO/BANGKOK CHICKEN WINGS

SERVES 4–6 AS A FIRST COURSE

For the Marinade:

⅓ cup soy sauce

3 tablespoons hot oil (available in oriental stores or food sections)

2 tablespoon rice wine vinegar

2 tablespoons peanut oil

1 tablespoon brown sugar

2 cloves garlic, pressed

3–4 slices fresh gingerroot, or ¼ teaspoon ground ginger

10–12 chicken wings

1 quart peanut oil for frying

1 daikon radish, scraped, cut into long sticks, and crisped in ice water

1 bunch scallions, tender green and white parts, trimmed, washed, chilled

1 small bunch cilantro

Peanut Satay Sauce (recipe follows)

Combine all the marinade ingredients in a large ovenproof bowl and set aside.

There are 2 joints in a chicken wing. Cut through both of them with a heavy knife or cleaver so that the wing is divided into the small "drummet" end, the middle section, and the small bony tip. Discard the bony tips, then rinse and dry the other sections.

Heat the oil in an electric wok, deep fryer, or any other deep-sided frying utensil of your choice. The temperature should be 375°F. (a cube of bread will sizzle, bob to the surface, and fry brown within a minute). Fry the wing sections in 3 batches for 8 minutes each. Strain out the chicken, blot the pieces briefly on paper toweling, and place in the marinade. Continue until all are fried. (The wings can be placed in a warming oven for 30 minutes at this point or gently rewarmed later. They need at minimum a 30-minute marination.)

Serve the wings slightly warm or at room temperature. Place daikon strips and scallions on each plate, add a garnish of cilantro, and give each person a portion of peanut Satay sauce in which to dip the chicken and vegetables.

—✂—

PEANUT SATAY SAUCE

2 tablespoons peanut oil

1 small onion, minced

2 large cloves garlic

1 tablespoon minced lemongrass (the tender inner portions, optional)

¼ teaspoon ground cumin

¼ teaspoon curry powder

1 teaspoon hot oil

2 tablespoons lemon juice

2 tablespoons sugar

Large pinch of cinnamon

1 tablespoon rice wine vinegar

3 tablespoons soy sauce

1 tablespoon sesame oil

1 cup skinless good-quality peanuts

Over low heat, heat the peanut oil; cook the onion, garlic, and lemongrass until the onion is limp. Add all the remaining ingredients *except* the peanuts and stir for 1 minute while the sugar melts. Remove from the heat.

Grind the peanuts in a blender or food processor. Feed in the onion mixture and continue to puree. Add about ¼ cup of water slowly as the machine works, and the sauce will come perfectly smooth. Add another tablespoon of water if necessary to bring the sauce to a dipping consistency that pleases you.

Here is a good and logical variation on coleslaw that uses all oriental ingredients. Even in the smallest of farmers' markets, it seems, there are orientals growing and sharing their native produce.

CHINESE "COLESLAW"

SERVES 8

For the Salad:

4 cups packed, shredded Napa (Chinese) cabbage

4 scallions, white and tender green parts, sliced thin

1 cup mung bean sprouts

1 carrot, grated

1/2 cup slivered almonds

10 snow pea pods, cut into long, thin shred

For the Dressing:

1 tablespoons peanut oil

2 tablespoons sesame oil

2 tablespoons rice wine or white wine vinegar

1 tablespoon brown sugar

1/2 teaspoon salt

3 tablespoons soy sauce

3 tablespoons toasted sesame seeds

Mix all the salad ingredients in a bowl.

Combine all the dressing ingredients and stir into the salad, mixing until the vegetables are coated. Refrigerate for 30 minutes.

Stir the ingredients (the vegetables will have watered out somewhat), then refrigerate for another 30 minutes. The salad will appear quite wilted. Strain the salad by pressing it down firmly in a colander and put all the expressed liquid in a small saucepan.

Boil the juices down to approximately 1/4 cup and restir it into the slaw.

A delicious make-ahead slaw-type salad, this takes on more character each day it ages.

CALICO CABBAGE

SERVES 10

1 medium head of green cabbage, quartered

1 small green bell pepper

1 large sweet red bell pepper

1 large yellow bell pepper

2 carrots, scraped

1 small bunch scallions, white and green
   parts, sliced (around ½ cup)

¼ cup minced chives

½ cup white wine vinegar

½ cup water

½ cup sugar

¼ cup olive oil

2 teaspoons salt

½ teaspoon black pepper

1 clove garlic, pressed

Remove a layer of outside leaves from the cabbage. Cut out the cores from each wedge, then slice the cabbage paper thin and place in the selected pot.

Seed all the peppers. Cut them into strips, and cut the strips into ⅓-inch diamonds or triangles. Add to the cabbage.

Cut the carrots to the approximate size of the peppers. Add the scallions, chives, and carrots to the cabbage mixture.

Place the remaining ingredients in a small saucepan and bring to a boil. Immediately pour the mixture over the cabbage, and stir to coat.

Place a plate down into the pot and press it over the cabbage. Add a weight (a small can or two of tomatoes will work), then cover the pot and place it in the refrigerator.

After 24 hours, drain half the liquid off the cabbage. The salad can be eaten at this point, but it is good the second day, even better the third, and best of all the fourth day.

Here's a piquant onion dish—sweet, sour, tart, that goes splendidly with lamb.

TAMARIND-ONION GRATIN

SERVES 6

2 large or 3 medium red onions, cored and
   sliced thin
½ cup orange juice
5 tablespoons tamarind paste (available in
   Indian sections of gourmet stores)
¼ teaspoon ground ginger

1 tablespoon brown sugar
½ teaspoon salt
Fresh ground pepper to taste
4 tablespoons (½ stick) butter
1 cup firm or dried bread crumbs

Bring a pot of salted water to a boil. Place the onions in the water, return to a boil, and cook for 4 minutes. Strain the onions out into a sieve or colander and press out all possible moisture.

Preheat the oven to 350°F. Butter a 10-inch gratin or baking dish.

In the same pot you cooked the onions, mix the orange juice, tamarind paste, ginger, sugar, salt, pepper, and 2 tablespoons of the butter. Cook over medium heat until the butter and sugar are melted. Stir in the onions and mix until evenly coated. Pour the onion mixture into the buttered baking dish.

Melt the remaining 2 tablespoons of butter, add the crumbs, and stir until coated. Scatter the crumbs over the top of the onions.

Bake for 45 minutes, at which point the onions will be nicely amber colored, with honey-gold slicks of caramel appearing along the sides.

This salad is a great way to use a summer's excess of cucumbers. Grated, salted, mixed with yogurt and Indian spices, the dish provides a cool counterpart to any piquant dish you might cook.

 RATED CUCUMBER SALAD

SERVES 6–8

4–5 cucumbers, peeled, halved lengthwise, and seeded
1 teaspoon salt
2 large carrots, scraped
1 1/2 cups plain yogurt
Large pinch of cayenne pepper
1/4 teaspoon paprika

1/4 teaspoon lemon zest
Juice of 1 lemon
Freshly ground pepper to taste
1 teaspoon lightly toasted cuminseed
1 teaspoon chopped mint or to taste, plus a sprig of mint

Grate the cucumbers through the thick blade of a hand grater or the medium-holed blade of a machine. Place the cucumbers in a bowl, sprinkle on the salt, and set aside for 20 minutes.

Grate the carrots into long, fine strands.

Place the yogurt in a bowl and whisk it smooth. Add the cayenne, paprika, lemon zest, lemon juice, pepper to taste, and toasted cuminseed. Stir in the grated carrots.

Place a colander or sieve in the sink. Taking up the cucumbers by handfuls, squeeze them out over the sieve as firmly as possible so that they release all their watery juices. Stir the cucumbers and mint into the yogurt. Refrigerate for at least 1 hour. Taste for seasoning before serving as coldness sometimes dilutes the effect of seasoning. Garnish the salad with a sprig of mint. This holds well for 2 or 3 days.

If you've never cooked cauliflower in good old French toast egg batter, you are in for a real treat—and you will find that even children like the vegetable in this golden form.

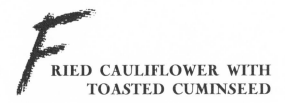

FRIED CAULIFLOWER WITH TOASTED CUMINSEED

SERVES 4–6

1 medium head cauliflower, washed and
   cored
2 eggs
3 tablespoons milk
½ teaspoon salt

¼ teaspoon turmeric
1 tablespoon whole cuminseed
Salt and freshly ground pepper to taste
¼ cup peanut or other vegetable oil for
   frying

Cut and divide the cauliflower into medium-sized flowerets around 1½ inches wide. Cook the cauliflower, preferably in a steamer to retain nutrients, until it is just tender, around 5 minutes. This step can be done ahead.

Combine the eggs, milk, salt, and turmeric. Place the cuminseed in an ungreased frying pan and toast over a medium-hot burner. Shake the pan and soon the seeds will turn a deeper shade of brown and start to pop and snap. Remove from heat. Add half the seeds to the egg mixture.

Heat the peanut oil in a frying pan. Dip the flowerets in egg and fry in 2 batches. The pieces should be browned on 2 sides.

Place in a serving dish, sprinkle lightly with salt and pepper, and scatter on the remaining cuminseed.

Here's an Indian vegetable dish that moves away from the usual preconceived notion of what to do with eggplant. Instead of olive oil, butter lends its nutty fragrance. Instead of parsley, a generous sprinkling of cilantro is used for garnish, and I think you will enjoy the little "smoking" technique at the end. Be sure to choose and reserve a good onion "skin" ahead of time.

SMOKY EGGPLANT

SERVES 6

2 medium-large eggplants
8 tablespoons (1 stick) butter
1 medium onion, sliced thin
3 cloves garlic, minced
2 large pinches of cayenne
1/4 teaspoon ground ginger

1/4 teaspoon paprika
2 teaspoons salt
Freshly ground pepper to taste
1 rounded cup onion skin
Fresh cilantro leaves

Place the whole eggplants in a pan in the oven. Turn the oven to 375°F. and roast for 1 hour, or until the eggplants look like pathetic wizened things, collapsed in upon themselves and completely soft.

When you can handle them, cut the eggplants in half and scrape out the meat from the skin. Discard the skin. (This can be done ahead of time.)

Heat 5 tablespoons of the butter in a large frying pan or saucepan with a tight-fitting lid. Add the onion and sauté over medium heat until the onion is completely soft. Add the garlic and seasonings and continue to stir and cook until the onion is browned. Add the eggplant, and stir and fry for 2 minutes. Turn off the heat.

Place a metal object (a knife sharpener, screwdriver, the end of a metal spatula, a small metal weight, or 2 quarters failing all else) over heat or in a pan under the broiler. Let the metal turn red hot (Indians might use a charcoal brick).

Form a small cup from the outer skins of an onion. You may need 2 or 3 layers of parchment skins in order to make as much of a seal as possible. Nestle the "cup" in the middle of the eggplant. Melt the remaining 3 tablespoons of butter to the sizzle point. Pour the butter into the onion-skin "cup," rest the hot metal in the butter (if you use coins, just drop them in with tongs) until it smokes, then immediately clap the lid on the eggplant (the knife sharpener or screwdriver will stick out the side). Leave covered for 10 minutes.

To serve, stir the smoked butter into the eggplant and discard the onion cup. Sprinkle with cilantro and serve at once.

— ❧ —

In Soulard market I finally found a cake that I had long heard about. Gooey Butter Cake is a St. Louis tradition, available in certain bakeries at certain times; never, it seemed, when I was there. At Soulard you can surely find it at least in the Saturday market. At the fund-raising booth run by St. Mary's Hungarian Church, huge pans of it sat in all their gooey golden glory and it was hard to walk by without feeling the sudden religious urge to contribute to the upkeep of that fine old St. Louis building. A young man who saw me purchasing a piece suggested that it was easy to make, then rattled off a recipe—one box of white cake, with pudding added, topped with one box of confectioners' sugar mixed with an egg and eight ounces of cream cheese. Claimed it was the finest tool of seduction he knew. I came back home and worked out this chocolate version, which I think is even better.

CHOCOLATE GOOEY BUTTER CAKE

SERVES 8–10

For the Topping:

8 ounces soft whipped cream cheese, at room
    temperature
3 ounces bittersweet chocolate, melted

1 egg
1 1-pound box confectioners' sugar, sifted

For the Cake:

1½ cups all-purpose flour
1 cup sugar
¼ cup cocoa powder
½ teaspoon salt
2 teaspoons baking powder

1 stick butter, melted
2 eggs
½ cup milk
1 teaspoon vanilla extract

Preheat the oven to 350°F. Butter a 9-x-13-inch cake pan.

Prepare the topping first. Whip together the cream cheese, melted chocolate, and egg. When smooth, stir in the sifted confectioner's sugar. Set aside.

To make the cake, mix the dry ingredients, preferably in the bowl of a mixer.

In another bowl, stir together the butter, eggs, milk, and vanilla. Slowly add the liquid ingredients to the dry ingredients and beat for 3 minutes. Pour the batter into the prepared cake pan. Gently spread the cream cheese topping over the cake. Bake for 40 minutes.

Cool the cake completely and then some (a good 4 hours) before cutting. This stays moist and delicious for 3 days.

Soulard market, the Last Days Pentecostal Church bake sale. The pastor's wife, Mae Johnson, makes a Lemon Cream Cheese Pound Cake that is delicious. Here's my version, with infused lemon sugar syrup for pockets of rich flavor.

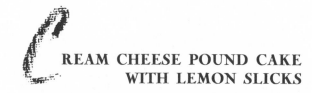

CREAM CHEESE POUND CAKE WITH LEMON SLICKS

SERVES 12–15

For the Cake:

2¼ cups sugar
4 ounces cream cheese, at room temperature
1 stick unsalted butter
5 eggs

Zest of 2 lemons
Juice of 2 large lemons, strained
Pinch of salt
2 cups flour

For the Glaze:

⅔ cup sugar

⅔ cup water

Preheat the oven to 325°F. Generously butter a 10-inch tube or bundt pan. Add a small scoop of sugar to the pan and rotate until a thick coat of sugar adheres to all sides.

Place the cream cheese and butter in a mixer and cream until blended and fluffy. Gradually add the sugar and continue beating. Let the sugar feed in slowly and whip it for 5 minutes to incorporate fully. Add the eggs one at a time and beat for 1 minute after each addition. Add the lemon zest, 1 tablespoon of the lemon juice, and the salt. At low speed, add the flour and mix just until blended.

Pour the batter into the prepared pan. Bake for 1 hour, or until a toothpick inserted in the middle comes out perfectly dry.

Ten minutes before the cake has finished baking, make the glaze. Place the sugar, water, and the remainder of the strained lemon juice in a small pan. Bring to a boil, then simmer for 5 minutes until the mixture is syrupy.

Take the cake from the oven and immediately poke some holes in the middle with a bamboo skewer. Drizzle half the lemon syrup over these holes and let it absorb. Cool the cake for 5 minutes, then run a knife around the mold and turn the cake out onto a cooling rack. Poke small holes in the top and patiently let the rest of the syrup sink in.

Cool completely, then wrap tightly. The cake should remain moist for days.

T E X A S

Dallas Farm Market

THE DALLAS FARM MARKET HAS BEEN MORE OR less in place since World War II. A new shed-style facility has been added from time to time so that there are now four great gray arms stretching under red, green, yellow, and orange roofs on either side of Pearl Street right in the heart of pricy downtown Dallas. It's a thumb nose kind of place—plain, squat, and gutsy over against the Mylar glitz of the shiny Dallas skyline above. It's another one of those markets that is threatened by proposed freeways, by a possible football stadium, by developers' fanciful schemes. But right now, on a late September day, it's looking "mighty sturdy" and "real fine" as Ted Langford, the market administrator, would say.

We stride the long stretches of covered stalls, me hurrying to keep up with his lope (they grow long men in Texas—men who can wear jewelry and still look like men; men who have to grow tall to fit into those Stetsons). Past strands of chilies, sweet potatoes, piles of muscadine and scuppernong grapes on the verge of fester, past pecans and plump southwestern produce we go while he points out the people I should talk to.

"We've been here since the late thirties. This is about as true a market as you can get these days. Way back then they planted those pear trees you see outside. They look right odd in the middle of all the concrete, but see all those pears up there? Those pears are symbols, and when they fall on people's heads I tell you it's an honor. Nobody's ever going to hurt those pear trees if I can help it. Bringing a market like this back to life if it ever got moved would be tough. I've watched my daddy and my granddaddy kill themselves over the years and die in debt farming. It would have saved their necks if they had this place. People come here from all over. We had a little old gal come in from Arkansas even, but mostly they're Texans. There's the Hollowells, they've been here forever . . . live here . . . sell sweet potatoes. There's Thomas Grimes and his sugarcane, and that guy who sells Noonday onions. Did you know they take Texas sweet onions and put them in Vidalia sacks, and take them to Georgia? Really, all those Georgia onions come from Noonday onion sweet stock." (That's a variation on a line I've heard before. New York farmers confide that unscrupulous Vermonters sneak across the state line, buy New York maple syrup, and sell it as Vermont's own; Washingtonians claim Vancouverites steal into the USA for most of their "Canadian" produce—love all these snippets of regional paranoia.)

"Let's see if old Billy Jack Lynch is there selling watermelons in the green shed—yup. You'll want to talk to him, but go holler at Linda Moreno there, first."

LINDA MORENO ON OKRA AND ONIONS

Right away you've got to like her, a mop of curly black hair, crinkly eyes, dangling earrings, glamour-girl smile and hard, hard-worked hands. All the time she talks she's sorting onions.

"I first started coming to the market when I was six. My parents would drop me to sell after school as I was the oldest of fourteen children. People in the market kind of took care of me, but the customers would sometimes take advantage on prices. I'd be here all Saturday and Sunday and every day after school until ten at night. It was all right that I was here, though men started to cause me trouble when I turned fourteen. It was a hard life. One year we'd make out real good, then next not so good. These days I get up at 2:30 A.M. every market morning. Get breakfast ready at 4:00, then drive from seventy miles east at Caddo Mills. First I sell wholesale, then I set up table to start retail by 8:00 A.M. I leave at three in the afternoon, go home, fix supper for six, eat at 7:00, and get to bed by 10:00. In between, I look after fifteen hands who do our field of sixty acres.

"We grow mainly onions and okra. The onions we raise from seed. We start pulling them when they're green. They get bigger and bigger and when the top blades fall over in the field, you know they're mature—that's when you can tell onions are completely dry. While they grow you watch out for onion thrips that make little spots on the top of the greens and turn the blades yellow and white. And then there are the cutworms that'll eat the plant bottoms.

"We put a blade on the cultivator, run it deep to loosen the onion roots, then workers pull them out and put them in piles to dry for a day in the field. Next day we clip off the blades and they dry in the field overnight. We put those old onions on big tables with runner belts on them. People size and grade and take out the stinkers, then we bag and tie them up.

"How should people store onions? Well, they'll put down for three or four months if you don't let sunlight hit them in storage. Keep them in dark, cool, dry places, not by windows where they will turn green and bitter tasting. When you buy them, pick yellow or white onions with no tint of green. Pick ones with lots of layers of skin. They keep better."

When the onions are neatly heaped, she opens a big sack of okra and starts to sort.

"Now, okra is an entirely different matter to grow. You plant okra, then side dress it, fertilize it on either side. The plants grow to three feet tall and up. Overnight one day you see it all blooms, then it seems the next day there are little okras. You break them off by hand, never cut them, but you better wear rubber gloves or the acid will eat your fingers.

"The leaves are scant first, and it's easy to pick, then it gets harder when the foliage grows thick and the okra grows under the leaves. It bears for four months, and the hotter it gets, the better. The more you pick, the more it keeps makin' and makin'. You go into the stands with a basket on each hip hanging from your belt. The plants will get so high in time, they'll cover you up.

"Now, okra is funny and I'm going to tell you its secret. When we were little my parents would say, 'Hey, kids, why don't you go play in the okra. Don't just walk around in there,' they'd say, 'bend down and touch the plants.' They taught us to stroke the leaves one by one. If you pay attention to it just like a little baby, it bears more. With fourteen kids in our family, we must have touched a million leaves.

"My mother fried lots of okra. She'd cut off both ends then leave them whole like potatoes. To this day I don't like it boiled, but I love okra gumbo and okra cooked with tomatoes and onions. Raw okra salad is good for ulcers . . . the slime settles the stomach.

"I'd like my boys to go into farming, but I don't think they will, and the girls were never like me. What's going to happen when we older farmers aren't here is everybody's question."

The earrings flash and sparkle as she shakes her head. By this time the okra sits in neat, scaled-by-the-eye one-pound heaps.

LINDA MORENO'S OKRA AND ONION GRATIN

SERVES 4–6

6 tablespoons (¾ stick) unsalted butter

1 large or 2 medium onions, halved, cored,
    and sliced thin

½ cup water

1 teaspoon sugar

1½ pounds small tender okra, rinsed,
    stemmed, halved

2 large tomatoes, coarsely chopped

½ teaspoon salt

3 tablespoons salsa, or 2 teaspoon hot sauce

2 cups firm but not dry bread crumbs

Freshly ground pepper to taste

Preheat the oven to 350°F. Butter a 6-cup gratin dish.

Melt 2 tablespoons of the butter in a large frying pan. Add the onion, water, and sugar. Cover and simmer until the onion is tender. Uncover and let the onion fry in the butter until it turns golden.

Add the okra, tomatoes, salt, and salsa or hot sauce. Cover the pan and simmer just until the okra is tender, around 2 minutes. The mixture should have a bit of juice to it.

While the okra is cooking, melt the remaining 4 tablespoons of butter in another frying pan. Stir in the bread crumbs and moisten them with the butter. Mix a good third of the bread crumbs into the okra mixture.

Smooth the okra mixture into the baking dish. Grind on fresh pepper. Scatter the remaining crumbs over the top and put the gratin to bake in the oven for about 25 minutes, or until the crumbs are crisp and lightly browned.

THOMAS GRIMES ON SUGARCANE

Down the row from Linda Moreno is Thomas Grimes, seller of sugarcane. As Linda is chatty, Thomas Grimes is terse, a tall man of few words. Surrounded by a small cut forest of bamboolike stalks, he condenses all of life and sugarcanery in a few short words:

"Growin'? You open up a furrow with a middle buster that throws the dirt both ways. October you plant cuttings eight inches deep. They stay all winter. Take a disk in February and cut 'um back. Three to twenty stalks come out of the eyes in each growth hill. They need lots of irrigation. We start stripping and cutting in September. Five feet or taller, we sell by the stalk. We take the short stuff and run it through the mill. Cook ten gallons of that juice down and you'll have one gallon of syrup. In World War II, they used that syrup for cakes, coffee, everything. Now it's just pancakes and waffles. Or you can take some syrup and mix it with corn chops and brew it up and you'll have twenty-seven-percent liquor that will knock your head off.

"In the oil boom days when I was six or seven, my daddy would drive us to Kilgore with a load of two hundred stalks. We'd sell one to a school kid for five cents. They'd peel it, cut off a little, chew it. Today Iranians like it. Mexicans and blacks like it too.

"Now we sell twelve stalks to a bundle. It's sweetest up top where the purple joints are. You can whittle on it, chew it, the darn stuff will stay good for six weeks. When it's knee high, them workers start chewin' on it. They cut it down with a machete and tote it —that's heavy work and they need the sugar, but you don't want to go drinking too much of cane juice now, ma'am. Take it gradual. It works worse than a laxative.

"In 1834, my family got a grant from Mexico for our land. We have two acres in cane. Half goes to make oh, four or five hundred gallons of syrup. The rest goes to chew. My great grandfather, my father, now me—we all grew cane. Today my son works in the oil field. When I'm dead and gone, it's over with. Guess that's about all I've got to say."

Thomas Grimes tips his Stetson and turns back to his wares.

If you see fresh sugarcane, buy it for the children in your life. Sniff the stalk if possible to see that it has a fresh, clean scent—there should be no odor of fermentation. If you have a choice, choose thinner sections, as sugarcane is sweeter at the top of the stalk. If you buy a big stalk, you can cut a slice three inches above and three inches below one of the joints. Plant it in a pot, cover it with soil, water it well, and leave it in a warm, sunny window. In most cases, green shoots will come up from the nodes at the ring around the joint.

TO EAT FRESH SUGARCANE

Cut in 4- or 5-inch sections between the joints. You can use a heavy cleaver or knife. Slap the knife down on the cane, then hit the top with a hammer to tap it through if you wish.

Peel off the outer green layer. Cut the interior into strips exactly like carrot sticks. They can be sucked and chewed on immediately, but I like to chill the strips first.

The residue, after you've chewed out all the juice, is called bagasse. (The same word is used for grape skins left after pressing.) You can make paper from this fiber, but you won't find a recipe for that in this book.

BILLY JACK LYNCH ON MELONS

"Hey come over here, girl," yells Billy Jack Lynch, teetering on a chair on the back of his melon truck. "Old Ted Langford says you want to know about melons, you come to me. There's three things I know—women, Holstein cows, and watermelons."

Billy Jack Lynch ("should be retired but isn't") is full of sayings like "I'm hell when I'm well and I ain't sick much," and when he's not talking faster than a mule can balk, he's singing me a little song and stamping out the rhythm with his high-heeled boot.

> *Watermelon, watermelon*
> *Good and juicy*
> *One for you and two for Lucy.*
> *Eat the meat,*
> *Pickle the rind,*
> *Save the seed to plantin' time.*

"See that man over there? He tried to grow melons but he ain't got no sense. People, they think you just throw seeds out and they grow. Well, four out of five years will be good, and on a watermelon ordinarily you'll get your money back, but this was the most difficult year I ever witnessed. Cost us $50,000 this year, ordinarily it costs $30,000. First off, the high water was bad. Too much water hurts a melon and the vines get long but no fruits get along, get it? Three rains in a season is what you want. We started with three hundred acres, planted and fertilized at the same time, then had to reseed the whole thing. I tell you we had to lay off them melons three times and still lost seventy-five acres with all that water. Then you hoe, weed, thin the plants, keep the little green beetle bugs off . . . nine times out of ten you need to spray for lice and aphids and prune off the little rotten melons. From the time you plant in March, it's 110 to 120 days to a ripe melon.

"Do I plant by the moon? That's like a black cat running across the street. I just don't pay no mind to it. When it's a good year, it cost 15¢ a pound to make melons and we eat melon every meal. When it cost $1.50 a pound, we don't eat them. If you have a bad year, you make $300 an acre and it's a sorry crop; $600 to $700 is middling; $1,000 an acre is good, and above that is gravy. If someone claims he makes $1,500 an acre, I think that's his braggin' price.

"How do you tell a melon is ripe? See that green shiny one with the dead stem? That means it's off a dead vine. Look for a good green stem that shows the mother vine is putting out good. Look for a nice light color in the long Jubilees. Little Black Diamonds you just have to hit or miss, but the redder the flesh the better. You want red meat with few white seeds. When you see 'um cut open, if it's cracked meat it's too ripe and the meat is grainy. Some people put a broom straw on the top of a melon. If it turns perpendicular they say it's ripe. Some people they'll thump 'um, thump 'um, punch 'um on the end. I just let them have their kicks.

"We Lynches are the biggest growers in Wise County. That's eighty miles from here. I had an uncle grew melons, his name was Sam, a father his name was R.S., and a brother his name was Jim, all raisin' melons.

"I get up three in the morning; get to bed at eight at night. Takes ten people to run three hundred acres and pick the melons, then I haul them here in a gooseneck trailer. I always have a load or two of melons parked out in front of the house and people know they're welcome to 'um. Hell, Wise County's only eighty miles from here. If you're ever out that way, stop and pick one up and holler at us."

WATERMELON PICKLES

MAKES 3 PINTS OF PICKLES

1 large watermelon
1 lemon, halved, sliced, seeded
2 cups light brown sugar
Juice of 1 orange
Juice of 2 lemons

2 cups cider vinegar
1½ cups water
1 cinnamon stick, plus 3 for jars
2 teaspoons whole cloves

Cut the melon into sections. Trim the flesh down to ½ inch of pink. Pare off the rind with a small sharp knife or a potato peeler. Cut the rind into rough squares and triangles approximately 1 inch large.

Cover the rind and sliced lemon with water, bring to a boil, and cook until tender, about 40 minutes.

While the watermelon cooks, combine the sugar, orange and lemon juices, vinegar, water, and cinnamon stick in a pan. Simmer until the mixture thickens slightly and forms a light syrup that drips with some weight from a spoon.

Refresh the watermelon under cold water until it is no longer warm. Drain well.

Add the melon to the syrup, bring to a boil, and cook for another 30 minutes, at which point the rind should have a translucent appearance and the liquid should have thickened further into a heavy syrup. Add the cloves.

Pour the watermelon into 3 sterilized jars (there should be a cinnamon stick in each), and seal. These pickles should be put away for 3 to 4 weeks before opening.

IVY AND ARLIE HOLLOWELL

Probably no one I met in any market stays in my mind anywhere as much as Ivy Hollowell. My breath still stops when I write about her six months later. Fragile, serene, crippled, she sits on a folding chair, blanket over her lap, on the open tailgate of the two-and-a-half-ton truck she calls home six months each year. Now no one in the whole Dallas market is neutral on the subject of the Hollowells. They either look askance ("I'd never allow my parents to live that way"), or they are staunch supporters ("It's better than sitting at home. I hope I can live my life that way"), but whatever their feelings, they look out tenderly for the elderly couple who sell sweet potatoes in the day and sleep each night on a mattress strewn with soft old blankets and worn, homemade quilts. There is a gentle mouse-nest look, a burrowed-animal smell to the truck. Inside, there's a small refrigerator, a hot plate, and a toaster; a television sits upon the refrigerator. They lie on the mattress at night and watch game shows ("We don't care much for the news any more"). Now Ivy looks inward and, talking of meeting her husband, bearing her children, working in the fields, she sweetly composes her life.

"When we were young, my husband and I lived half a mile from one another. One night when I was nineteen and he was twenty-one, we went to the same party. They played a game called Knock. Every girl got a number. The boys guessed a number, then they got to walk the girl around the house in the dark. Well, Arlie fixed it and found out my number so no boy would get a chance, and when he walked me around the house, he asked if he could walk me home, and we walked out ever since then. I've been putting up with him a long time now. We'll be married fifty-seven years on September 16. Maybe we'll go eat at Lubeys on our way home to celebrate. My son picks us up every Saturday night and brings us back every Sunday. I spend Sunday doing washing, going to church, and going grocery storing.

"We've been sleeping here four years now because the eighty miles each way from Grand Saline got to be too much for us. We haven't had any problems with sleeping here. Lots of people come and go every day but we can't anymore. Our son comes once a day with sweet potatoes, twice a day when we have squash. Back when we started coming here in 1940 and 7, I was digging potatoes regular, and let me tell you, potatoes is a little bit of hard work. You bed them out in March, cover them with dirt, put on some plastic topping to hold moisture and create heat, then they grow and push up out of the paper. You pull

81

out the green slips and plant them. If you get them settings in by June, the last of July you can go pulling potatoes come August. You store them and they'll last till January.

"We used to have some good eating off those sweets. There was sweet potato chips and casserole with butter-mashed sweets, corn flakes, pecans, and plenty brown sugar on top. We had regular cow butter then from our own cows. What we didn't eat we'd feed to the cows. Of course, we ate other things, too, because you'll get gas if you eat too many sweets. I can't eat a lot of things now. Six years ago I came up with Arthur Itis. Dr. Gold told me my knees just wore out and that was no surprise after setting out all those potato slips. I can eat fruit and angel-food cake and applesauce. I like my corn bread, but it's bad for me. I boil a mess of meat on Sunday at home and bring it back to the icebox. Sometimes we go over to Frank's Restaurant when it opens at 4 A.M. or we go to the Farmers Grill.

"We'll keep coming every year as long as our health hangs out. My husband had a heart attack in '59. Farmers didn't pay in social security as soon as public works people did, so he's been on disability since. Coming here helps my son and gives us extra money even though we can't work the field anymore, and there's a lot of entertainment here. There's all kinds of people, all kinds of dress, sometimes not enough clothes on. I've seen marriages break up here, made a lot of friends, most of them nice. Sometimes people aren't so nice though. They'll go through the produce and tear it up till it gets on your nerves. My mother, she taught me how to cook and do my work and treat people right, but once a lady came in and was handling and handling the squash. She said, 'These are soft.'

"I said, 'Lady, that's because you've been a-mashing on them,' and she stalked off like her tail had been bit, but that's the only time I ever said anything in forty years."

If you get to the Dallas market, walk two blocks over to the Farmers Grill on Park Avenue. It's in the fine tradition of populist restaurants. The cook, sixty-seven-year old Ruby Watson, comes in at five fifteen every morning to make cream gravy, corn biscuits, and buttermilk pie, and she can put five of any other cooks in her pocket as far as I'm concerned. The Farmers Grill is famous. Local politicos tend to congregate at breakfast, and it's always a stop in election years when candidates visit the market. Clever they are at knowing where the hearts and souls of the electorate can be found.

If you cannot visit the Farmers Grill, you can make this classic buttermilk pie. I added the cinnamon crust, and the whole smacks of Mother Love more than just about any other dessert I can think of.

BUTTERMILK PIE IN A CINNAMON CRUST

THIS IS A RICH PIE
THAT SERVES 8 TO 10

For the Crust:

1 cup all-purpose flour
1 teaspoon ground cinnamon
Pinch of salt

6 tablespoons (¾ stick) butter, chilled and
   cut into cubes
2–3 tablespoons ice water

For the Filling:

¼ cup flour
1⅔ cups sugar
¾ cup buttermilk
1 stick butter, melted

1 teaspoon vanilla extract
3 eggs
Ground cinnamon

To make the crust, in a bowl blend the flour, cinnamon, and salt. Cut in the butter with your fingers until a coarse meal is formed. Add enough water to form a smooth but not sticky dough. Compact the crust, flatten into a 6-inch circle, cover with plastic wrap and refrigerate 30 minutes.

Preheat the oven to 350°F.

Roll out the dough on a floured surface to ½-inch thick. Place the crust in a 9- to 10-inch pie plate. Cover with foil and fill with pie weights or beans. Bake for 10 minutes, then remove the foil and weights and bake for another 5 minutes. Remove from the oven, stick a knife point in any bubbles that have formed, and press the crust down to expel any air pockets.

While the crust cools, prepare the filling. Combine the flour and sugar in a mixing bowl. Whisk in the buttermilk, melted butter, vanilla, and eggs. (Never mind if some of the butter looks a bit congealed.) Pour into the baked crust. Sprinkle the top with cinnamon. Bake in the preheated oven for 45 to 50 minutes. The filling should be dark gold. Cool to room temperature before serving. Delicious with coffee.

For this Farmers Grill recipe, have your butcher cut a strip of top (inside) round beef that is thick enough (a generous ½-inch) for cubed steak. Have the steak run through the tenderizer three times (twice the long way, then cut the steak in half to feed it through the machine crosswise).

FARMERS GRILL-STYLE CHICKEN FRIED STEAK

SERVES 4

4 4-ounce portions tenderized top round beef
1 cup flour
1 teaspoon sugar

For the Gravy:

2 slices bacon
3 tablespoons butter
6 tablespoons flour
½ teaspoon sugar
1 bay leaf

1 egg
2 tablespoons milk
2 quart peanut oil for frying

1 chicken bouillon cube, crushed
2 cups canned chicken stock
2 cups milk
Freshly ground pepper

Have the meat at room temperature if possible. Spread the flour on a plate. Mix it with the sugar and a light sprinkling of salt. Combine the egg with the milk on another plate. Press each steak first into the flour so that it is heavily coated, then into the egg mixture. Turn to coat all sides. Return the steak to the flour and dredge it heavily, pressing in as much flour as possible.

When all the pieces are coated, place them on a wax paper–covered platter and refrigerate while you make the gravy.

Fry the bacon in a medium-large skillet until just crisp. Do not overbrown. Discard the bacon.

What you want here is around 1 tablespoon of rendered fat. Add the butter to bring the amount to 4 tablespoons.

Add the flour to the fat and whisk it over low heat for 2 minutes to cook the "roux." Add the sugar, bay leaf, bouillon cube, and stock. Stir until smooth, then add the milk. Whisk gently until the gravy starts simmering. Let it cook over medium low heat for 15 to 20 minutes while you fry the steaks. The end result should be a fairly thick gravy.

Heat the peanut oil in a deep fryer, electric fry pan, or wok. Fry the steaks 2 at a time until they are golden brown, about 4 minutes altogether. Turn over as they brown.

Place the steaks on plates. Remove the bay leaf, grind lots of pepper into the gravy, and ladle a cup over each steak. Serve at once, with steamed potatoes on the side.

I went to San Antonio not to see the large commercial Tex-Mex festival market that most tourists visit but to go with Marilyn Magaro, a market specialist for the Texas Department of Agriculture, to see a WIC farm market program in action.

The WIC (Women, Infants, Children) program has been around since the mid-seventies as an economic support to low-income mothers and children at nutritional risk. They received WIC coupons for eggs and milk, cereals and fruit juices, and nutritionists told them which brands were the healthiest. You could get natural Cheddar but not Velveeta. You could get unsweetened juices but they had to have at least 89 percent of the US RDA (recommended daily allowance) for vitamin C. You could get Kellogg's Product 19 but not Fruity Pebbles with Marshmallows. Made sense. What the program didn't offer was fresh produce.

Then, in 1988, someone came up with a spectacular plan so simple, so right that one could only wonder why it had not always been with us (it's of the magnitude of letting retired folks take care of children and brighten both their lives, that sort of thing). Why not, someone reasoned, let low-income mothers buy directly from farmers. The farmers needed the financial support; the mothers needed the optimal nutrition of fresh produce—everyone would be a winner. Texas was one of the ten states to have a pilot program federally funded under the Hunger Prevention Act in 1988, and a year later, when I visited during the first "official year," the program was running smoothly.

Each WIC qualifier received from ten to twenty dollars' worth of coupons over the summer of 1989. The farmers brought their just-picked produce to the public health clinics of the area on rotating days, and the mothers and children came to buy. They earned the coupons by attending nutritional classes twice during the summer. The class I saw had thirty-five adults and what seemed like four times that many children. The mothers came a long way and with some sacrifice to attend the class. They listened to the lecture in Spanish and held wiggling children. It was not the easiest way to earn.

Bill Kinsey from Dilley sells at two or three of San Antonio's clinics. A solid, earnest man of middling years, he gives good value to his customers:

"Two bunches of greens, ma'am? That's seventy-five cents each. What do you want to make up the extra fifty cents, a few peppers? Good, and here's an extra onion. When we started last year, we had people lined up back to that fence over there. The coupons were issued to people who are at nutritional risk—lactating mothers, small children, and babies. Sometimes I wondered how people got here. They had to take public transportation, they had two or three kids hanging on them, then they had to carry food back on the bus. We charged the standard price that we would sell at any farm market, we just changed our language from dollars to WIC cards. We had little kids coming up at the beginning of the clinic market. They'd grab a yellow squash and try to peel it like a banana. I tell you, these young girls come and they don't know how to cook green beans. They know meat, bread, and potatoes. I tell them the nutritional value of lots of this stuff that people have never tried, like these cream peas here—see the eye of the pea is lighter than a black-eyed pea.

"I've enjoyed meeting people all over town. You gotta get down with everyone. I've learned a lot of Spanish in the process. You learn that you sell greens and okra on the east side, hot peppers on the west. Whites eat pickling-sized cucumbers because they are sweeter; blacks like the big cucumbers; Mexicans put lemon, salt, and Tabasco on theirs for a snack.

"Sometimes I have to educate customers about the produce. When it's grown healthy, there may be spots on it sometimes. Look at these little dents on this apple. That's nothing but where it got hit during a hail storm, but it's still going to taste better and be better for you because it was just picked. Women will be grabbing and pinching things and discarding them; I'll say, 'Look, lady, you going to hang it on the wall or eat it? You're not going to get perfection straight out of the field but you're going to get a hell of a lot better nutrition.'"

An ancient car pulls into the parking lot, a pregnant woman leading a small child, the woman's husband, and an older relative get out, come over to the table and start talking rapidly in sign language.

"They want tomatoes and some of those over there," says the older relative, pointing to some pale green ovoid squash.

"That's tatuma," says Bill. "Ask 'em if they know how to cook it. No, well here's a recipe from the Texas Department of Agriculture. Never knew about tatuma until I got a demand for them here. Had a lady come one day and she looked at them and looked at them and said what's that then. I said tatuma, and I told her how to fix it. We farmers may not always like to eat what we sell but we know how to cook it. Well, she bought some and took it home along with this recipe and cooked it for a bunch of relatives, and the next week she was back, waiting when we pulled in to set up market. She was so excited she bought all I had to sell for the day. She said that was the only time ever she got her husband and son to eat a vegetable.

"We must have given out two hundred of these. Here's one for you. See how it's got the nutrition printed right on it."

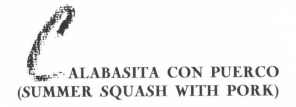

CALABASITA CON PUERCO (SUMMER SQUASH WITH PORK)

SERVES 8

2 tablespoons peanut oil

1½ pounds loin of pork, fat removed, cut into ½-inch cubes

2 cloves garlic, mashed

1 large onion, chopped

5 heaping cups cubed tatuma squash or small zucchini

2 cups fresh corn kernels

4–6 whole serrano peppers

2 cups pureed tomatoes (1 pound)

Salt and freshly ground pepper to taste

Heat the oil in a large skillet or Dutch oven. When the oil is hot, add the pork and brown well on at least one side. Remove the meat from the pan and add the garlic and onion. Cook and stir until the onion is tender. Return the meat to the pan, then add the squash, corn, peppers, tomato puree, and seasoning. Turn the heat to low, cover, and simmer for 20 minutes.

The Texas Department of Agriculture Nutritional Analysis per serving is:

368 calories

26 grams protein

23 grams fat

16 grams carbohydrate

465 milligrams sodium

83 milligrams cholesterol

From San Antonio it's pretty much a straight two-hour shot of a drive up Interstate 35 to Austin. Lots of what seems to me like archetypical Texas along the way: big game preserves advertised every three miles; huge revolving billboards on stilts high above the flat land as if all Texans were so tall their eyes must surely be level with the clouds; big Baptist convention centers; towns that look like they've been started then stopped; and always cars whizzing past so fast you can hardly read the TEXAS DOES IT BIGGER, TEXAS DOES IT BETTER bumper stickers.

I was headed to the capital to visit the Texas Department of Agriculture's John Vlcek, something of a legend back East where he had set up a farm market program in Tennessee (it started with food fairs in church parking lots) that was so successful he had been hired away to do an even bigger (and no doubt better) project in Texas.

The capitol complex looked like an inflated university and the Texas Department of Agriculture seemed to be in the biggest building of them all. I could see why John Vlcek got the job. Full of bounce, toes tapping, legs jiggling, he had just the kind of energy Jim Hightower, the progressive former Commissioner of Agriculture, liked to surround himself with. John was wearing, among other things, red argyles, a red tie, and an inverted "V" mustache like a little thatched roof. If you wanted a game plan for establishing a farmers' market, he was the man to give it to you.

JOHN VLCEK ON CREATING A FARMERS' MARKET

"When I came here ten years ago, Jim Hightower was campaigning on farm markets and it became politics at its best . . . that is, people were supporting the idea, government wanted it, and a network of nonpartisan people combined to implement it, but nobody had the bigger picture as to how to go about establishing markets, so I came in as a catalyst and said yes, you can do it, and here's what has to happen. Now, back then we were working against the state instead of with it, and what worked in Tennessee didn't necessarily work here. I'd try something and they'd say 'That's nice, boy, but you're in Texas now.' It's much more diverse here; people think big, there's a swagger to them, and lots of diversity in the cities. We hit dry holes that first year, spent a lot of effort here and there.

"We went to town meetings to get civic support. When we had that, we went to county agents and convinced them, then they in turn went out and found farmers who formed a steering committee. Then we looked for sites. It took lots of driving around. I'd say, 'Take me to your car lots, your churches, drive-in movies, and parks.' We wanted places that were highly visible and had easy access. When we found the site, we set an opening date, sent out publicity, and asked the Chamber of Commerce for support. With them behind you, you can do a market in three or four months. We learned that farmers want more permanent sites. They need to feel that commitment. If it's in a parking lot, they wonder, will it be here next year? Each community was a fight.

"In 1983, we established four markets, now there are ninety. We've gotten Texas melons and sweet potatoes in chain supermarkets rather than letting them buy from Florida or California. The Department of Agriculture has gained legitimacy and clout, with consistent institutions that both farmers and consumers can depend on. Markets provide diversity to small farmers that get missed in larger government agricultural programs. Young folks can start farming with us; older retirees can supplement social security. The disappointment is that people are not going into farming, so there's no exponential growth. We need more permanent facilities, and there are a lot of communities out there that want to develop markets. What better way to foster civic pride or revitalize a dead main street or simply return to the quality of what we used to have."

AUSTIN'S TRAVIS COUNTY FARMERS' MARKET

Austin's market is more the product of individual entrepreneurship than state funding, but it is entrepreneurship of the most foresightful kind. Here is a jolly market if ever there was one. It's young now, just getting a toehold, but I hope it thrives and prospers, because it's doing things right. You take an idiosyncratic set of buildings in a discarded maintenance yard and fill them full of tiny businesses, all food related. You encourage a good barbecue restaurant next door, invite farmers to set up shop, plant a teaching garden for children, tap into the Austin City sound for music on weekends, and invite the community.

David Winsberg's organic red peppers
at the Marin County Farmers' Market

Ivy and Arlie Hollowell at the
Dallas Farm Market

Cactus, cucumbers, and varieties of chilies at the Dallas Farm
Market

Thomas Grimes, seller of sugarcane, at the Dallas Farm Market

Melon varietals and sunflowers in abundance at the Tasting of Summer Produce, Oakland, California

The Dane County Market literally surrounds the State Capitol building in Madison, Wisconsin

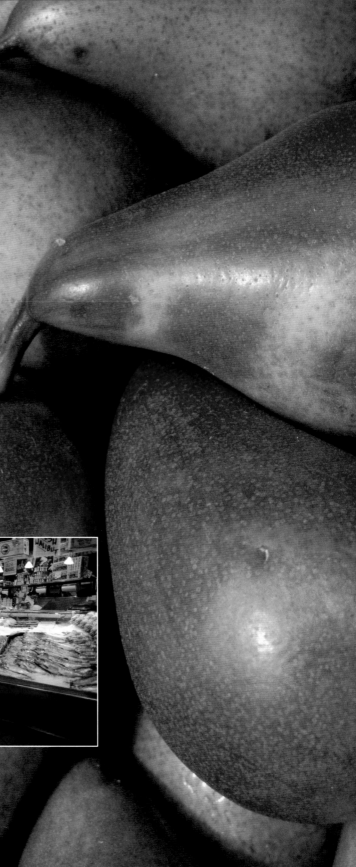

Early fall apples at the Lansing Farm Market

Setting up early in the morning at a Pike Place fish store, Seattle, Washington

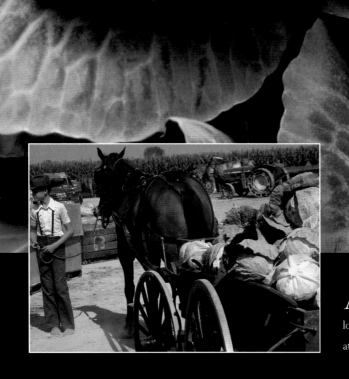

A Moravian boy waits for his
load of cabbage to be auctioned
at the Leola Farm Market

As developer Hill Rylander tells it, "When the starting bell rings at eight on a Saturday morning, our elderly hard core head for the fresh tomatoes. They buy in small amounts then have tea and croissants. The Yuppies move in midmorning—have brunch, drink Yellow Blossoms, eat tamales. Families come along with kids who watch the bean sheller and pet farm animals, then go to lunch at the barbecue joint. By noon, it's seriously crowded. We have music—musicians play for the tip buckets, a free meal, and, at the end of the day, a fresh vegetable donation from the farmers."

I came away from the market with new food inspirations. What a change from the forced "festival market" atmosphere that some ill-fated developments fall into. Those tend to depend on tired franchises for their feed, but here was a cheesecake "cupcake" store that played with Texas themes and ingredients for its flavorings; a store selling fajita "cones" to eat on the move, and sausage on a stick. You can have fresh sopaipillas and honey with your coffee, wondrous Tex-Mex breakfasts, and visit the Mirth Food Company for all sorts of exclusive Taste of Texas products (see Market Finds).

AN AUSTIN FARM MARKET BREAKFAST

I love the combination of ingredients in this gutsy breakfast dish. If you don't know smoky-flavored adzuki beans, they are worth searching out. To cook the beans, bring a quart of water and 1 cup of dried adzukis to a boil in a covered pan. Turn off the heat and let them sit for 45 minutes. Drain, place fresh water in the pan, and season with ¼ teaspoon salt, then simmer until just tender, around 20 minutes. If you can't find them, use pinto or black beans.

EGGS WITH SALSA, CHIPOTLES, AND ADZUKI BEANS

SERVES 6

3 cups cooked adzuki beans (see above)
6 tablespoons (¾ stick) butter
1 clove garlic, peeled
6 eggs
¼ teaspoon salt
Freshly ground pepper to taste
½ cup salsa, heated (this can be purchased, or make Golden Salsa, recipe follows)

Handful of cilantro leaves
Tortilla chips
Chipotles (canned hot peppers in adobo sauce available in Mexican food sections of gourmet stores)
Tabasco Lemon Cucumbers (optional)— (page 94)

Place the beans in a frying pan with 3 tablespoons of the butter and let them heat gently while you make the eggs.

Melt the remaining 3 tablespoons of butter over hot water in a double boiler (or simply place a medium saucepan in a large pot containing 3 inches of water).

Spear the garlic onto a fork. Break the eggs into a bowl, add salt and pepper, then whisk the eggs together with the fork to add just a hint of garlic. Discard the garlic.

Place the eggs in the double boiler and whisk over hot, never boiling, water until the eggs turn the consistency of a thick hollandaise sauce. They won't scramble in the clotted American sense, but they will be cooked in the manner of the French *brouillés*. Just when the eggs are thick and smooth, add the heated salsa.

Place a serving of beans on each plate, top with eggs, and garnish with a few cilantro leaves. Serve extra salsa on the side if you wish, and certainly some tortilla chips. Have the chipotles on a side dish and let people serve themselves if they wish to garnish their eggs with hot, hot peppers. Tabasco Lemon Cucumbers also make a great accompaniment.

— ✿ —

OLDEN SALSA

MAKES 3½–4 CUPS; SERVES 6 TO 8

5 medium large yellow tomatoes
2 yellow bell peppers, seeded and diced
1 small red onion, minced
1 fresh serrano chile, seeded and minced
1 teaspoon salt

Juice of 1 lime
2 teaspoons white wine vinegar
1 cup fresh cilantro leaves, coarsely chopped
1 tablespoon olive oil

Core the tomatoes, cut them across through the middle, then squeeze out the seeds. Dice the tomatoes.

Combine all the ingredients but the oil. Refrigerate for at least 30 minutes.

Drain off any accumulated juices, stir in the oil, and serve.

A favorite way for Hispanic Americans to eat cucumbers is to chill slices then sprinkle them with salt, lemon juice, and Tabasco. Here's the combination in a delicious salad.

TABASCO LEMON CUCUMBERS

SERVES 6

2 burpless English cucumbers, or 3–4 regular
   cucumbers
¼ teaspoon salt
3 tablespoons sour cream

Juice of ½ lemon
Freshly ground pepper
¼ teaspoon Tabasco sauce, or to taste

Peel the cucumbers. Slice them lengthwise down the middle. With a small spoon, scrape out the seeds. Slice the halves crosswise, paper thin. Place in a bowl, add the salt, stir briefly, then refrigerate for 30 minutes.

Whisk the sour cream, lemon juice, pepper, and Tabasco together.

Take up the now limp cucumbers by the handful and squeeze as hard as possible to rid them of their water. Stir the cucumbers into the dressing and serve.

— ⁂ —

These irresistible rounds of fried dough found in the Austin market (and at most festivals in the Southwest) are easy to make and fun to eat. I like to do most of my deep frying in an electric wok . . . if you have one, put it to good use here.

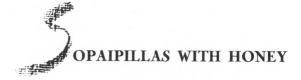

SOPAIPILLAS WITH HONEY

MAKES 8–10 PASTRIES

2 cups all-purpose or cake flour

1 tablespoon baking powder

1¼ teaspoons salt

2 tablespoons margarine or vegetable shortening

⅔ cup plus 1 tablespoon water, at room temperature

1 quart oil, preferably peanut, for frying

¾ cup sugar mixed with 1 tablespoon ground cinnamon

Honey

Mix the flour, baking powder, and salt. With your fingertips, cut in the margarine or shortening until it disappears into the flour. Make a well in the middle of the flour and slowly pour in the water; stir around the edges of the flour as you pour so that the liquid incorporates smoothly. Gather the dough together and give one quick knead. Try not to work the dough any more than is necessary. Wrap tightly in plastic or foil and refrigerate for 45 minutes.

Heat the oil to 375°F. Use an electric wok, a deep fryer, or simply pour the oil into a large heavy pot with tall sides. (The oil will be hot enough when a small piece of dough sizzles immediately on contact, bobs back to the surface, and browns within 1 minute.)

Roll out half the dough on a lightly floured surface. It should be around ¼ inch thick. Cut out rough rounds approximately 8 to 9 inches in diameter and let the shapes be odd and interesting. Fry the dough rounds one at a time. Let them blister and begin to turn brown, then turn once in the oil—the entire cooking time will be around 1 minute.

Have ready 3 or 4 sheets of paper toweling on a plate. Spread the cinnamon sugar on another plate. When a sopaipilla is cooked and crisp, lift it out and onto the paper toweling. Brush 2 or 3 swipes of honey on top and immediately place the pastry, honeyside down, in the cinnamon sugar. Continue frying, honeying, and sugaring the pastries. These are best eaten immediately.

You'll see people walking happily around the Austin market, fajita cones in hand, with juices dripping down their hands. This finger-licking twist on fast food will be the hit of your next informal gathering or children's party. Make the cones up ahead of time and simply warm them as needed.

FAJITA CONES

MAKES 12 CONES:
SERVES 4–6 ADULTS; 12 CHILDREN

12 fresh 8-inch flour tortillas
1 quart peanut oil for frying

For the Filling:

Shredded lettuce
Shredded cheese
Chunky Guacamole (recipe follows)
Pico de gallo sauce or salsa

Toothpicks; aluminum foil

Slivers of grilled chicken or beef that have been marinated in commercial fajita spices
Sour cream

To form the cones, shape each tortilla into a cone with as crisp a point as possible and secure the folded-over side with 1 toothpick. Cut a wide strip of aluminum foil, double or triple it over on itself, and form into a cone shape that will fit inside the tortilla to hold it open.

Heat the oil in a medium-sized saucepan or deep-fry unit to around 375°F. (A piece of tortilla will brown rapidly when the oil is hot enough.) If using a saucepan, the heat will most likely be turned to medium-high.

Using a pair of kitchen tongs, place 1 cone in the oil seam side down. It will fry quickly, so turn the cone around to all sides; it should be crisp and golden in about 30 seconds. Remove the foil, and tip it up so the oil drains out, then remove it from the pan. Tip and drain the cone and place it on paper toweling to crisp. Remove the toothpick.

Continue frying the cones one at a time. (These can be done a day ahead and rewarmed.)

To assemble, place some shredded lettuce in the bottom of a cone. Top with cheese, guacamole, pico de gallo sauce, and meat, then top with a few shreds of lettuce and a scoop of sour cream.

—❦—

This guacamole makes a nice tableside presentation. You will need a mortar or heavy bowl and a pestle for this bit of theater.

CHUNKY GUACAMOLE

SERVES 4, BUT 2 PEOPLE COULD
ALSO POLISH IT OFF.

1 *small fresh chile pepper*

1 *medium small red onion, chopped fine*

1 *teaspoon salt*

1 *medium tomato, halved, juice and seeds squeezed out, cut into small cubes*

1 *cup coarsely chopped cilantro*

Freshly ground pepper

2 *small ripe black fuerte, or 1 large green avocado*

1 *lime, halved*

Tortilla chips, warmed

Cut off 2 or 3 slices of chile pepper (or more if you like hotness) and discard all the seeds. Place the pepper, 2 tablespoons of the chopped onion, and the salt in a mortar and pound to a paste. Stir in half the tomato, half the cilantro, and grind in pepper to taste.

Cut the avocado in half and remove the seed, but do not peel. Holding one half in the palm of your hand, cut the flesh into large cubes by running a knife in criss-cross lines. Gently scoop the cubes into the tomato mixture, then cube the other half. Add the rest of the tomatoes, the remaining onion, and the juice of half a lime, and carefully turn the mixture with 2 large spoons. Sprinkle on the juice from the other lime half, and top with the remaining cilantro.

Serve at once with warm tortilla chips.

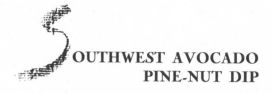

SOUTHWEST AVOCADO PINE-NUT DIP

SERVES 8

1 ripe Hass avocado (with dark black rough skin)
1 cup pine nuts
1 teaspoon salt
Juice of 1 lime
1 clove garlic, minced
2 tablespoons mayonnaise

Large pinch of cayenne pepper
Freshly ground black pepper to taste
½ teaspoon chili paste (optional)
1 small jicama
¼ cup coarsely chopped cilantro, plus whole leaves for garnish
Tortilla chips, warmed

Peel the avocado and scoop its meat into the bowl of a food processor or blender. Add the pine nuts, salt, lime juice, garlic, mayonnaise, peppers, and chili paste. Blend until smooth.

Cut a thick peel from the jicama (that plump round buff-colored root found with the Mexican produce in most supermarkets these days). It is crisp and rather like a water chestnut inside. Slice the jicama into ¼-inch-thick rounds, then cut the rounds into thin matchsticks and the matchsticks into small cubes.

Stir the jicama and chopped cilantro into the avocado by hand. Scoop the mixture into a rustic serving dish, smooth the top, cover with foil, and chill for at least 1 hour.

Garnish with a few whole leaves of cilantro and serve with crisp, warm tortilla chips.

This combination of jalapeños, pecans, and salsa–flavored cream cheese is particularly good for a luncheon dish, with a green salad on the plate alongside. The dish can be composed ahead, refrigerated, then placed briefly under the broiler.

TEX-MEX CANNELLONI

SERVES 2–4

2 fresh 8-inch tortillas
1 8-ounce container soft cream cheese,
  preferably Philadelphia, at room
  temperature
2 teaspoons chopped jalapeño peppers
1 cup coarsely chopped pecans
½ teaspoon salt

Freshly ground pepper to taste
⅓ cup salsa
1 tablespoon butter, melted
2–3 tablespoons grated Parmesan or
  Monterey Jack cheese

Straighten 1 edge of each round tortilla by cutting off a strip that will be 1-inch at its fattest point.

Stir the cream cheese, jalapeños, pecans, seasoning, and salsa together until smooth. Place half the mixture on each tortilla, spreading it gently out to the edge (use wet fingers to pat the mix if the tortillas seem particularly fragile).

Roll up the tortillas. (You may refrigerate them at this point, or even freeze them if desired. Warm or thaw to room temperature before use.)

Heat the broiler. Brush the melted butter over the top of the tortilla rolls, then sprinkle grated cheese down their length. Place under the hot broiler until the cheese is golden brown.

Cut each roll in half. They are fairly rich.

These pancakes are wonderful with leftover cooked corn cut from the cob. They can be an interesting Southwest-style breakfast, brunch, or lunch dish, or they can accompany grilled chicken.

SMOKY CORN PANCAKES WITH SALSA BUTTER

MAKES ABOUT TWELVE
4-INCH PANCAKES

For the Pancakes:

½ cup boiling water

½ cup cornmeal (I prefer yellow, but white will do, also)

½ cup flour

⅓ cup sugar

2 teaspoons baking powder

1½ teaspoons salt

2 tablespoons butter, melted

2 cups cooked corn kernels

2 eggs

¼ cup milk

¼ cup hot salsa

1 teaspoon finely minced jalapeño peppers

¼ teaspoon Liquid Smoke

2 tablespoons cooking oil or more as needed

For the Salsa Butter:

4 tablespoons (½ stick) unsalted butter

¼ cup salsa

Torn cilantro for garnish

To make the pancake batter, start by pouring boiling water over the cornmeal. Let it sit for 10 minutes while you measure and prepare the other ingredients.

Place the dry ingredients in a bowl.

Stir the butter, corn, eggs, milk, salsa, jalapeños, and liquid smoke into the cornmeal. Stir in the flour mixture.

Heat the oil in a frying pan and when it has sizzled again, ladle in the pancakes. Use about ¼ cup of batter for each cake so that the pancakes will be slightly larger than normal. Fry until dark golden brown edges develop, and bubbles start to form and burst on top of the cakes. Turn each cake gently and fry on the other side. Continue frying pancakes, adding more oil as necessary, until all are cooked.

To make the salsa butter, melt the butter, remove from the heat, and whisk in the salsa. Serve on pancakes with a generous sprinkling of torn cilantro for garnish.

—❧—

MARKET WISDOM ON CORN

"Worms know more than we do. Worms go to the sweetest corn—that's why it's smart to buy corn with worms."

"If it ain't good raw, it ain't good anyway. When I'm hungry out in the field I'll just pull off an ear and eat it."

"Grow Silver Queen in the South; Illini Extra Sweet in the North."

"Every kernel of corn has a silk and every silk has to be pollinated by a seed from those tassels on top of the corn. If there's too much rain, the corn doesn't get pollinated right because the bees can't smell it. Well, for every one of those silks that doesn't develop or it blows off, you lose a kernel of corn on the cob. That's why some ears look like my mouth of old teeth."

"See piles of corn and want to know which ears are freshest? Turn the shuck back and press a fingertip gently on the kernels. If the kernel gives slightly under pressure it should mean sweet juicy corn. Harder, less yielding kernels have not had a chance to ripen and develop sugar content."

You could use several different vegetables in this presentation, but I think that cauliflower, pattypan squash, and firm small zucchini are the tastiest grilling items to accompany this sauce. Serve it as a first course or luncheon dish. It smacks of either salad or vegetable.

GRILLED WHITE VEGETABLES WITH BOILED PECAN DRESSING

SERVES 3–4

For the Dressing:

3 eggs

1 teaspoon sugar

½ cup white wine or champagne vinegar

⅔ cup water

½ teaspoon salt

1 small clove garlic, pressed

Freshly ground pepper

½ cup broken toasted pecans

1 tablespoon minced fresh parsley and/or chives

Vegetables:

Choose one or a mixture of:

1 head cauliflower, trimmed, partially steamed, cut into thick slices

Pattypan squash, halved, scored lightly with a knife tip, steamed

Small new potatoes, boiled

Small zucchini, trimmed, halved lengthwise, and partially steamed

Olive oil

Salt

To make the dressing, place the eggs, sugar, vinegar, water, salt, and garlic in a saucepan over medium-high heat, and whisk continually until the mixture rises up in a boil. Whisk hard, then remove from the heat. The dressing should be thick and smooth. Cool to room temperature, add pepper to taste, then refrigerate.

Parboil or fully cook the vegetables. Drizzle olive oil over them and sprinkle lightly with salt. Heat the grill, brush it with oil, and briefly cook the vegetables. Let them get grill marks.

Arrange the vegetables on dinner plates. Stir the toasted pecans and herbs into the sauce and serve on the side or ladle over the vegetables, as you choose.

— ✂ —

This bread should be sliced thick, "Texas Toast" style, slathered with butter, and toasted to bring out its pecan flavor.

TEXAS PECAN TOASTING BREAD

MAKES 2 LOAVES

1½ envelopes yeast
2 tablespoons sugar
2 cups warm, not hot, water
2 teaspoons salt
1 tablespoon walnut oil
2 cups whole pecans, lightly toasted, cooled, ground in a food processor, plus 8 large pecans

Around 5 cups flour
1 egg yolk mixed with 2 teaspoons water for glaze

Dissolve the yeast and sugar in the warm water. Stir in the salt, walnut oil, and ground nuts. Add around 3½ cups of flour and stir into the water. Add flour as necessary to form a dough that is firm enough to turn out of the bowl onto a floured surface. Knead, adding more flour as necessary, until the dough is elastic, soft, but not sticky. (This should take a good 6 or 7 minutes.)

Place the dough in an oiled bowl (walnut oil would again be nice). Cover with a towel, place in a warm place, and let rise for 1 hour.

Divide the dough into 2 loaves and place each in an oiled 4½-x8½-inch bread pan. Cover with a towel and allow to rise again for 30 to 40 minutes, or until the dough mounds slightly over the rim of the pans. Preheat the oven to 375°F.

Brush the loaves with the egg yolk glaze. Arrange 4 pecans decoratively at the center of each loaf. Bake for 50 minutes. Cool. Cut into thick slices and use as toast.

— ❦ —

If you like the flavor of scuppernong wine, this is a delightful, not-too-sweet cake just right for tea.

SCUPPERNONG WINE CAKE

MAKES 1 DENSE CAKE; 10–12 SERVINGS

¾ cup sliced almonds
2¼ cups sifted all-purpose flour
1 tablespoon baking powder
1 teaspoon salt
1 cup sugar
4 eggs, lightly beaten

1 stick unsalted butter, melted
1 cup scuppernong wine
Juice of ½ lemon
1 teaspoon lemon zest
½ cup confectioners' sugar for glaze
  (optional)

Preheat the oven to 350°F. Grease and flour a standard bundt pan or 10-cup ring mold. Spread the sliced almonds evenly on the bottom of the pan and set aside.

In a bowl, mix the dry ingredients together. Stir in the eggs and melted butter and beat for 2 minutes. Add ½ cup of the wine, and gently fold it in by hand. Add the remaining wine, the lemon juice, and zest and stir until smooth.

Pour the batter over the almonds. Place immediately in the preheated oven and bake for 50 minutes. Cool completely before glazing, if desired.

To make a light decorative glaze for the cake, sift the confectioners' sugar into a small bowl. Whisk in about 3 tablespoons of scuppernong wine or water to make a thin glaze. Drizzle the icing back and forth over the top of the cake with a small spoon.

— ❧ —

You might want to serve Scuppernong Wine Cake with the following apple slush. This is also delicious on a summer's day in a tall frosted glass with a wedge of lemon on the rim, a sprig of mint trailing over the side . . . you get the idea.

APPLE SLUSH

SERVES 4

3 cups natural pressed apple juice (the cloudy kind, not the see-through kind)

1 cup scuppernong wine
Juice of 1 medium lemon

Mix the liquids together and freeze in a shallow nonaluminum pan. As the mixture starts to freeze, rake a fork through it at intervals to dislodge the setting sides.

When all is icy, scoop into 4 tall frosted glasses. You can also freeze this in cubes, of course, and whiz it up in a blender or food processor.

The Austin farmers' market has one small store where you can get all sorts of homemade cheesecakes in cupcake form. They have irresistible names like Pecan Praline, Texas Turtle, and Key Lime. Here is a "turtle" cupcake full of chocolate, pecans, and caramel. You know perfectly well that cheesecake tastes better if it ages a day after being made, so try and act upon this principle.

TEXAS TURTLE CHEESECAKE CUPCAKES

MAKES 12 CUPCAKES

For the Cheesecake:

1 pound cream cheese, cut into cubes

3 eggs

¾ cup sugar

1½ teaspoons vanilla extract

Large pinch of salt

For the Topping:

1 3-ounce bar bittersweet chocolate, such as Lindt, coarsely chopped

12 caramels, quartered (I recommend Borden's Eagle Caramels)

½ cup pecan halves

Preheat the oven to 350°F.

Place all the cream cheese ingredients in a food processor and blend for 3 minutes, until perfectly smooth. Stop and scrape down the sides once or twice. You can also whip this up by hand, but a machine makes shorter work.

Place 12 foil baking cups on a baking sheet or place cupcake liners in a muffin tin. Ladle the cheesecake batter into the cups.

Combine the topping ingredients in a bowl and generously top each cheesecake with this mixture. Try and keep the pieces of caramel toward the center.

Bake in the preheated oven for 35 minutes. Cool completely, then refrigerate. Let come to room temperature before serving.

HEIGHT OF SUMMER

CALIFORNIA
Santa Monica Market

YOU WANT A LITTLE GLITZ WHEN YOU HIT A southern California market, you get a little glitz.

"Keep your eyes peeled," says Laura Dingle, manager of the Santa Monica Market by the sea. "You might see Kirk Douglas. . . ."

I can believe it in this bright market along Arizona Street, so close to the ocean that the Spandex crowd is here—girls looking fit in midriff-baring tops the color of nectarines, mangoes, and Persian melons; hulk-bodied beach boys with bicycle pants and roller blades and Great Danes pulling them along on leashes.

". . . or Lloyd Bridges. He's here a lot. . . ."

Lots of retired folks under the mellow sun, sorting through the fruit piles, purchasing a peach. Mounds of oriental vegetables, a spectacular collection of mushrooms—morels, porcini, sponge, oysters so pungent they smell almost truffle-strong.

". . . Go up to Santa Barbara tomorrow and you might catch Kevin Costner or Jonathan Winters. That's Julia Child's market you know."

What is amazing is the close, strident questioning of growers by customers. They want to know about residues, about chemicals, how the soil was fed, if the crops were fumigated. The alar scare, the watermelon fiasco, the cucumber botch put fear into everyone in California, growers and customers alike. The "nozzle heads" (growers quick to use chemical panaceas for every ill) were caught short by the vociferous consumer demand for safe food. Chemically poisoned water wells in Fresno and a seven-million-dollar water-treatment plant to remove pesticides in Lodi, both in the prime heart of growing country, galvanized the public. And if the general tenor of conversation I heard around me was any indication, people were taking charge of their lives when it came to the food that they put in their bodies.

"Quick, turn around, there's Suzanne Somers."

Lo, there she is. Leggings, turquoise pullover, sunglasses big as Betty Boop's eyes, long straw hair. Turns out she has a family rendezvous with her son here each Wednesday morning while she buys and orders up food to take on the road for her cabaret act. "I can't find food this pure and good on the road," she says, "so I arrange with farmers I know to send me care packages in different cities where I'm appearing."

She heads to the mushroom stand to arrange an order, then waits in line to buy spectacular strawberries.

"No sprays? she asks. "Organic?"

"You better believe it," answers the grower.

Farm markets in California are serious business. In the past ten years their numbers have grown from 5 Certified Farmers' Markets to over 120. Considered a bellwether in so many other matters, perhaps California's concern for sustainable agriculture, its nurturing policies toward farmers, and its general market-oriented ethos will spread across our country like a fortifying balm. Nowhere else in America are markets such celebrations of food, health, nutrition, community, good fellowship, and a sense of mission.

Now, you would expect a state that is one-third farmland and that grows 50 percent of the nation's food to have a vested interest in its crop economy. With growing fields so plentifully at hand in most of the state, it seems almost ironic that alternative markets are springing up everywhere. As one farm market manager explained it, "Produce in California stores may look better, but for the most part it's no better than back East, because supermarkets buy unripe here, too. If you want truly fresh, you have to go to the farm market."

What small growers in California and elsewhere are finding is that there is increasing public discontent with supermarket produce. Why, thinking consumers ask themselves, are there so many pesticide scares? Why are my foods gassed and dipped, sprayed, radiated, waxed, and trucked from so far away? Why are they wrapped in plastic and placed under pink lights to make them look sunlit rosy? If trendsetting California is any indication, more and more farmers will be growing foods for local stores, devoting their acreage to new varietals and "boutique" farming for restaurants; they will use ecologically and environmentally sound agricultural methods. In time, this movement could permanently affect agricultural policy, the supermarket industries, and the way we all shop, eat, and thrive.

Marin County Farmers' Market

One of the best places to catch a glimpse of the idealist future is at the Marin County farmers' market. Located on the Civic Center fairgrounds in San Rafael, it provides a welcome humanizing counterpoint to the squat, modernistic, Frank Lloyd Wright–designed Marin Civic Center that sits sternly behind. It boasts more Certified Organic Gardeners than any other market in America. I walked the grounds with Lynn Bagley, who manages the market with passionate dedication, and I found her, like the very best managers around the country, tenacious, devoted, and concerned:

"I was interested in nutrition and alternative healing, and studying Chinese medicine when farm markets took over my life. It seemed to me that we as a society desperately needed ways to bring people together in community. We needed to save downtowns, we needed healthy food affordable to everyone. When we started here, the turnout was extraordinary. It's so important to choose the right location and do the right kind of publicity. We have a billboard out on Highway 8o, we got the telephone company to let us put inserts in phone bills, we placed display ads in the newspaper. The grocery-store chains felt threatened initially and formed a committee to thwart us. They told the newspapers they would pull their advertising if they did a story on us, and refused to buy from farms who sold in the market. Then we started up, and they calmed down, but everything right you have to fight for. Now people have a place to see friends and neighbors. It changes their mindsets about food. You pay eighty cents for a candy bar then balk at forty cents for a fine organic heirloom varietal plum. If you're intelligent you have to say whoa, there, what's valuable here."

Thursday morning we walk the rows of brilliant produce under the lustering sun (no cosmetic lighting here), and the hand-lettered signs tell the story.

ORGANIC FARMERS ARE MORE FERTILE

FREE RUN FRESH RANCH EGGS, FED ONLY CRACK CORN AND GREENS

MANY PESTICIDES ENHANCE THE APPEARANCE OF PRODUCE. THE PRICE OF PERFECT-
LOOKING FRUITS AND VEGETABLES IS OFTEN MORE RESIDUES.

FEED THE SOIL, FEED THE WORLD. SUPPORT SUSTAINABLE AGRICULTURE.

THIS IS THE ONLY PRODUCE IN THE WORLD GROWN AT THE BOTTOM OF A DRAINED FISH
POND FREE OF WEEDS AND ENRICHED WITH THE BY-PRODUCTS OF FISH.

SUE'S STRAWBERRIES—ORGANICALLY GROWN IN ACCORDANCE WITH CALIFORNIA HEALTH
AND SAFETY CODE #26569-11

DON'T TREAT OUR EARTH LIKE DIRT

Snippets of conversation overheard tell more:

"Excuse me, do you sulfurize your almonds?"
"Yes, but we rinse them off."
"No thank you, then."

Many of the farmers who are not as yet Certified Organic have signs above their tables that read IN TRANSITION. They are weaning their land away from herbicides, fertilizers, pesticides, and moving toward organic. It costs a hundred dollars more an acre than regular farming, you have to weed four times a season, but the demand for organic has quadrupled since the alar scare, and some experts think that if a small farmer is not in transition these days, he probably won't be in business in five years.

Garlic grower Bill Reynolds explained his crop in organic terms:

"I have two acres of garlic. It takes nine months for garlic to mature, and during that time three sets of pests attack and you have to weed three times. Five people go through it, ten days each time, and it's hard work down on your hands and knees. You take out pigweed in spring, lamb's-quarters in summer, and fescues and grasses in winter. Now the commercial garlic comes up cheaper from Mexico and undercuts our price. It's common knowledge that we send our banned pesticides to Mexico and South America, but down there they can fly over eight times a season with herbicides so strong they damn near kill the stuff, which means that they have to fly eight *more* times with fertilizer to bring back the growth. Now garlic should be a medicinal herb. It's good for the health, purifies the blood, the Russians use it as an antibiotic replacement for penicillin, but garlic is a storage bulb. If it soaks all those chemicals up, it's poison. If you don't eat it organically grown, you're deceiving yourself."

There's all sorts of cooking inspiration to be had from the produce and growers at the Marin market, starting with David Winsberg and his pepper stand. PEPPER POWER, reads the sign. His father is a pepper grower in Florida, and five years ago, after David had a fling in the corporate world, he returned to his roots and started growing peppers. He also does experimental plantings for Sun World, an international seed company. The day I met him, he had a load of "chocolate" peppers, a new varietal, though he explained that red peppers are called "chocolate" when they have that brownish state before they turn to green. Want a good recipe? he volunteered. Cook a soup of peppers and carrots and you'll have the full spectrum of vitamins and minerals.

This thick, bright red soup, nutritionally loaded, is a good alternative to gazpacho, but you can treat it the same way if you wish and garnish it with diced sweet Spanish onions and croutons. Or swirl in a bit of crème fraîche.

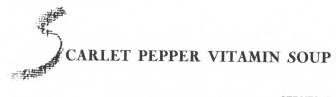

SCARLET PEPPER VITAMIN SOUP

SERVES 8

3 large red bell peppers, seeded and diced

3 carrots, scraped and sliced thin

3 medium tomatoes, cut across the center, seeds pressed out, coarsely chopped

2 cups chicken stock

3 tablespoons olive oil

2 cloves garlic, minced

1 medium onion, minced

Salt and freshly ground pepper to taste

2 tablespoons balsamic vinegar

For Optional Garnish:

Minced parsley

Croutons

Crème fraîche

Place the peppers, carrots, tomatoes, and stock in a nonaluminum pot and set over medium heat. Simmer for about 30 minutes, or until the carrots are soft.

Meanwhile, heat the olive oil in a frying pan. Add the minced garlic and onion. Sauté over medium heat until the onion is limp and begins to turn golden. Add the onion to the soup.

Season with salt and several grindings of fresh pepper, then puree the mixture for a generous time in a blender or processor, until the soup is silken.

When the soup has cooled to room temperature, add the balsamic vinegar.

Serve lightly chilled. Add a bit of water to thin the soup, if so desired, but I like it very thick, like a healthy potage.

Garnish with minced parsley, croutons, crème fraîche or all three.

—⚬—

If you have a grill, cook these peppers under a closed lid until blistered. Otherwise, use a broiler. Serve with good bread and sweet butter to sop up the juices.

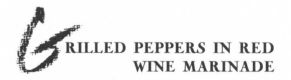

GRILLED PEPPERS IN RED WINE MARINADE

SERVES 6 AS A FIRST COURSE

6 large red bell peppers
1 cup red wine
1 bay leaf
1 clove garlic, peeled and flattened with a knife blade
2 sprigs fresh thyme (optional)

¼ teaspoon sugar
1 1-inch piece of orange peel
⅓ cup olive oil
Salt and freshly ground pepper to taste
Fresh basil leaves for garnish

Place the peppers on a grill or under the broiler and let them cook until blackened on all sides. You will have to keep a watch and turn them as necessary, even up on end. Immediately when the peppers are soft, place them in a bowl and cover with a plate for 15 minutes while you prepare the marinade.

To make the marinade, place the wine, bay leaf, garlic, thyme, sugar, and orange peel in a small nonaluminum pan and bring to a simmer. Cook until the wine has reduced to ⅓ cup. Strain off the wine, remove the bay leaf and orange peel, and press the garlic through a strainer into the wine. Whisk in the olive oil, then add salt and pepper.

As soon as the peppers are cool enough to handle, peel them, keeping all refuse (cores, peelings, juice that escapes from the peppers). Lay the strips in a rustic dish. Put a colander or sieve over a larger bowl and press the refuse in big handfuls so that all the juices are collected. Add the pepper juice to the marinade. Whisk briefly, taste for seasoning (more salt? oil? a pinch of sugar?) then pour the marinade over the peppers.

Cover and refrigerate for at least 2 hours, though overnight is better. The peppers hold well for 4 to 5 days.

Let them sit out of the refrigerator for 1 hour before serving. Garnish with fresh basil.

This rich "bread salad" is one of the very best uses for red peppers, and it tastes of summer even when made in the winter. Note that the tomato-pepper mixture can be prepared a day or two ahead, but once the croutons are added, the salad should be served immediately.

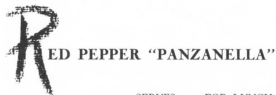

RED PEPPER "PANZANELLA"

SERVES 4–5 FOR LUNCH;
6–8 AS SIDE DISH

About 4 large fresh tomatoes (16 smaller Italian plums are also good in this dish)

3 large red bell peppers

1 medium red onion

2 large cloves garlic, peeled and sliced

4 tablespoons olive oil

1 tablespoon balsamic vinegar

½ teaspoon salt

Generous grinding of fresh black pepper

For the Croutons:

About ½ cup olive oil

2 cups stale French or Italian bread, cut into ¾-inch cubes

1 large clove garlic, peeled

Handful of chopped fresh parsley

Fresh basil leaves

Leaves of romaine lettuce

Core the tomatoes. Cut into quarters and then in half again. Core and seed the peppers and cut the flesh into 1-inch squares. Cut the onion into medium slices.

Heat 3 tablespoons of the olive oil in a large saucepan (it should be big enough to hold all the ingredients). Sauté the onion and garlic until translucent, then add the tomatoes and peppers. Turn the heat down, cover the pan, and cook over medium-low heat until most of the liquid has evaporated. This will take around 20 minutes. Stir frequently, and during the final 5 minutes, cook uncovered so you can watch and prevent scorching.

Remove from the heat. Add the remaining tablespoon of olive oil, the vinegar, salt, and freshly ground pepper. Cool to room temperature. (The peppers can be refrigerated at this time for a day or two.)

Prepare the croutons by heating ⅓ cup of the olive oil in a large frying pan. Add the bread cubes and turn each one to coat with oil. Add more oil as necessary so that the bread absorbs as much as possible and turns into succulent crisps (the trick is to let all the oil possible absorb but not allow any excess). Brown the croutons on all sides. Tend the fires here so they don't burn.

Turn off the heat and give each one a swipe with the garlic clove.

To assemble the salad, gently stir the croutons, half the chopped parsley, and some torn basil leaves into the pepper mixture. Arrange a leaf or two of romaine on a plate and add a mound of the salad. Sprinkle with additional parsley and add a sprig of basil.

This makes a hearty rustic luncheon dish (I can't think of anything else needed except a glass of wine and dessert). Or you can serve it as an accompanying salad, though I could easily eat half the bowl myself if left to my own devices.

There's a certain amount of showmanship at the Marin market, a savvy sense of display. Heaps of purple green grapes, vines and tendrils curling from the massive bunches, spill from vineyard baskets against an azure cloth. Garlic braids entwined with dried flowers hang from drying racks. Duck and quail and hen's eggs nestle on straw at Stell Caramucci's stand, and John Carlson of J C Farm in Kenwood fills huge baskets full of ten varieties of lettuce then scatters in whole flowers and petals and tosses the greens with his hands. He keeps up a constant chatter—"no sprays, no chemicals here"—and exhorts us to think of lettuce in both raw and cooked terms. All right then.

BRAISED RADICCHIO

SERVES 4

4 medium radicchio de Verona (the kind with a tight head like a small cabbage)
About ½ cup olive oil
⅓ cup water
Salt

2 tablespoons balsamic vinegar
Pinch of sugar
Freshly ground pepper
Minced parsley

Trim any rust off the stems of the radicchio. Cut them in half lengthwise. Cut out most of the core from each half and remove any wilting outer leaves.

Place 3 tablespoons of the olive oil in a large frying pan. Add the water and radicchio, cut sides down. Place over medium heat, add a light sprinkling of salt, and cover. Let the liquid come to a simmer and regulate the heat as necessary to keep it that way. Let the radicchio cook until a knife tip penetrates easily and the lettuce is tender, 12 to 15 minutes.

When you braise correctly, you want the object first to simmer its way to tenderness in the water, then fry its way to a browned edge in the remaining oil. You can hear the difference between the two cooking processes. Add water if necessary to keep the tenderizing simmer going.

When the radicchio is tender, press it down flat with the back of a spatula. (If there is any excess water now, simply pour it off and add a little more oil so that a fry can commence). Let the vegetable fry another 3 to 4 minutes, or until the cut edges turn a dark crisped color,

Remove the pan and place the radicchio, cut sides up, in a dish that will just hold them.

Return the cooking pan to the heat. Add the vinegar and sugar and swirl the pan until the vinegar reduces by half. Stir in the remaining olive oil then pour the contents of the pan over the vegetable. Sprinkle lightly with salt, generously with pepper, and decoratively with chopped parsley. May be served hot (good accompanying grilled duck breasts), or as a cool antipasto.

— ⅌ —

GIVE PEAS A CHANCE, reads the sign over the table.
"Pop the top . . .
Peel the string . . .
Eat the whole thing . . ." chants the vendor.

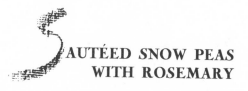

SAUTÉED SNOW PEAS WITH ROSEMARY

SERVES 2–4

¼ pound snow peas, stemmed
3 tablespoons olive oil
1 clove garlic, pressed
1 tablespoon fresh rosemary needles

6 ounces cremini or regular mushrooms,
*   clean, stemmed, and halved if large*
Salt and pepper to taste

Cut the snow peas in half diagonally lengthwise. Heat the olive oil in a medium-sized frying pan and add the garlic, rosemary, and mushrooms. Sauté, shaking the pan, until the mushrooms are just tender (around 2 minutes).

Add the snow peas and continue cooking until they turn bright green and are just crunchy-tender (less than a minute). Add salt and pepper and serve at once.

This is a handsome salad and a good way to use fresh farm-market berries in a nondessert guise.

CHEF MARK DAY'S SNOW PEA AND BERRY SALAD

SERVES 3–4

Generous ¼ pound crisp snow peas, stemmed
½ pint raspberries
2 tablespoons raspberry vinegar
2 tablespoons olive oil

Pinch of sugar
Salt and pepper to taste
½ pint blueberries

Steam the snow peas until they are a bright translucent green. Do not overcook. Rinse immediately under cold water to set the color and stop the cooking.

To make the dressing, press a heaping tablespoon of the raspberries through a sieve. Add the vinegar to the raspberry puree, then the olive oil, sugar, and salt and pepper.

Place the snow peas and blueberries in a bowl and add the dressing. Turn gently. Add the remaining raspberries and again gently turn the ingredients. Refrigerate for at least 30 minutes before serving.

— ❧ —

Producer Richard Hambright guarantees that you too can become an organic farmer if you purchase one of his mushroom-growing trees. The five-pound logs made from pressed black walnut, four different grains, cotton, seed hulls, and nutrients have been sterilized in an autoclave then inoculated with a clone culture of oyster or shiitake strains. There's a strange tree of Blue Oyster mushrooms that he's going to show off at the Tasting of California Produce on Sunday. There's also a Golden Oyster. All are available for home fruiting, and the taste of the just-grown fresh mushrooms almost convinces me to pack a log on the plane back home. Fortunately, they are available for mail order. (See Market Finds.)

When you get your shiitake log rolling at full production, you might want to make this intense soup. You can thin the soup with a bit of water before serving, but I like it very thick, so that you almost spoon it out of rustic bowls rather like a mousse. Shiitake are usually clean mushrooms. Simply discard the stems, then wipe with a damp cloth.

BED OF THE FOREST MUSHROOM SOUP

SERVES 8–10

2 tablespoons butter
1 large leek, cleaned, trimmed, and sliced
8 cups chopped shiitake mushrooms (around 1¼–1½ pounds)
2 cups chicken stock
½ teaspoon salt

2 tablespoons vermouth
2 cups heavy cream
Sour cream or crème fraîche (optional)
½ cup sliced toasted almonds
Minced fresh parsley

Melt the butter in a large pot. Add the leek and stir over medium heat for 2 minutes. Add the mushrooms, stock, salt, and vermouth. Simmer and stir until the mushrooms are cooked, around 3 minutes. Add the cream, cover, and simmer over low heat for 20 minutes. Stir once or twice.

When the soup has finished cooking, puree around two thirds of the mixture in a blender or food processor, then stir back together.

I like this soup warm but not piping hot. To serve, spoon into rustic bowls. Add a swirl of sour cream or crème fraîche, if so desired. Top with toasted almonds and a sprinkle of minced parsley. Refrigerates well, but do reheat before serving.

If you have a bountiful crop of mushrooms, try this delicious play on pâté.

SHIITAKE "PÂTÉ"

SERVES 8–10

1¼ pounds fresh shiitake mushrooms, wiped
  and stemmed
1 large leek, trimmed and washed
4 tablespoons (½ stick) butter
Juice of 1 medium lemon
1 large clove garlic, pressed
⅓ cup pine nuts
2 eggs

¼ cup plain yogurt
1 teaspoon salt
Generous grindings of fresh coarse black
  pepper
Pinch of ground mace
¼ teaspoon fresh or dried thyme
Minced fresh parsley for garnish

Preheat the oven to 350°F.

Reserve 1 large handsome mushroom specimen for decoration, then dice the mushrooms, preferably by hand. Slice and mince the tender white part of the leek.

Melt the butter in a large frying pan. Add the lemon juice, garlic, mushrooms, and leek and sauté until the mushrooms are dry and just cooked (you will hear them squeak in the pan when done).

Place half the mushroom mixture, the pine nuts, eggs, and yogurt in a food processor and blend to a fine pulp. Stir the blended mushrooms back into the coarse mixture. Add the salt, pepper, mace, and thyme.

Place the mixture in a rustic 7- or 8-inch terrine or other baking dish. Press the handsome reserved mushroom (it can be fluted if you wish) into the middle of the mixture. Bake for 30 minutes. Cool to room temperature and refrigerate. (This is good made 2 or 3 days ahead.)

To serve, sprinkle a fine mince of parsley around the edge of the dish. Accompany with toast points or crackers.

Roesti potatoes, the crusty national potato dish of Switzerland, can be made particularly well with the firm, waxier new types of potatoes that farmers have to offer in markets these days. The Swiss maintain that boiling the potatoes and chilling them overnight does wonders for the texture of this dish.

ROESTI POTATOES WITH SHIITAKE MUSHROOMS AND CHIVES

SERVES 4–6

4 medium potatoes (do not use baking potatoes)
7 tablespoons butter
⅓ pound shiitake mushrooms, cleaned, destemmed, diced

3 tablespoons minced fresh chives
Salt and freshly ground pepper to taste

Boil the potatoes in their skins for 15 minutes. Remove from the heat and rinse under cold water. The potatoes should stay firm. Let the potatoes cool, then refrigerate them for at least 2 hours but preferably overnight.

The Swiss have a hand grater with large round holes that is made especially for roesti potatoes, but you can use the largest blade for a Mouli-julienne or the largest holes of a standard hand grater. Peel the potatoes then grate them.

Melt 1 tablespoon of the butter in a frying pan. Sauté the mushrooms until they "squeak" in the pan. Gently stir the mushrooms and 2 tablespoons of the chives into the potatoes.

In a clean 9-inch frying pan, melt 3 tablespoons of the butter. Tip the pan so the sides are well coated. Spoon the potato mixture into the pan and gently press it down. Salt the top of the potatoes. Cook the pancake covered, over medium heat, for 15–20 minutes, at which point you should see a golden brown crust forming up the sides and the pancake should feel loose when you shake the pan.

Uncover the pan and press the cake down with a spatula from time to time. Place a dish over the top of the pan, and reverse the pancake out onto it.

Melt 2 more tablespoons of the butter in the pan and slide the pancake back in, pressing it into shape as necessary. (If bits of crust stick to the pan on either turn, they can be pressed back onto the top.) Run the remaining tablespoon of butter around the edge of the pan, then place what's left of the butter on top of the potatoes. Salt and pepper the top and continue cooking, uncovered, over low heat, for another 10 minutes, or until nicely crusted on the other side. You can hold the potatoes on low warming heat for another 15 minutes if necessary.

Reverse the potatoes out onto a serving dish, sprinkle on the remaining tablespoon of chives, and cut into individual portions.

—✀—

Right away you have to like peach farmer Martin Glashoff. A rugged, older man, he's one of those fellows who looks a bit stern, no nonsense, until you see the sparkle in his eye. The hat with CRIME DOESN'T PAY, AND NEITHER DOES FARMING, gives him away too.

"We have four acres and there's a hundred trees on each one. Peaches are a poor man's crop. Almonds and cherries have to be cross-pollinated but peaches almost always self-pollinate. I have such joy in seeing the barren trees blossom in spring, and then watching the little peaches in bloom to see what kind of set they have. You can tell a few days after the trees have fertilized. You tap a twig the bloom is on, the petals fall, and there's the little peach smaller than a pea. You stimulate the tree, thin off crowding branches, don't overload with flowers and fruit, leave the top shoots long.

"It takes a pruning crew a month to go through the orchard. We have real spasms of activity. There's probably six hundred peaches a tree, twenty-five tons an acre. We start picking the tenth of June. Pack the fruit in Los Angeles Lugs and put a shim in between layers so the fruit won't bruise. Wish customers would give a thought to bruising and keep their little fingers to themselves. They go around squeezing and squeezing—it just burns me. All you have to do is look at the stem end. When it's a clear, greenless yellow all around, it's ripe. And you can tell by the suture (the indent) what type of peach it is. That Rio Oso over there is famous for deep sutures and warts; that pretty smooth one is a Faye Alberta, the Cadillac of peaches."

One of the most refreshing summer cocktails is the famous Bellini perfected at Harry's Bar in Venice. A mixture of fresh pureed peaches and Asti Spumante, the "champagne" of Italian wines, it is a beautifully hued tribute to the family of fifteenth-century Venetian artists, Iacopo, Gentile, and Giovanni Bellini. You might want to freeze some puree when the peaches are at their ripest so you can re-create this drink out of season.

PEACH BELLINIS

SERVES 6

4 ripe, peelable peaches, preferably white
Juice of ½ lemon
Sugar to taste

2 teaspoons grenadine syrup
1 bottle Asti Spumante, well chilled

Peel the peaches and cut them into slices. Place the peaches and lemon juice in a blender and puree. To be perfectly elegant, press the puree through a sieve. Taste, and if the mixture is at all tart, add just a minimum (around ½ to 1 teaspoon) of sugar to make it mildly sweet. Stir the grenadine syrup into the peaches.

(**I**f you have time, stick the peach puree and Asti Spumante in the freezer for 30 minutes and let the puree turn to half-frozen slush.)

Mix the cocktails in the proportion of 1 part peach puree to 3 parts Asti Spumante. (Spoon the puree into champagne glasses. Stir in a bit of Asti Spumante and mix well, then top up the glasses and give a gentle stir.)

PEACHES

"**A**lways can peaches with the pit in them. When you slice them and freeze them, include a few pits in the container—it makes for sweeter-tasting peaches."

—Rene Postam Siek, Jamaica farmers' market

There's a long line of customers at jovial Bill Adamson's Happy Haven ranch stand. They buy his beautiful strawberries, of course, but the big cooler next to the stand holds the best treat in the market on a sweltering day—cups of dense strawberry ice cream, with some unusual ingredients.

"I started thirteen years ago when I had a massive stroke and had to retire. Got mad at myself and everyone else when the doctors told me I'd never walk or talk. I told them hell with that. My wife had twenty-four strawberry plants. I started tending those, and being out in the garden was healthy, so I started mending. We have seventy-five thousand plants now, three acres of strawberries. I go to seven farm markets in the area each week. People probably think I'm mad.

"Strawberries are lots of work. There's sow bugs, those roly-poly ones with a million legs, and slugs. You have to pick off all the first blossoms and let the second bunch come, and that's the start of the berries. Takes three men full time to keep the plants clean. Then there's blackbirds and starlings. The wine vineyards suffer there, but I luck out because the boys in the fields act like scarecrows all day.

"When strawberries are ripe and ready to pick, you look at the color, you taste 'um, but the seeds are the real give away because they need to be ripe. When they're ripe, they get dark and that's when we make our ice cream. Here, have some."

STRAWBERRY ICE CREAM "HAPPY HAVEN RANCH STYLE"

MAKES 1½ QUARTS

3 ounces cream cheese
¼ cup pineapple juice
Juice of 1 lemon

¾ cup sugar
2 pints ripe strawberries, washed then hulled
2 cups heavy cream, chilled

Place the cream cheese, fruit juices and sugar in a food processor. Blend until smooth. Add the strawberries and run the processor as long as necessary to make a very smooth mixture. Scrape the bowl down once or twice during the puree.

Scrape the strawberries into a bowl and stir in the chilled cream. Pour the mixture into an ice cream maker and churn according to the manufacturer's directions.

— ⚘ —

By 1 P.M., everyone is packing up. Lynn Bagley makes the rounds collecting the last of the day's dues. Lots of bartering goes on:

"You want some corn?"

"Here, have some apples then."

"Trade you some figs."

"See you tonight at Santa Rosa."

"See you at Davis on Saturday."

"See you at the California Tasting on Sunday."

"See you here next week."

Santa Rosa
Thursday Night Market

Thursday-night markets are becoming something of an institution in cities all over California. The most famous one is the 6:30 to 9:00 P.M. bash in San Luis Obispo that started the tradition. Faced with the problem of "cruising" teen-agers speeding up and down the main street of the night-dead downtown area, a forward-looking commission studying the problem came up with the bright idea of closing the street and holding a public festivity that would bring everyone positively into city center. Now five to seven thousand people turn out each week to stroll the street, buy farm produce, celebrate.

This Thursday night I spent in Santa Rosa, one of the cities that studied San Luis Obispo and used it as a blueprint. Main Street is cordoned off, restaurants have moved sampling stands out in front of their doors, merchants have tables of merchandise; groups of bands, dancers, acrobats tune themselves up to perform. The fire department has parked a truck in the middle of the street on official call. Nobody can quite think why it might be needed, but that's the law, and meanwhile kids can clamber on it. The scene reminds me a bit of Friday night "jump-ups" in the Carribean—informal gatherings around produce that lead to dance and music—but market manager Hilda Swartz tells me that not so long ago you could have thrown fifty bowling balls down Main Street and never hit a soul.

The farmers are bunched at one end of the street doing a brisk business.

"Hi." They grin at me. "Saw you this morning."

We are friends by this time.

"See you at Davis on Saturday, too," I say.

Davis Market

The Saturday Davis market stretches out along a leafy central park. There are tables where you can sign up to Save the Blue Heron or have your pet spayed, children on the park swings and slides, an organ grinder in lederhosen. Elderly-lady produce buyers pull up on motorcycles wearing biker helmets; people picnic on their purchases, and always-spectacular mounds of sun-dappled produce arrayed under the trees. Randii MacNear, another committed manager, speaks of the market as a living, breathing force. "I'm totally passionate about it. I want it to be an addiction, a healing part of people's lives, a tonic for their souls." A powerful word, addiction, but in truth that's what a good market becomes. You develop proprietary interests, expand your circle of sociability, become a market "groupie."

"Hey, Judith," yells one of my farmer friends, "what time will we see you at the Tasting tomorrow?"

Tasting of Summer Produce
The Oakland Museum
Oakland, California

Every August since 1983, when Sibella Krause first organized the event to find buyers for farmers' crops in the San Francisco area, a spectacular tasting of height-of-summer produce has been arrayed on tables up and down the terraced gardens of the Oakland Museum. Over one hundred growers now showcase their produce at this event, which Alice Waters, the "mother" of California cuisine, calls the "most important food event in the country." Starting early in the morning, the farmers set up overflowing tables of the season's prime produce, and long tasting tables with cut samples of peaches, melons, tomatoes, raw sweet corn, figs . . . so that people can know and taste varietal differences.

Writer Rosalind Creasy is there with her camera, and any way she points it there's picture-perfect produce she'll include in one of her spectacular books. The owners of the best seed companies all over America are there studying. Renee Shepard of Shepard's Seeds, Ellen and Shepard Ogden flown in from Vermont in search of new items for their "Cook's Garden Seed Catalogue"; cameras follow Alice Waters as she tastes tomatoes and tells interviewers in her no-nonsense way, "I hope in the future that people reconnect with food and its source. I want them to understand purity, how we should be treasuring our farmers. They are the stewards of the land and they're all going broke."

Everyone is taking about the new bug-sucker machine that vacuums a thirty-foot wide swathe of plants and draws in all the bugs—a dream answer to an organic farmer's needs.

Awesome legends are discussed . . . "Do you know broccoli breeder X? He can drive by a field at sixty miles an hour and tell you what varietal is planted." Did you taste X's lettuce? I can't believe he fertilizes with ground river rock."

The vibrant setting, the colorful crowds would make Matisse happy, and I am struck by what a boon farm produce might be to designers and decorators. Tumescent yellow cone flowers are played against the aubergine of eggplant; peaches are piled in blue and white bowls. Endless varietals of tomatoes, striped green, pale, medium, dark gold, salmon red, and dark fat burgher German Johnstons stun the crowd. That is another of the good deeds small farmers do us . . . producing and protecting heirloom nonhybrid varieties that without their cherishing care might disappear forever.

TOMATOES

Gold Nugget,
    Green Grape,
        Red Pear,
            Red Plum,
                Yellow Plum,
                    Early Girl,
                        Better Boy,
                            Celebrity,
                                Sun Drop,
                                    Golden Jubilee,
                                        Marvel Stripe
                                          Green Zebra . . .

—Tasting of Summer Produce

— ✿ —

I'm not sure whether the name "cobble" comes from the sense of the word meaning lumpy; put together hastily, or from the more archaic iced drink, as in whiskey cobbler, but both meanings could apply here. This is a delicious and unexpected use for peak season tomatoes on a hot August day. Half soup, half salad, and an icy slush to boot, try it with German Johnston beefsteaks if you get a chance.

FRESH TOMATO COBBLE

SERVES 6

4 ripe medium tomatoes, or 2 large
  beefsteaks
1 small sweet red onion, minced
1 tablespoon finely minced fresh parsley
2 teaspoons minced fresh chives

½ teaspoon fresh thyme
½ teaspoon salt
Good grinding of fresh pepper
¼ teaspoon sugar

For the Garnish:

Sour Cream

Parsley sprigs (optional)

If the tomatoes are fully sun ripened, they may peel easily. If not, bring a large pot of water to a boil, slip in the tomatoes, cover, and let them steam for half a minute. Strain out and peel when cool enough to handle. Cut out the stem end.

Place a sieve over a bowl. Holding the tomatoes stem end up, cut them crosswise through the center. Squeeze both halves so that the seeds are expelled. Press the seeds and collect all the juice.

Place the tomatoes, onion, herbs, seasonings, and sugar in the bowl of a food processor or in a blender and blend on/off until the mixture is juicy but still coarse—rather like a chili or salsa in consistency.

Place the tomatoes in a stainless-steel or glass bowl in the freezer. About 1½ hours along, the mixture will have frozen to the sides of the bowl. Scrape down, break up the chunks, and return to the freezer for at least another 30 minutes. At any point from 2 to 5 hours after freezing, the mixture will be a wonderful slush.

To serve, mash to a good slushy consistency with a fork. Place in mugs, bowls, or tall wineglasses. Top with a small spoonful of sour cream and an herb sprig if so desired and eat with a spoon.

Here's a pretty cooked use for both red and yellow cherry tomatoes. You can use one or the other color or mix them, and the skinning process can be done a day ahead if you wish. Serve this just slightly warm or at room temperature with roasted lamb.

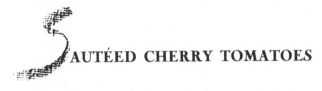

SAUTÉED CHERRY TOMATOES

SERVES 4–6

2 pints red or yellow cherry tomatoes
  (or 1 pint of each), stemmed
¼ cup olive oil
1 large clove garlic, minced
Large pinch of sugar
1 tablespoon balsamic vinegar, or
  2 tablespoons red wine vinegar

½ teaspoon salt
Freshly ground pepper to taste
¼ cup basil leaves (preferably small-leafed
  Greek basil)

Bring a large pot of water to a boil. Dump in the cherry tomatoes, cover the pot, turn off the heat, and let them sit for 30 seconds. Lift the tomatoes out gently and as soon as you can handle them, slip off all the skins. (The peeled tomatoes can be put in a single layer on paper toweling and refrigerated over night if need be.)

Heat the oil and garlic together in a large frying pan. When the garlic is just starting to brown, add the sugar, vinegar, and salt. Shake the pan over the heat until the vinegar stops foaming. Slip in the tomatoes and gently roll them about in the fragrant oil to just barely heat through. Add pepper to taste and a dense sprinkling of basil.

This has been one of my favorite ways to use fresh, ripe tomatoes ever since I saw a cook prepare the dish in a small New Delhi restaurant. It's splendid for entertaining because you can marinate and roast the chicken ahead of time and simply rewarm it in the sauce. If you wish, you can take the garam masala, ginger, and cuminseed out and turn the dish from Indian to Mediterranean (niçoise olives, oregano, sautéed zucchini, and peppers) in a flash.

TOMATO BUTTER CHICKEN

SERVES 6

1 large chicken, cut into serving portions

For the Marinade:

Juice of 1 lemon
1½ cups plain yogurt
1 small onion, minced fine

1 teaspoon salt
1 teaspoon garam masala (Indian spice mixture)

For the Sauce:

5 medium-large fresh tomatoes
1 stick unsalted butter
2 teaspoons cuminseed, toasted brown
1 inch fresh gingerroot, grated
1½ cups heavy cream
2 teaspoons garam masala
1 teaspoon salt

¼ teaspoon sugar
Cayenne to taste
Freshly ground black pepper to taste
Juice of ½ lemon

Handful of coriander leaves for garnish

Rinse and wipe the chicken pieces. Remove the skin (except for the wing pieces). In the thickest portions of breast, thigh, and leg, make 2 or 3 shallow scoring marks with a small knife so that the marinade can penetrate.

Mix all the marinade ingredients. Place the chicken in a pan and add the marinade. (This must be done 1 hour ahead at minimum, but it's even better to give 12 or even 24 hours to this step.) Cover and refrigerate, then let the chicken come to room temperature 30 minutes before the time to bake it.

Turn your oven as high as it will go (that's 525°F. on mine). When the oven is fully hot, roast the chicken for 30 minutes. This will give a tandoori-oven look to the portions. The chicken can be roasted an hour ahead of time, then gently rewarmed in its sauce).

To make the sauce, core out the tomatoes and cut them in half across the middle. Squeeze out the seeds, then coarsely chop the tomatoes. Melt the butter in large sauté pan. Add the tomatoes and all the rest of the sauce ingredients. Let them simmer until all is smooth, 10 to 12 minutes.

Place the chicken in the sauce, spooning some up over the portions, and gently heat together for 5 minutes on top of the stove or in the oven before serving. Top with coriander leaves.

You may think of uses for this summer "gravy" other than as an accompaniment to drop noodles, but none this tasty, I suspect. This is wonderful by itself for lunch, or you might want to serve it along with roast chicken.

BROWN TOMATO GRAVY WITH PAPRIKA DROP NOODLES

SERVES 4–6

For the Gravy:

2 medium-large firm, ripe tomatoes
4 tablespoons (½ stick) butter
Around ½ cup flour
2 tablespoons sugar

1 teaspoon salt
1 small onion, minced
1 cup hot water
Freshly ground pepper to taste

For the Drop Noodles:

4 teaspoons salt
½ teaspoon paprika
Pinch of baking powder
Around 1 cup quick-blending flour (such as Pillsbury's Shake & Blend)

2 teaspoons olive oil
3 eggs, lightly beaten

For the Garnish:

1 plastic Baggie
Lots of minced parsley

Freshly ground pepper to taste
Butter

Bring a large pot of water to a boil. Skin the tomatoes by dropping them in the water and letting them simmer for 2 minutes. Remove the tomatoes with a slotted spoon. (Cover the pot of water and keep it to poach the noodles later.)

Peel the tomatoes and cut out the core. Cut each one into 4 thick cross slices. Melt the butter in a large frying pan. Place the flour on a plate, add the tomato slices, and flour each side generously. When the butter has sizzled up then subsided, add the tomatoes and quickly fry each side brown.

Add the sugar, salt, onion, and water to the tomatoes; turn the heat to low, and continue to cook for 20 minutes. Stir 2 or 3 times and mash down on the tomatoes with a fork to break them up as smoothly as possible. Just before serving, add pepper to the "gravy."

While the tomato gravy simmers, make the noodles. Add 3 teaspoons of the salt to the reserved poaching water and bring back up to a boil, then regulate the heat to a barely moving simmer.

Mix the remaining teaspoon of salt, paprika, baking powder, and flour in a bowl. Make a well in the center and stir in the oil and eggs. Add a little more flour if necessary to make the consistency of thin peanut butter.

Scrape the batter into a plastic Baggie and twist tie the top shut. Cut off a ¼-inch corner of the bag. Hold the bag over the simmering water and squeeze out half the batter in driblets. They will sink then float to the surface. Cover and poach for 1 minute. Strain out the noodles and cook the remaining batter.

Gently mix the noodles, gravy, and parsley. Grind on more pepper and serve at once with a lump of butter on each portion.

Under the garden trees at noon we have a box lunch (Armenian cracker lavash rolls; Bruce Aidells' Andouille, Sweet Corn, and Rice Salad; raw vegetables and dip; a brownie; a crisp Orange-Almond Bar); and a discussion with garlic grower Rich Knoll. White-blond hair, a suntanned surfer-boy look (he *does* go surfing in January, his farmer's month off) Rich is a state-of-the-art California farmer—that's a bit of Zen, a little mysticism, an overwhelming concern for the plight of the land.

"I'm an astro-organic farmer. The moon is important and every professional farmer should plant on the moon. It helps pull and draw seed upward. Check the almanac and plant on lunar phases. If the plant fruits aboveground, plant on a waxing moon. If it roots —like garlic, onion, beets—wait until the moon wanes.

"A lot of people think that farmers are bumpkins, but as a matter of fact we're intelligent, tenacious, and a lot of us have come back to the land from office jobs. We're not a social community anymore. We don't have grandfather farmers tell us 'watch this, do this, learn that,' so we may fail at half the things we try. Back in the 1800s, if your crops failed, the community would gather 'round and support you, but now if too much goes wrong, farmers just go under.

"We really tore up our land . . . harvested all the trees, planted grain, burned out the topsoil . . . raped it so continually that after the past hundred years of abuse it will only support houses. But the earth is dynamic enough to reverse itself. What organic farmers do is help maintain the Green Belt. We rebuild the soil that past generations have trashed, experiment with production, produce nutritious, nondestructive food. We could use some subsidies, maybe we shouldn't have to pay taxes at all.

"When the traditional farmers plant, they put a lot of nitrogen, water, fungicides on the seeds—in effect, they drown the plant. When it is not left to its own genetic material's devices, you stress the plant beyond belief. Most of the world lives on stressed-out food. Between that food and the stressed people living off the stressed-out food, we're in a mess. That may be a bizarre theory, but if we don't get our food production straight and real and authentic, America's in trouble."

Lavash Armenian cracker bread is particularly popular in California as a rolled hors d'oeuvre. The cracker is moistened, spread with a variety of fillings, rolled up, chilled, then cut.

CALIFORNIA TASTING SMOKED TURKEY LAVASH

MAKES 20–24 SLICES

1 large (15-inch) round of lavash
1 stick butter, softened
8 ounces cream cheese, at room temperature
¼ teaspoon Liquid Smoke (LiquaSmoke)
2 tablespoons mayonnaise
1 clove garlic
⅔ pound smoked turkey, thinly sliced then
    cut into shreds

6 large black olives, drained and minced
5 sun-dried tomatoes, minced
2 stalks celery, strings removed, minced
3 tablespoons minced fresh parsley or parsley
    and chives

Thoroughly wet and wring out 2 clean dish towels. Spread 1 towel on a counter. Hold the lavash under a trickling faucet and gently wet it on both sides. Place on the dish towel, then cover with the other wet towel. Allow to soften for at least 45 to 50 minutes (you may have to sprinkle on a bit more water or, if the cracker is too moist, wait a bit for it to dry out). The easily-rollable stage should be apparent.

To make the filling, place butter, cream cheese, liquid smoke, mayonnaise, and garlic in the bowl of a food processor and puree until smooth. Stir in the smoked turkey.

Scrape the mixture into a bowl. Add the remaining ingredients and mix well.

When the lavash is perfectly limp but in no danger of tearing apart, spread the mixture over the cracker. Roll up very tightly and place in the refrigerator to harden for at least 2 hours.

Slice thin and serve as an hors d'oeuvres.

Bruce Aidells, the Bay Area's premier sausage maker, made and donated this hearty salad to the Tasting. He originally test-marketed his spicy Cajun andouille in the Marin County market, but now he sells all over the country.

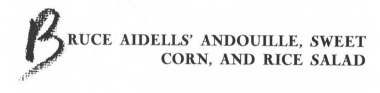

BRUCE AIDELLS' ANDOUILLE, SWEET CORN, AND RICE SALAD

SERVES 4–6

For the Salad:

1 pound andouille sausage, sliced into thin rounds

2 ears corn, kernels cut from cob

2 cups fresh cooked rice or rice-shaped pasta (orzo)

⅓ cup toasted pine nuts

½ cup Mustard Vinaigrette (see below)

1 bunch watercress, stems removed

3 scallions, both white and green parts sliced thin

1 red bell pepper, roasted, peeled, and cut into strips

For the Mustard Vinaigrette:

¼ cup red wine vinegar

2 tablespoons Dijon mustard

1 teaspoon minced garlic

¾ cup olive oil

Salt and freshly ground pepper to taste

In a skillet over moderate heat, fry the sausage for 3 to 4 minutes. Add the corn and cook, stirring constantly, for 2 minutes.

Combine the sausage, corn, and remaining salad ingredients in a large bowl.

Mix the dressing, toss the salad, and serve.

Here's a delicious cookie bar that shows two of California's best-known crops to advantage.

ORANGE-ALMOND BARS

MAKES 16 PORTIONS

2 sticks unsalted butter

1 cup sugar

1 pound (an entire box) light brown sugar

4 eggs, separated

3 tablespoons Grand Marnier

2 teaspoons orange extract

Zest from 2 large oranges

1¾ cups all-purpose flour

2 teaspoons baking powder

¼ teaspoon salt

1 cup slivered almonds, toasted light brown

Confectioners' sugar

Preheat the oven to 350°F. Butter and flour a 9-x-13-inch baking pan.

Melt the butter in a medium-large saucepan. Stir in the sugars, egg yolks, Grand Marnier, orange extract, and zest.

Stir the flour, baking powder, and salt together, then mix it into the liquid ingredients.

Beat the egg whites until stiff but still glossy. Stir half of them into the batter. Fold in the remaining whites, then pour the mixture into the prepared baking pan. Scatter the almonds over the top.

Bake for 35 minutes. The mixture will puff up then settle back down into a dense compact bar. When completely cool, sift a bit of confectioners' sugar over the top. Don't cut the bars for at least 2 hours.

Here's a recipe given to me at the California Tasting by Jesse Cool of the Flea St. Cafe in Menlow Park. It puts a spin on melons, turning them from sweet to savory.

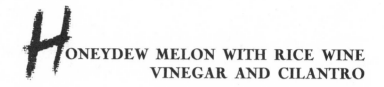

HONEYDEW MELON WITH RICE WINE VINEGAR AND CILANTRO

SERVES 4

1 honeydew melon, seeded, peeled, cut into fork-sized chunks
⅓ cup rice wine vinegar

1 small chile pepper, seeded and cut into thin strips
¼ cup torn cilantro leaves

Place the melon chunks in a bowl. Sprinkle with the vinegar, pepper strips, and cilantro, then place in the refrigerator to chill for 20 minutes.

Drain off any juices that have collected, and serve the melon for breakfast or brunch.

MELONS

Green Pearl

    Tiger Baby

        Ambrosia

            Crimson Sweet

                Old-Fashioned Barrel

                    Yellow Baby

        —at the Tasting from Hungry Hollow Farm, Yalo County

— ∘ —

"Cut off water to melons the last three weeks they're growing. It improves and concentrates the taste."

"As watermelon matures, the stems get less hairy. Choose the smoothest stem for the sweetest melon."

        —words of wisdom from Renee Shepard of Shepard Garden Seeds

— ∘ —

I've gotta melon that's sweet to the rind,
Ya can't find a melon that's sweeter than mine.

        —Melon "rapper" in Detroit's Eastern market

Maxine Sessoms, with her extraordinary display of edible flowers, is one of the highlights of the California Tasting. For flower products you order by mail, check the sources at the back of the book. If you have lots of roses growing, or you can find them in profusion at a farmers' market, make this glamorous pink sauce.

MAXINE SESSOMS' ROSE PETAL SAUCE

MAKES ABOUT 1 PINT OF SAUCE

2 packed cups rose petals (highly scented
    Deep Red, or Chrysler Imperial if possible)
1 teaspoon lemon juice
¼ cup white wine vinegar (do not use
    distilled vinegar)

½ cup light corn syrup
1 cup sugar
2 tablespoons corn starch dissolved in
    2 tablespoons water
½ cup water

Cut off the white tips of the petals, as they tend to be slightly bitter. Cut the petals into large shreds.

Combine all ingredients in a nonaluminum saucepan and bring to a boil. Simmer for 8 minutes. Strain and cool.

Cover and store in the refrigerator. This sauce can be kept for several weeks, and it can be used with fresh fruits such as pears and white nectarines, or over a warm bread pudding. Try it on ice cream (scatter on a few fresh rose petals for garnish), or with fruit ices and sorbets.

A pretty summer's compote:

RHUBARB IN ROSÉ

SERVES 4–6

2 pounds rhubarb

1 cup rosé wine

1½ cups sugar

¼ teaspoon fine orange zest

2 large pinches of ginger

3–4 drops vanilla extract

½ cup heavy cream or crème fraîche

Rose petals and mint sprigs for garnish

Trim the ends from the rhubarb and lightly string the stalks. Cut them into thin slices.

Bring the wine, sugar, orange zest, and ginger to a boil. Add the rhubarb and simmer for 10 to 12 minutes, or until tender.

In the saucepan slice the mass through with a small knife so that the slices are uniformly smooth, with a consistency the size of large cottage cheese curds. Add the vanilla. Cool the compote.

To serve, whip the cream until lightly thickened but not dry. Spoon the compote into bowls (glass ones are pretty), stir in a small swirl of cream, and garnish with a few rose petals and a sprig of mint.

INTO THE FUTURE

One of the best agricultural futurists on the California landscape is Bob Cannard, teacher/philosopher, practicing farmer, and grower of much of the produce used by Alice Waters's Chez Panisse restaurant. His Sonoma farm uses controversial methods of tillage—crushed river rock as a fertilizing base; weeds thick between rows; thick interplanted crops (sage under grapevines; strawberries beneath the pear trees); but everyone agrees that the methods result in aromatic, intensely flavored, superior produce.

Ask Bob Cannard for a glimpse into the visionary future of farming and farm markets and he grows passionate and intense:

"You talked to Rich Knoll about garlic today. That's a good crop to talk about because there is a documented history of its cultivation in the area. One hundred and fifty years ago, garlic was growing in downtown San Francisco where the Bank of America sits now. When the town expanded, garlic growing moved out to the suburbs, and when that soil got depleted, people just moved on to the virgin soil of the Sierra foothills. America has been a spendthrift country where we used up the land, pulled stakes, and went in search of the great fertile soil over the next mountain. Then we'd dominate that soil with chemicals and pollute it, rather than embrace nature and cooperate with it.

"Recently we've had a change in consciousness. We've realized there is a hunger, an incompleteness in the process of living, which we are starting to respect both in and out of person. Our levels of respect for nature are growing, and that in turn leads to a sense of personal, communal, and earthly responsibility. We are moving back to a nurturing system; we are realizing localness and community are important. We are asking why nature has to be denied us if we abide in cities. Why can't that garlic grow nearby where people live? If you grow vegetables locally, you have ease in transportation. Small growing plots are more operative than big farms, which are notoriously inefficient.

"What I would like to see in the future are vacant lots in towns or small edges of cities given over to agriculture. A community might have a bond issue, buy or lease the property, break it up into family-sized sections, and let young farmers grow for local consumption. Children won't be segregated from the rural experience that way.

"We could make use of grocery-store locations that chains desert as they move on to bigger facilities. Bash out the fronts of the empty stores so that small trucks could get inside and you'd have perfect protected buildings in which to hold farmers' markets.

"As more and more people in desk-bound professions are leaving stale jobs to embrace nature, I think small farming will become prestigious and small farmers local heroes, for they can actively demonstrate earthly responsibility.

"That farming fields can be close to all of us is not as farfetched as it might seem. Less than a hundred years ago there was no preserving National Park system in place, but as our levels of respect for nature grow, as our own natures grow 'sweeter' and demand greater sweetness from life, so can we make all things happen."

"Wouldn't it be wonderful if there were a national 'convenience store' chain of farm markets as big as 7-Eleven?"

—Steve Evans, Pike Place Market

LATE SUMMER

THE PACIFIC NORTHWEST

Pike Place Market
Seattle

PIKE PLACE IS PROBABLY THE MOST STIMULATING
and sensuously appealing market in America. Stretched along the bank right above Puget
Sound, tangled in amid industry, shipping, neon lights, blue movies, upscale hotels, shops,
derelict hotels, spectacular mountain-range vistas, and city-center bustle, the market
breathes, respires, inspires, flows, delights.

It was organized in 1907 as a city council experiment. (At the time farmers were
forced to sell to consignment houses that bought cheap, charged a commission, and had a
monopoly on resale.) Five farmers drove up to the old pike in wagons in August of that
year, sold out their wares within an hour, and the place soon became a city institution.

Like many other city markets, Pike Place was at its heyday during the Depression.
Over six hundred farmers regularly sold there during the thirties, and the jobless could
spend their days in the nurturing, friendly environment that the market did and still does
provide.

Waves of immigrant vendors from Europe and Asia opened businesses under the
long, sheltering sheds and in the expanding covered markets and underground areas.
Italians started grocery stores; Japanese farmed and sold impeccable produce; Greek brothers opened a luncheonette called the Athenian Inn; Dave "Good Weight" Levy bought the
City Fish market. During World War II the market lost about half its farmers when
Japanese-Americans were interned. The fifties brought a flight from the city center to the
industrial parks and suburbs.

In the 1960s, developers began to eye the now-crumbling neighborhood. Wouldn't a nice row of high-rises, some Mylared office buildings be better here, they proffered. Fortunately, it was not to be. A grass-roots campaign saved the market and an initiative measure turned the seven-acre site into an historical district.

Recently, two hundred representatives from every state and Canada came for a conference at the market. They studied the senior center, the low-income housing units, the medical clinic, and the food bank that are active units of the market. They viewed the 46,500 bricks stamped with caring citizens' names that cost ten dollars each and paved the floor of the Market Arcade. They saw the day-old bread shop in the prime space across the street, which could have been a yuppie store but is preserved as an outlet where the poor can purchase loaves. They saw the street people hanging about and the "baby brigade" from a nearby nursery that gets wheeled through the market three abreast every Tuesday and Friday. They heard Steve Evans, the market manager, talk about his active recruitment of farmers and how the nonprofit development corporation actually lends money to new farmers for equipment, seed, travel expenses. They tasted the bounty of the produce, visited the restaurants, and came away inspired to create or re-create the experience in towns across the continent.

One of the good things about Pike Place market is that nobody attempted to gussy it up too much. There are light bulbs screwed into sockets, old white glass light fixtures, the same green-and-white color scheme that was there in the thirties. There are lots of old neon signs. It's simple and plain—no fake "ye olde" business, no quaint reproductions. The heart of the central market building houses the fish stores. At Pike Place Fish Company you can catch an act that has been going on for years but still seems to stop people in their tracks. Someone buys a whole salmon—a king, silver, pink, chum, or sockeye—and the seller heaves the big fish through the air to the back of the stand where it will be weighed. The fish flies and lands with a big slap in the hands of the catcher, not an easy feat given the freshness, size, and slipperiness of the fish. And there's a wonderful curiosity, the Puget Sound geoduck. Pronounced "gooey-duck," this largest-clam-in-the-world (about five pounds) sits on ice while its siphon neck oozes from the shell like an alien's nightmare limb. "Gooey-ducks, get your gooey-ducks here," the vendors cry. "Take them home for pets."

There's mahimahi, tuna, shark, sea bass, sturgeon, orange roughy, smelts, butterfish, and Dungeness crab; while at the food stalls and restaurants you can buy seafood and shellfish cooked a score of ways.

Kathy Lewis of Martin's Farm
packs up edible flowers to take to
Pike Place Market

Pat Sterling's peach kuchen displayed at Carrboro Market nose-to-nose with a Mercedes

Martin Glashoff, peach farmer, at the Marin Market

Historic Soulard Market with the famous St. Louis arch visible in the background

Two farmer's sons proudly display their wares at the Travis County Farmers' Market in Austin, Texas

Suzanne Somers examines sponge mushrooms during one of her frequent visits to the Santa Monica Market

Deliciously sweet Amsterdam-style carrots beautifully displayed at the Union Square Market

 A vegetable seller at the Richmond, Virginia, Farmers' Market

One of my favorite places in the market is the Athenian Inn, which has been in operation since 1909. You can sit and look out at the waterfront while no-nonsense ladies serve you clam hash, broiled kippers, and classic Northwest salmon preparations.

—❦—

The Athenian Inn serves sides of salt salmon (as in salt cod), which they soak to revitalize, then sauté and cover with egg sauce. Here is an ersatz version of more delicate flavor than actual salt salmon.

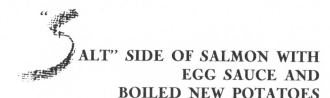

"SALT" SIDE OF SALMON WITH EGG SAUCE AND BOILED NEW POTATOES

SERVES 4

1 side of salmon, around 1½–2 pounds (Have the fishmonger cut the fish through at the back tip of the dorsal fin, then slice the tail section through along the backbone. Have him bone one side.)

½ cup dry white wine

For the Egg Sauce:

6 tablespoons (¾ stick) unsalted butter
Juice of 1 lemon
3 tablespoons minced fresh parsley
3 eggs, hard-boiled and coarsely chopped
Freshly ground pepper

6 allspice berries
2 tablespoons coarse salt
Coarsely ground fresh pepper
Olive oil

Hot boiled new potatoes dressed with a bit of butter and minced parsley
Lemon wedges

Whole parsley sprigs for garnish

Place the salmon flesh side up in a broilerproof baking dish. Pour the wine over the fish. Crush the allspice berries with the flat side of a large knife blade. Sprinkle the crushed berries, salt, and ground pepper over the fish. Leave at room temperature for 1 to 1½ hours before broiling (or you may refrigerate overnight).

Preheat the broiler. Ten minutes before you want to eat, turn the fish over, skin side up, and brush the skin with a coating of olive oil. Place the baking dish under the broiler, and cook for 10 minutes. There will be black blisters on the skin.

While the fish cooks, prepare the egg sauce. Melt the butter in a saucepan, add the lemon juice, parsley, and the eggs. Pepper to taste and keep warm.

To serve, transfer the fish to a serving platter skin side down. Place the hot boiled potatoes and lemon wedges around the fish. Spoon the egg sauce down the center of the salmon and garnish with a sprig or 2 of parsley. With a sharp knife and a spatula, cut the fish into 4 portions and slide the spatula under the flesh to separate it from the skin.

At the Athenian Inn these Yugoslavian Potatoes captured my imagination. I like both how they look (sliced big, gutsy with specks of black pepper and rosemary, a patina of golden brown) and how they taste. This is a great dish for dieters, as it satisfies the eye's need for a fried look without using any fat.

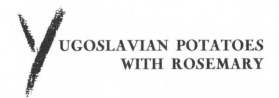

YUGOSLAVIAN POTATOES WITH ROSEMARY

SERVES 4

3 large, nicely oval Idaho potatoes, peeled
Oil
1 tablespoon fresh rosemary

½ teaspoon cracked or coarsely ground black pepper
Salt to taste

Start some water heating in a vegetable steamer.

Slice the potatoes through the long way into 3 long, thick slices. Cut each slice into oversized "French fries."

Steam the potatoes for around 12 minutes. You want them "al dente"—just at the point where a knife tip pierces without resistance, but don't let them get mashing soft.

Lightly oil a baking sheet. Turn the broiler on full blast and let it heat completely. Place the potatoes on the baking sheet in a single layer. Sprinkle with the rosemary, pepper, and salt. Place the potatoes under the broiler and let them turn deep brown, brown/black even in some spots. Turn the potatoes and let them brown on the other side.

Only 2 sides need be spotted this way. Serve at once.

I think you would like Yugoslavian Potatoes alongside this shrimp—a delicious combination. You could steam up one extra potato and use it as the mashed potato for the cakes.

IKE PLACE SHRIMP CAKES

SERVES 4

1 pound peeled, deveined shrimp, coarsely chopped

1 egg

1 cup sieved or smoothly mashed cooked potatoes

1 small onion, coarsely chopped

2 stalks celery, diced

Zest of 1 lemon (about ½ teaspoon)

1 teaspoon salt

1 teaspoon Old Bay Seasoning (or other comparable seafood seasoning)

Large pinch of cayenne

Generous grinding of fresh black ground pepper

⅓ cup chopped fresh parsley

For Frying:

⅔ cup flour

1 egg beaten with 2 teaspoons water

1 cup fine dry bread crumbs

Around 3 tablespoons each of oil and butter

Lemon wedges

Tartar sauce (optional)

Place half the shrimp and the egg in a food processor or blender and process to a fine puree.

Stir the shrimp, mashed potatoes, and all the remaining vegetables, spices, and seasonings together.

Line a cookie sheet with a piece of wax paper or foil.

On 3 separate plates place the flour, beaten egg, and bread crumbs.

With oiled hands, form the shrimp mixture into 8 patties. Dredge each patty in flour, then transfer it to the egg plate with a spatula and let the liquid adhere to both sides of the cake. Finally, place each cake in the bread crumbs and make sure they thickly coat both flat sides and the rim of each patty. Place the cakes on the paper-covered cookie sheet as each one is finished. Refrigerate for at least 30 minutes (or up to 3 or 4 hours).

Heat the oil and butter in a large frying pan and fry the cakes in 2 batches over medium-low heat. Let them slowly brown to a deep gold on one side, then turn and brown to a crisp on the other side.

Serve immediately with the lemon wedges. Tartar sauce goes nicely, also.

—❦—

SALMON STEAK AND FENNEL SALAD WITH GAZPACHO DRESSING

SERVES 4

4 small or 3 medium fennel bulbs
4 cross-section salmon steaks
Flour
2 tablespoons butter

2 tablespoons olive oil
Large green romaine lettuce leaves and a few
    tender leaves spinach for each plate
Cherry tomatoes

For the Dressing:

1 large ripe tomato, dipped in boiling water,
    skinned, pressed to expel seeds
¼ cup chopped red onion
½ small red bell pepper, seeded and minced
⅓ cup olive oil

3 tablespoons balsamic vinegar
1 clove garlic, pressed
½ teaspoon salt
Freshly ground pepper to taste
Pinch of sugar

Cut off the fennel tops and reserve 4 sprigs of leafy green for garnish. Remove the tough outer stalks, then halve and slice the fennel. Place the vegetable in a steamer and steam until softened but still slightly crunchy (test with a knife tip). Rinse under cold water, drain well, and refrigerate.

Dry the salmon steaks, then press each side heavily into the flour. Melt the butter and olive oil together and fry the salmon, 4 minutes on each side, over medium heat. The flour will form a crisp crust and keep the flesh inside moist.

Arrange a bed of romaine and spinach leaves on 4 large dinner plates. Place a salmon steak in the middle, and steamed fennel around the steaks. Garnish with a few cherry tomatoes. Let the fish cool while you prepare the dressing.

Place all the dressing ingredients in a blender or food processor. Pulse on and off until the mixture is liquid but still a bit chunky. Taste for seasoning. You may wish to add more vinegar.

Spoon the dressing over the salmon and place a fennel sprig atop each portion. Serve cold or at room temperature.

There's a wealth of fast foods to be had in the market. A miniature donut machine turns out hot fried cakes before your eyes; there are Swedish pancakes, tempura haystacks, and you are sure to spot two or three stores selling HoJos—irresistible-looking planks of seasoned fried potatoes. This is a very West Coast "fast food," but it adapts nicely to home use.

HOJOS

MAKES 12 SLICES, SERVES 4–6

3 large, nicely ovaled Idaho baking potatoes, peeled
¾ cup flour
2 tablespoons Lawry's Seasoned Salt, plus extra for sprinkling

½ teaspoon cayenne
1 quart oil for frying (preferably peanut)
1 egg white beaten with 1 tablespoon water
Salt

Cut the potatoes in half the long way, then cut each again the long way so that you have 4 large "planks" of potato. Place the planks in a bowl and cover with cold water. Soak for 30 minutes.

Mix the flour, Lawry's salt, and cayenne together and spread on a plate.

Heat the oil in a deep fryer, electric fry pan, or electric wok, to 375°F.

Remove 2 potato slices from the water and pat dry. With your fingers, rub egg white lightly over the potato slices, place them in the seasoned flour, and press a thick coating onto both sides. Fry the potatoes, 2 slices at a time, until they are a rich golden brown.

Remove from the fat and drain on absorbent paper toweling. Sprinkle again generously with Lawry's salt and with plain salt. These may be kept warm briefly in a holding oven.

TEMPURA HAYSTACKS OF BEETS, CARROTS, AND HERBS

SERVES 3–4

2 medium beets, peeled

3 medium carrots, scraped

4 small, tender zucchini, trimmed

1 quart olive oil for frying

2–3 tablespoons mixed fresh herbs (sage leaves, rosemary, small sprigs of tender thyme)

½ cup flour

1 egg white beaten with 1 tablespoon water

Salt and freshly ground pepper to taste

Large handful of Italian (flat-leaf) parsley

Lemon wedges

Cut all 3 vegetables in a julienne (matchstick) slice. A Mouli-julienne machine, or the grater blade on a food processor works well, or you can hand-slice if you have patience.

Heat the oil to 375°F. in a deep fryer, electric fry pan, or wok.

Rinse the herbs and shake off most but not all of the water. Place the flour in a small bag and add the vegetables and herbs. Shake to coat the vegetables with flour. Dump the contents of the bag into a sieve and shake off the extra flour.

When the oil is hot, pick up loose handfuls of vegetables in one hand. With the other hand, dip your fingers into the egg white and drizzle it onto the vegetables to dampen the mass slightly and allow it to compact at the center. Place a "haystack" loosely in a mesh strainer or skimmer and lower it into the fat. The haystacks will crisp and brown in about 1 minute.

Lift the vegetable clumps out onto a paper towel–covered plate and continue until all are fried. Sprinkle with salt and pepper.

Throw the handful of Italian parsley into the hot fat (it will sizzle and bubble up). Strain it out almost immediately and use it as a crisp garnish for the haystacks. Serve with lemon wedges.

Away from the tempting smells of restaurants and frying foods, and down the long, open hallway, you pass the high stalls where wholesalers sell a variety of produce . . . lots of cherries today and varietal potatoes. Continue toward the open arm of the market that looks out over the Sound, and you come to the real farmer/producers. There's Sue Verdi, solid and serious in glasses, standing behind a bountiful display of carrots so thin, sweet, so brilliantly orange that they stop you in your tracks. And she has fresh fava bean pods that look like common peas on steroids. As she talks to me she organizes the carrots into bunches by folding the tender greens back over and around the carrots like the leafy fringe around a floral nosegay.

"My husband dropped me at the market this morning at 8:00. He drives an hour back home to Snohomish to tend the crops while I sell, then he'll drive back to pick me up at 6:00 P.M. We'll wholesale the leftovers at the end of the day and give some to the senior center. Back home I'll cook a quick supper, then we'll tend the fields till 10:00 at night— midnight even during high season, and that's six days a week. We set an alarm and get up between 3:30 or 4:00 A.M. to start picking. We wear miner's hats with flashlights strapped to either side to pick the rows. Certain weeks you just go on willpower only. Come our winter months off, we hibernate—sleep twenty hours at a stretch sometimes to conserve strength for summer. We're farmers because we're workaholics, passionate, nonmaterialistic. We like the independence and we're sure not money oriented. We could grow things to wholesale and get a better price, but we like our crops to be interesting to us. Things like purslane, broccoli rabe, baby carrots, fava beans are sure more fascinating than potatoes.

"We are just moving to a new farm. Next week is our farm-warming and we invited our good customers and lots of the growers to help us celebrate. I'll cook for the occasion, but usually when we get home at night, I'll make a quick stir-fry . . . something like pole peas and potatoes cubed, hot sausage, and zucchini—just fry them all up and sprinkle on Parmesan.

She gave me the recipe for broccoli rabe on the following page.

SUE VERDI'S BROCCOLI RABE IN THE ITALIAN MANNER

Choose 4 to 5 tender stalks per person. Trim and peel any coarse stems toward the bottom. Steam for 10 to 12 minutes, or until tender.

Heat some oil in a frying pan and press in a good clove of garlic. Add the broccoli and sauté until lightly brown on one side. Add salt and pepper and a tablespoon each of grated Parmesan, Pecorino, and Romano cheese.

—&—

You can do the same thing with fava beans if you like, or you can eat them like the Europeans do:

RAW FAVA BEANS

Place on each person's plate some unshelled beans, some freshly dug radishes, and some niçoise olives. There should be good bread and sweet butter and a salt grinder on the table. Let each person shell his or her own beans, then peel the beans. The skins slip off easily when punctured with a knife or fingernail. Grind a little pile of salt on the plate and use it to dip the beans and radishes. Serve as an appetizer with cold white wine.

FAVA BEANS

You will want to use an inoculant for peas and beans when you grow them. This special culture, completely organic, coats the seed with nutrients that allow increased nitrogen fixation and therefore higher yields. Order it along with legume seeds from a reputable company (see Market Finds).

– ❧ –

Midweek I took Kathy Lewis up on her invitation to come out and visit Martin's Farm. She sells near Sue Verdi on the same wing of the market and again the radiance of her produce is breathtaking . . . a tessellated mosaic of verdigris broccoli, miniature cauliflower, herbs and flowers in bouquet, sun-struck zinnias. My son and I drove Interstate 5 down south to exit 137 at Fife. After that, Kathy had given me a labyrinthian set of left and right turns to bring us into the Puyallup Valley road where "the left field is ours. Turn in by the Porta Potty."

Martin's Farm is a six-year-old project of the Martin Luther King, Jr., Ecumenical Center in Tacoma, which shelters the homeless. The United Way donates seed money each year, and the farm then offers inner-city disadvantaged people the opportunity for work. In addition, the farm donates fifty thousand pounds of produce to local food banks. Money for daily living comes from the crops sold at Pike Place and Puyallup farm markets and specialty crops raised for Seattle restaurants. This is one of a growing number of "boutique" farms around the country. Furthermore, all the produce is organic.

As Kathy puts it, "Selling wholesale is more lucrative than selling at a farmers' market, but we make wonderful connections there. Chefs tell us things to grow and that makes it more interesting for us. We have an immediate cash crop at the market. We can walk home with money rather than wait six weeks for some hotel to pay its bills."

While my son picks and packs edible flowers to be sold that evening to a restaurant, Kathy and fellow farm manager Steve Lospalluto cut into candy-striped chioggia beets that swirl like Van Gogh's sun at the center. There are vitelline yellow beets and small lime-green heads of Romanesque broccoli, a sort of sci-fi vegetable with a pointed head that doesn't yellow and has a sweet, mellow flavor. There are cardoons, salsify, other sturdy root vegetables growing in rows for Bruce Naftaly, one of Seattle's best-known chefs. There are cabbage, squash, and cauliflower rows set aside for the food bank . . . altogether a state-of-the-art and state-of-the-heart garden.

This is a delicious, brilliantly hued soup that you will want to make at least one day ahead.

AGENTA SOUP

SERVES 6

5 large beets, with tops
5 cups lightly salted water
2 large ripe tomatoes
Juice of 1 lemon
1 tablespoon red wine vinegar

1 cup buttermilk
1 cup cream
1 small onion, finely minced
Around 1/2 teaspoon salt
Freshly ground pepper to taste

For the Garnish:

1 small cucumber, peeled, seeded, and diced
2 eggs, hard-boiled and minced
6 tablespoons minced fresh chives (preferable)
   or parsley

Sour cream

Wash the beets, scrubbing them well. Cut off the tops, rinse the leaves, and chop them coarsely.

Place the whole beets and chopped greens in a pot and cover with the water. Bring to a boil, then regulate to a simmer and cook for 20 minutes, or until the beets are tender.

Lift out the beets, strain the cooking water, and reserve 3 cups.

Rub the skin off the beets and chop them coarsely. Core the tomatoes, then cut them crosswise and squeeze out the seeds.

Place the tomatoes, beets, and 2 cups of the beet water in a blender and puree until perfectly smooth.

Pour into a bowl and stir in the lemon juice, vinegar, buttermilk, and cream. Add the minced onion, then taste for salt and add pepper.

At this point you can add more of the reserved beet water as necessary to make a soup, either thick or thin, to your own liking. Refrigerate for at least 24 hours. Taste again for lemon juice and salt.

Serve with small bowls of diced cucumber, hard-boiled egg, minced herbs, and sour cream on the side.

— ❧ —

Slightly caramelized orange zest gives these beets a unique flavor, and if you've never cooked grated beets, you will like the almost sweet corn freshness of their crunch and flavor.

GRATED BEETS WITH ORANGE ZEST

SERVES 4–6

1 medium orange
1 tablespoon sugar
1 cup water
3–4 large beets
¼ teaspoon salt

3 tablespoons butter
⅓ cup cream
A few drops of lemon juice
Freshly ground pepper to taste

With a small, sharp knife, cut off long, thin, spiraling peels of orange skin. Turn the peel strips over and gently scrape off any white that adheres to the orange. Cut the orange zest into long, needle-thin julienne strips.

Place the strips of zest, the sugar, and water in a frying pan and barely simmer over low heat while you prepare the beets.

Peel the beets. Either grate them through the large holes of a hand grater, the medium blade of a Mouli-julienne, or use the large blade attachment of your food processor.

Turn the heat up on the orange zest and let the water reduce to just a moistening tablespoon or two. Add the beets, salt, and butter. Cover the pan, reduce the heat back to a simmer, and let the beets cook for 5 to 7 minutes. Stir from time to time and taste the beets. When they are just cooked but still slightly crunchy, add the cream, and cook and stir until the cream reduces and barely coats the beets in a moistening sauce. Stir in the lemon juice and add the pepper.

$-\text{\%}-$

As to those rows that belong to Bruce Naftaly, they're sacred. A nuturing link between producer and consumer, Naftaly is known up and down the rows of truck farmers at Pike Place. He encourages farmers, visits their farms, spends time with the Indo-Chinese farm project that Pike Place backs. (A group of Laotian refugees who settled in Seattle in 1972 were mainly farmers in their homeland. With help from HUD and technical assistance from farmers at the market, the refugees are now fully functioning and independent farmers. They sell green leafy tatsoi for stir fries and salad, edible pea vines and chrysan-themum, and Chinese broccoli.) Eating at Naftaly's small, wheat-colored restaurant, Le Gourmand, is like visiting the house of a friend who's an excellent cook.

BRUCE NAFTALY

"Cooking for the restaurant is like a game I play to see if I can always eat off the season. I stick with just what is available, but I sit down with seed catalogues and farmers and ask them to grow cardoons, celery root, salsify, kohlrabi, and other odd items. What I would really like is a restaurant where sweet corn grew right outside the door so customers could pick an ear like they choose lobsters from a tank in a seafood restaurant. Right now, Martin's Farm delivers two times a week and I go to Pike Place twice a week. Every grower, every cheesemaker who contributes to the menu, is listed on the back like the credits at the end of a movie. Why shouldn't farmers get starring credits? Why shouldn't diners know who produces their food?"

Cardoons are strange creatures—rather like hoary celery run amuck. They are difficult to grow, but if you find some, try this simple, delicious recipe. As cardoons discolor like artichoke hearts when cut, they need to be cooked in a "blanc" (a white stock) to keep them pretty.

BRUCE NAFTALY'S CARDOONS IN CREAM

SERVES 4–5

For the White Stock:

3 tablespoons flour

6 cups water

1 teaspoon salt

Juice of 1 lemon

3 tablespoons butter

Small bundle of parsley sprigs with stems wrapped around a bay leaf and tied with string

1 large cardoon

2 cups heavy cream

Grated nutmeg

1/2 teaspoon salt

Freshly ground pepper to taste

2 tablespoons minced fresh parsley (preferably Italian)

Place the flour in a small bowl and slowly, smoothly, whisk in 1 cup of water so that there are no clots. Pour the mixture into a large saucepan. Add the 5 remaining cups of water, the salt, lemon juice, butter, and parsley bundle, and bring to a boil.

Prepare the cardoon while the stock is coming to a boil. Pull the vegetable apart into stalks. Discard any wilted, discolored outside stems. Trim the tops and bottoms of the tender stalks and pull the strings back lightly on the larger stalks. Cut into 3-inch-long slices. Trim the heart and cut it into rounds.

Reduce the heat under the stock to a simmer and add the cardoons. Cover and cook until they are tender, 25 to 30 minutes.

Place the cream in a pan over medium heat and reduce it by half. When the cardoons are tender, drain well and add to the reduced cream. Add a grating or two of fresh nutmeg (or a small knife-tip point of ground nutmeg), the salt, and the pepper to taste. Shake the pan over the heat until the cardoons are coated with cream and the vegetable seems to be covered with a sauce of medium consistency. Throw on the handful of parsley and serve.

–❦–

This is a dish from my German grandmother. She always called white sauce by its old fashioned name, "milk gravy."

KOHLRABI BAKED IN MILK GRAVY

SERVES 6–8

6 kohlrabi
4 tablespoons (½ stick) butter
3 tablespoons flour
2½ cups milk
1 teaspoon salt

1 bay leaf
Freshly ground pepper to taste
2 tablespoons grated Parmesan cheese
3 tablespoons fine dry bread crumbs
2 tablespoons finely minced fresh parsley

Trim the kohlrabi stems to 1 inch. Place in a large pot, cover with water, and bring to a boil. Simmer until a knife point stuck into the top meets only tender resistance. The bottom "root" end will always feel pithy.

While the vegetable cooks, prepare the white sauce. Melt 3 tablespoons of the butter and the flour together over medium heat, stirring all the while. Let it simmer and bubble for 2 minutes, then add 2 cups of the milk and whisk hard. When the sauce is smooth, add the remaining ½ cup of milk, the salt, and the bay leaf. Simmer, stirring every 2 or 3 minutes, while the kohlrabi is cooking.

When the vegetable is tender, rinse it under cold water and peel (kohlrabi are strange, uneven beasts). Stick a small knife point into the "root" and core out the pithy part. This may almost produce a donut shape in some of the vegetables. Cut each kohlrabi into 4 slices.

Butter a 6-to-8-cup gratin dish. Arrange the slices in the dish, then pour white sauce over the vegetable. Center the bay leaf and give the dish a shake to cover the slices with sauce. Add the pepper.

Mix the cheese, bread crumbs, and parsley and scatter the mixture over the surface. Place 7 or 8 thin shavings of cold butter on top and bake in a 350° oven for 25 to 30 minutes, or until the surface is nicely browned.

Delicious with lamb or other red meat.

— ❦ —

Sautéed Jerusalem Artichokes with Garlic and Rosemary

SERVES 4

½ pound Jerusalem artichokes
3 tablespoons olive oil
2 cloves garlic, sliced paper thin

¼ teaspoon minced fresh rosemary
Salt and freshly ground pepper to taste
Handful of minced fresh parsley

Wash the chokes but leave them unpeeled; slice them ¼ inch thick. Heat the oil, garlic, and rosemary in a large frying pan. Just as the garlic begins to turn golden brown, add the chokes and sauté, shaking the pan and tossing the contents over medium heat until all are browned, 4 to 5 minutes.

Sprinkle with salt and pepper, toss in some parsley and serve at once.

If you have not yet tried any of the new yellow potato varietals, you are in for a treat. Not only are they richer in hue than white potatoes, but also they taste more of the earth —and they contain more vitamins. This dish is too good *not* to make, so give it a whirl with red new potatoes rather than forego it. It is one of my favorite recipes in this book.

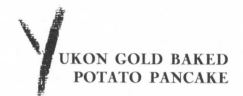

YUKON GOLD BAKED POTATO PANCAKE

SHOULD SERVE 6,
UNLESS I'M INVITED TO DINNER

6 medium Yukon Gold (or Yellow Finn)
  potatoes

2 eggs

2 tablespoons flour

1 large clove garlic, pressed

1 tablespoon grated onion

2 teaspoons salt

Lots of freshly ground pepper

1¼ cups milk

3 tablespoons butter, melted

Sour cream and minced fresh parsley for
  garnish

Preheat the oven to 350°F. Butter an 11-inch quiche or other baking dish.

Peel and grate the potatoes with a medium-holed grater. (The middle blade of a Mouli-julienne is perfect; otherwise use the large holes of a hand grater.) Add all the remaining ingredients except the melted butter, sour cream, and parsley and mix well—your hands are most effective here. Put the potatoes into the prepared baking dish and press the surface down flat.

Drizzle the melted butter over the top and bake for 1 hour.

Serve immediately with a bowl of sour cream and another of minced parsley on the side. I suppose you could have some apple sauce too if you are a real purist.

This combination of purple Caribe and red new potatoes makes a colorful hash.

HARLEQUIN HASH BROWNS

SERVES 4–6

1 pound red new potatoes
6 tablespoons (¾ stick butter)
1 small onion, minced

1 pound purple Caribe potatoes
Salt and freshly ground pepper
Around ½ teaspoon thyme leaves

Peel the red potatoes and cut them into ½-inch cubes. Melt the butter at medium heat in a large skillet and add the red potatoes and onion.

Peel the caribe potatoes, cut them into cubes, and add them to the skillet. Sprinkle with ½ teaspoon of salt and gently turn the potato mass to mix the 2 colors. Regulate the heat to medium low and continue to make tender turns of the potatoes every 2 to 3 minutes as they brown on the bottom.

The potatoes should cook slowly over a period of 15 minutes and the result should be a crisp, browned-on-all-sides checkered potato cake. Sprinkle with a bit more salt, pepper to taste, and the fresh thyme, then serve immediately.

Walk along the street in front of Pike Place market and you will probably see provençal inspired "fougassa" prepared. I stood in a crowd and watched while the baker vigorously chopped away at the dough. You can bet that when it came out of the oven, we were all milling nearby to purchase a share. This break-apart bread is wonderful looking and tasting. Serve it for lunch with a salad, or pass large baskets of it at a party if you like.

GARDEN FOUGASSA (CHOPPED VEGETABLE BREAD)

SERVES 12–15

For the Dough:

1 cup milk

2 tablespoons butter

2 tablespoons sugar

1½ tablespoons chili paste or tomato paste (or enough ketchup to turn the milk a pretty salmon color)

1 large clove garlic, pressed

3 teaspoons salt

¾ cup lukewarm water

1½ packages active dry yeast

Around 6¼ cups unbleached flour

1 generous cup chopped red onion

1 large red bell pepper, seeded and cubed

2 small zucchini, halved and sliced

1 cup sliced mushrooms

1½ cups cubed sharp Cheddar cheese

Olive or walnut oil

Scald the milk, then add the butter, sugar, chili paste, garlic, and salt, and let them dissolve. When the milk has cooled to lukewarm, dissolve the yeast in the water and add it to the milk. Stir in around 5½ cups of flour and, as soon as possible, turn the dough out onto a floured surface and continue kneading and working in more flour until a very elastic consistency has formed. Place the dough in an oiled bowl, cover with a towel, and let it rise in a warm place for 1 hour.

Place the dough on a floured board and pat it out with your hands. Scatter approximately ¼ of the vegetables and cheese over the surface of the dough. Using 2 stiff metal-bladed scrapers or spatulas, chop the vegetables into the dough until they are nicely mixed in. Sprinkle on a few drops of oil and knead the dough together. Pat the dough out again and continue working in the vegetables and cheese until all have been incorporated. The dough will be stringy and barely contain its load of vegetables. Do one last fine chop through the mass.

Oil a large cookie sheet. Place the dough in its *chopped state* on the sheet. Do not tamp it down or attempt to smooth it. It should have a rough, chopped quality and be allowed to spread over the top of the sheet even if there are occasional small holes.

Let the dough rise for 30 minutes. Bake in a preheated 350°F. oven for around 50 minutes. Bread will be firm and golden brown.

This bread is easily broken apart and delicious reheated or toasted.

If you like making Garden Fougassa (there is something both addictive and therapeutic about the procedure for that bread), you will also like this chopped apple bread. It looks quite like its inspirational loaf, which I spotted in St. Louis's Soulard market.

CHOPPED APPLE STREUSEL BREAD

MAKES 2 LOAVES

For the Dough:

1 cup milk

2 tablespoons butter

1 teaspoon salt

1 cup baby-bottle warm water

1½ envelopes active dry yeast

Around 6 cups all-purpose flour

For the Streusel:

4 tablespoons (½ stick) chilled butter, cut
    into cubes
2 teaspoons ground cinnamon
1⅓ cups sugar

2 large Granny Smith apples
Juice of 1 lemon

To make the dough, scald the milk, remove it from the heat, and add the butter and salt. While this mixture cools to lukewarm (you may want to help it along by placing it briefly in the freezer), put the warm water in a bowl and dissolve the yeast. When the milk is tepid, combine the 2 mixtures.

Add 5 cups of the flour, mix briefly, then turn the dough out onto a heavily floured surface. Knead in more flour until the dough is no longer sticky. Continue kneading until elastic. Put the dough in a clean, oiled bowl, cover it with a towel, and let it rise in a warm place for 1 hour.

Just before the rising time is up, make the streusel by mixing the butter, cinnamon, and sugar with your fingertips until it is the consistency of oatmeal.

Peel, core, and coarsely chop the apples; sprinkle them with lemon juice to keep them white.

Gather up the dough, place it on a well-floured board, and pat it out flat.

Scatter half the apples and one third of the streusel over the dough. Using 2 pastry cutters or large spatulas, chop the apples repeatedly into the dough. Cut, cut, cut, fold over, and cut some more. Sprinkle on the remaining apples, and another third of the streusel and continue cutting. The dough will be quite wet. Divide the dough in half and put it, as roughly cut as possible, into 2 oiled loaf pans.

Sprinkle the remaining streusel over the 2 loaves, cover the pans, and put the dough to rise for at least 1¼ hours. It should top the pan.

Bake in a preheated 350°F. oven for 50 minutes. Let the bread cool in the pans for 10 minutes before turning the loaves out into cooling racks.

These breads may be drizzled with a simple frosting of confectioners' sugar moistened with water, but it is hardly necessary.

In Pike Place market the apple-growing Woodring family sells applesauce made from a frontier recipe of their great-grandparents. A touch of cider vinegar makes this slightly tart sauce unusual.

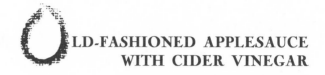

OLD-FASHIONED APPLESAUCE WITH CIDER VINEGAR

MAKES 1 QUART OF APPLESAUCE

1 dozen medium apples, preferably Winesaps, Cortlands, Empires (around 3½ pounds)

1 tablespoon ground cinnamon
½ cup apple cider vinegar
⅓–½ cup sugar

Quarter and core the apples but do not peel them. Place the apples in a nonaluminum pot and add the cinnamon and vinegar. Taste a bit of apple and, depending on whether it is sweet or tart, add sugar accordingly.

Cook over medium low heat, stirring occasionally, until the apples are soft, about 45 minutes. Uncover and cook for another 15 minutes. The sauce should be thick, so if there appears to be too much liquid, stir the apples over high heat the last 5 minutes to evaporate the excess juice.

Press the sauce through a food mill or sieve. Serve warm, with thick cream if you wish.

— ❧ —

(. . . Mr. Woodring endeared himself to me by calling out after my Pepsi-toting teen-age son: "Hey, kid, apple cider's lots better for you than soft drinks." Those things help a parent.)

Show off dark, ripe Washington State Bing cherries to delicious advantage in this recipe.

FROZEN CHERRIES JUBILEE "BRÛLÉE"

SERVES 4–6

1½–2 pints rich vanilla ice cream (depending on the size of your gratin dish), softened

¼ cup kirsch, or to taste
2–3 cups halved and pitted Bing cherries
⅓ packed cup light brown sugar

Place the softened ice cream and kirsch in a bowl and work it with a heavy spoon until smooth. Stir in the cherries. Spread the mixture into a gratin or quiche dish and press the ice cream as flat as possible.

Return the dish to the freezer for at least 1 hour (overnight is better).

At dessert time, preheat the broiler until very hot. Press the brown sugar through a sieve in a light fluffy covering over the ice cream. Place immediately under the broiler just long enough for the sugar to caramelize into a brown crust, less than a minute—keep a close watch.

To serve, crack the crust and spoon portions of crisp sugar and cold cherries in cream into serving dishes.

CHERRIES

"Cherries should have lots of shine, and the stems should be on because they keep better that way. The lighter the cherry, the tarter the flavor. Buy black ones. We pick our cherries by hand. Elevating machines take us up to the crown of the trees, but we fight the birds for those sweet top ones. Cherries need lots of cross-pollination. We keep six hives for a hundred trees on our one-and-a-half-acre grove."

—Second generation Washington State cherry farmer, Ewald Hapke

Granville Island Market
Vancouver, British Columbia

The Granville Island Market is one of the many public developments that has taken Pike Place as a role model. In 1972, Granville Island was a collection of rusty warehouses and factories largely abandoned after World War II. Huge shipbuilding and ironworks factories stood vacant and derelict.

Located on False Creek, surrounded by water, with snow-capped mountains in the distance and modern downtown Vancouver just across a spanning bridge, the island offered the government of Canada and progressive planners a chance to build and think creatively. You can read some of the premises on which the market was planned in the information building where the whole intellectual process behind the development of the market is displayed in architects' models, and memos like:

> As soon as you put in curbs, you divide the street into zones. We don't want that. We want the street level to be like wall to wall carpet. There are cities around the world where the interaction between cars and people isn't a threat but actually adds a kind of life. Pedestrians walk in the middle of the street, there are urban sparks rubbing together. We want the heart of the market dense, European, robust.

And so you can arrive at Granville from across the water on an aquabus, or from farther away on a ferry. Temporary moorage is available in front of the Public Market. In an attempt to overcome the "dead" hours that seem to plague so many downtown renovations, planners filled the buildings with art centers, theaters, restaurants, evening activities, music, craft studios, and probably the most complete food-shopping selection in the area.

What Granville faces now is the need for a diversity of ethnic groups and socioeconomic levels. The market is filled with middle- to upper-class customers spending freely. I like the fact that the powers that be encourage industry (there's a cement factory running at full tilt in one of the buildings); that they plan for low-income housing; that there is a social commitment to children and the elderly. The historic industrial heritage shows in the cranes, rail tracks, and tin sidings that have been allowed to remain. And the farmers are starting to come to the side of the food market, which tends now to be full of middlemen, not producers. It's remarkable how different the feel is between the two groups of food purveyors. Something's missing when real farmers are absent.

Granville Market is evolving, and the east end of the island is still ragged and undeveloped ground. I can't help wondering what would happen if they plowed under those remaining acres and let farmers have a go at cultivating gardens where urbanites could pick their own produce.

When you stroll along the tempting walkways of the Granville market you notice the English-style baked goods. Sweet rolls, pastries, cakes are distinctively plumper, doughier looking than their American counterparts for the simple reason that they are meant for tea. The name "scrumpets" caught my eye in Granville and I came back home to create this mix of crumpet and scone that's lightly cooked on a griddle. They're delicious for breakfast.

BACON AND CHEESE "SCRUMPETS"

MAKES 8–10 SCRUMPETS

2 cups sifted all-purpose flour

2 teaspoons baking powder

1 tablespoon sugar

½ teaspoon salt

6 slices bacon, fried crisp and blotted

½ cup diced extra-sharp Cheddar cheese

4 tablespoons (½ stick) butter, melted

1 egg plus 1 egg white

½ cup milk

Place the dry ingredients in a bowl and mix well. Crumble the bacon and add it and the cheese to the flour. Stir until blended.

Beat together the butter, eggs, and milk and, in a few swift strokes, stir them into the flour mixture. Handle the dough as little as possible.

Scrape the dough out onto a generously floured surface. With floured fingers, pat it into a circle approximately ⅓ inch thick. Cut the dough into 4-inch rounds.

Place a large frying pan on medium-high heat and grease it very lightly. Add the scrumpets and immediately turn the heat down to medium. Cook for 5 minutes, then turn the scrumpets over and lower the heat. Cook for another 5 minutes. Continue until all are done. Serve warm.

Here is another English-style pastry—this one is a fairly healthy bar that is vaguely reminiscent of Fig Newtons. Children and adults like them. There really isn't any substitute for pearl sugar, that lovely crispy bit of sweet that looks like the salt on a pretzel. Either don't sprinkle anything on the bars, or send away for a box of Parl Socker from the address source in the back of this book.

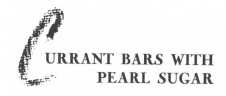

CURRANT BARS WITH PEARL SUGAR

MAKES 12 BARS

For the Crust:

1 tablespoon brown sugar
1 cup all-purpose flour
Pinch of salt

1 stick unsalted butter, chilled, cut into cubes
½ teaspoon vanilla extract
3–4 tablespoons ice water

For the Filling:

6 tablespoons (¾ stick) unsalted butter
⅓ cup brown sugar
1½ cups currants (raisins may be substituted)

1 teaspoon ground cinnamon
1 egg yolk beaten with 2 teaspoons water for glaze
3 tablespoons pearl sugar

To make the crust, mix the brown sugar, flour, and salt in a bowl. Cut the butter into the flour until it disappears. Sprinkle the vanilla over the flour, then sprinkle on the ice water until the dough is moistened enough to hold together well. Gather it into a ball on a floured surface, give it one quick kneading turn, then pat it out to a rough rectangle. Wrap in plastic and chill for at least 1 hour.

To make the filling, melt the butter and brown sugar over medium heat. Place the currants and cinnamon in the bowl of a food processor, add the melted butter, and blend until the mixture is smooth.

Preheat oven to 350°F. Lightly grease a 9-x-13-inch baking pan. Roll the dough out into a rectangle around ¼ inch thick and press it gently into the baking dish. Leaving about ⅓ inch of dough rising on the sides, cut off the excess dough. Use wet fingers to spread the filling gently over the dough.

Gather the dough scraps and roll them out into a long narrow strip. Brush the strip with egg yolk glaze and slice the dough into ½-inch-wide strips with a knife or pastry cutter. Lattice the top of the filling with 2 strips lengthwise and 3 strips crosswise to divide the pastry into 12 sections.

Pinch and flute the sides and strips together and cut off any excess lattice stripping. Sprinkle pearl sugar over the top, especially on the lattice, as that's where it will show up the most.

Bake for 30 minutes. Cut when cool. The whole pastry should easily lift out of the pan in one piece.

A popular item at the Granville Island market is Spaghetti Ice Cream. Let the person with the strongest hands in the house help make this. You will need a potato ricer, the kind that looks rather like a giant garlic press.

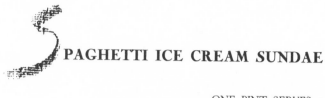

SPAGHETTI ICE CREAM SUNDAE

ONE PINT SERVES 2

1 pint good-quality vanilla ice cream
Fudge sauce

2 Maraschino cherries

Get the ice cream frozen as hard as possible. Scoop some out into the bowl of the potato ricer and press the ice cream out in long spaghetti strands into serving dish. Run a knife under the ricer to slice off the ice cream.

Top quickly with fudge sauce, place a cherry on top, and delight some small child.

A UTUMN

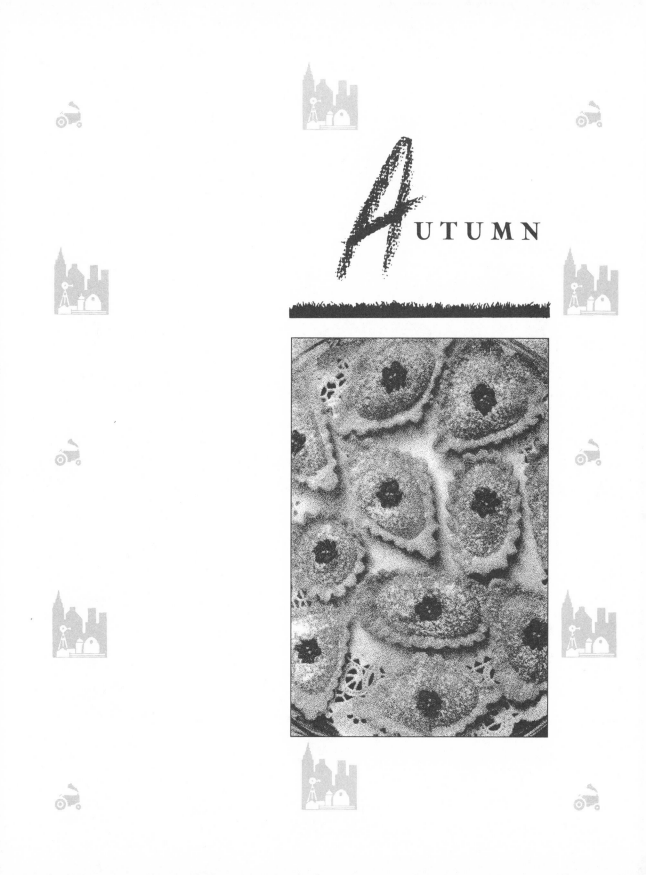

MICHIGAN

*The Lansing
Farm Market*

PRESERVING

"**Y**OU'RE NOT GOING TO RECOGNIZE IT," SAID Doug Wiley, the market manager. "If you haven't been here in twenty-five years you'll see a whole new place."

It was with some worry that I went back to my birthplace to visit the Lansing Farm Market. When I was young, my mother and I went faithfully every Thursday. I remember armloads of pink peonies, baskets of cucumbers, and peaches to make pickled peaches. We bought eggs always from Mrs. Hofstra, and I scavenged and came away with treasures— single gladiola flowers that had dropped from their stems, gum balls, a fresh Parker House roll from the bakery lady. The big event was weighing myself on the 500-pound scales— hardly made a dent on its face in those days.

What I didn't want to see was one of those slicked-up jobs that makes an unappealing megamess of something that used to be wonderful. You start modernizing those old places, start forcing the festive gaiety, and everybody loses. But there it was, two long, narrow buildings on the corner of Shiawassee and Cedar streets still showing the old Electric Car Barn heritage from which they had sprung.

Inside, I was momentarily thrown till I dropped to my knees. What had changed was my vision of the market. My tall adult height skewed proportions, but it was still there.

189

We should all drop to our knees from time to time to see things from a child's viewpoint. When you are close to the cement floor, the dark green park bench runners in front of the tables seem high and endless; the produce is heaped like Eden; there are apple red, yellow pear mountains far as the eye can see and forests of flowers. Stand up and it is smaller than I'd remembered; the tables and benches are too low, as if made for a shorter generation. About the only thing really different was a covered ramp connecting the two buildings, and the fact that the pointer on the 500-pound scales under the ramp now gave swift confirmation of adulthood.

Ask the sellers how the market has changed and you get an encapsulated vision of time passing, mores evolving:

"People cook different than their mothers did. They used to take produce out of here by the bushel. Today's customer doesn't shop the same—a few of this, a few of that."

"People are fussier than they used to be—see what I mean—that lady with the press-on-nails will spill that whole pile of peppers to find one. The least they take, the more they pick."

"We used to sell fifteen dozen eggs to a family, then three dozen, now its half a dozen. People have changed their diets, they aren't eating meat anymore, it's all those advertising gimmicks on the TV about low cholesterol. Milk used to be the most perfect food, now it's a danger. Customers go with the times. We used to tap two thousand maple trees a year, now we tap five hundred. The local trade is not eating the syrup—they want all that 'lite' stuff and you can't take calories out of real maple sugar."

"People used to can a little bit, make a little jelly, now they go down to the supermarket."

"For the last five years the market has just been holding its own. Now the young housewives seem to be coming back. There seems to be a swell of people in at lunchtime. Guess we're a good alternative to all those junk-food lunch places."

The longer I walk in the market, the more it comes back to me, and I finally recognize faces I know from somewhere long ago . . . they don't remember me, but I remember them. There's a sharp, white-haired old man who looks just like a white-haired old man deep in my mind.

"Yah, yah," says Jimmy Hnetynka. "Sure I was here. Been here since 1922. We came from Austria in 1909 and landed at Ellis Island. You had to have twenty-five dollars for each family member to get into the country. Dad said, let's get out of this New York, so we went to Chicago. Dad wanted to farm but he didn't know whether potatoes grew on trees. Land was a hundred dollars an acre near Chicago, so we came to Michigan where my dad heard there was work on the sugar-beet farm. He started with a wooden shovel pitching those beets into the hopper, then mechanizing came and push buttons. My father led a strike against the company, but all the workers went, yah.

"So we started growing sugar beets under contract, then pickles under contract. We would haul the pickles to the pickle station, and they would give you scrip that wasn't worth a tinker's darn. Someone said go try the Lansing market, so we came, but the manager said, I don't let foreigners inside. They put us to sell out in the street, backed up against the curb. Rain and sun and shine we sold there. We put twenty-five cents a bushel on our pickles; inside it was fifty cents and it was good to us. We started here in 1922 and it was 1925 before they let us under the roof.

"I'm ninety years old now. Last night I put on my boots and hitched the trailer to the tractor. I got more boots at home. You come home with me and help me pick tomorrow, would you sleep good tonight, yah."

The whole market is vivid now—apple, peach, pear colors, the last of muskmelons, the last of corn. There's that smell that hits both markets and seasons—of time ripening, culminating, of life about to change. If my mother were here, we'd be buying those peaches, those cucumbers; probably buy some makings for homemade chili. I'll always remember the two of us together here.

Back from the Lansing market of my childhood, my mother and I would come with a half bushel of pickling cucumbers and a big bunch of dill, which would always set the nose tingling. My mother would send me down to the cellar to bring up quart mason jars, and I would watch as she brought them to a boil in a large pan over the stove. She'd take each one out with tongs, settle it neck down on clean dish towels, then empty the water from the pan and fill it with pickling liquid.

Into the bottom of each jar would go a bit of alum, then the cucumbers packed in layers, spiky heads of dill, and that one red pepper showing just so. She'd funnel the hot liquid over the cucumbers, place a grape leaf on top, seal them up, listen for the soft pop of each lid as it correctly secured its vacuum tight seal. Then there was what seemed like an interminable wait for my mother to pronounce them edible, though she swears it was only two weeks.

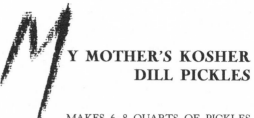

MY MOTHER'S KOSHER DILL PICKLES

MAKES 6–8 QUARTS OF PICKLES

For Each Jar:

Around 24 small fresh cucumbers

1 teaspoon alum (available at most drugstores)

1 clove garlic, peeled

2 dill flower heads

1 small hot red pepper

1 grape leaf

For the Pickling Brine:

1 quart cider vinegar

1 cup noniodized salt

3 quarts water

6–8 quart mason jars with lids

Wash the cucumbers. Cover them with cold water and let them stand overnight to firm and crisp.

Sterilize each jar and lid by bringing them up to a boil in water. Drain the jars upside down on a clean towel. When dry, add the alum and garlic to the bottom of each jar. Pack in the cucumbers, arranging the dill flowers and red pepper at the outside of the jar if possible. Place a grape leaf over the top of the pickles.

Bring all the brine ingredients to a boil in a nonaluminum pot. Place a funnel into each jar and top the contents with brine. Screw on the lids and secure them tightly. There should be a gentle popping that bulges the lid on each jar. If you can't detect this on one or two, place those jars in the refrigerator when they are cool, and use them up first. Pickles are supposed to age for 3 to 4 weeks, if you can wait that long, but you can open a jar at 2 weeks for a whining child.

. . . and her chili sauce, which filled the kitchen with a wondrous pungency while it cooked and then brightened up baked beans all winter long.

TART CHILI SAUCE

MAKES 3 PINTS OF SAUCE

4 pounds ripe tomatoes
2 medium green bell peppers
2 large red bell peppers
1 cup sliced celery (do some stringing before cutting)
2 cups chopped red Bermuda onion
2 firmly packed cups light-brown sugar
1 tablespoon salt
1 cinnamon stick

½ teaspoon crushed cloves
2 teaspoons mustard seeds
1 small jalapeño pepper seeded, and minced (or to taste)
Freshly ground pepper to taste
1½ cups cider vinegar

3 pint mason jars with lids

Core the tomatoes and slice them. Squeeze out the juice into a bowl. Chop the tomatoes coarsely and place them in a large nonaluminum pot. Strain the tomato juice back over the tomatoes.

Remove the seeds from the peppers and cut them into large dice. Add the peppers, celery, and chopped onion to the pot. Stir in the sugar and salt.

Place the pot over medium heat and stir until the sugar is dissolved. Bring the vegetables to a simmer and cook uncovered for 35 minutes.

Add the remaining ingredients and continue cooking, with an occasional stir, for 1 hour more, or until the vegetables appear thick and most of the liquid is gone. The chili should have a certain jamlike quality, though it is possible to have a soupier version if you so desire.

Place the 3 jars and their lids in a large pan of water and slowly bring to a boil. Turn off the heat and leave the jars in the water until you are ready to fill them.

Fish out the cinnamon sticks. Ladle the hot chili sauce into the jars, and put the lids on at once.

– ❧ –

This is a good, old-fashioned, quickly made pickle that basically needs no cooking. Use small young cucumbers (five or six inches) and small white onions.

BETTY'S BREAD AND BUTTER PICKLES

MAKES 4 PINTS OF PICKLES

6 cups paper-thin cucumber slices
2 cups paper-thin onion slices

1 small red bell pepper, seeded and slivered
1/4 cup salt

For the Brine:

1 cup brown sugar
1/4 teaspoon ground turmeric
1/4 teaspoon ground cloves
1 teaspoon white peppercorns
1/2 teaspoon celery seed

2 teaspoons white mustard seed
2 1/2 cups cider vinegar

4 pint mason jars with lids, sterilized

Prepare the vegetables a day ahead so that they can "salt out" overnight: Combine the cucumbers, onions, and pepper. Sprinkle on the salt and mix. Cover the bowl with plastic wrap and refrigerate at least 6 hours—overnight is preferable.

After the salting period, make the brine: Combine all the ingredients in a nonaluminum pan and bring to a boil. Regulate the heat to a brisk simmer and cook, stirring frequently, until the mixture is syruplike. Remove from the heat but leave the burner on.

Rinse the vegetables briefly under cold water and press them gently to expel any liquid. Add the vegetables to the hot syrup, return the pan to the burner, and let the vegetables heat just to the point when they threaten to break into a boil.

Have the clean, hot pint jars ready (they can be standing filled with hot water and emptied at the last minute). Ladle the pickles into the jars with enough brine to cover them completely. Seal and let stand for 2 to 3 weeks before using. Refrigerate jars after opening.

— ✁ —

This is not a true preserve, but you can make spectacular presentations with these vegetables if you care to spend a bit of time layering them artfully in a large glass jar. This is particularly effective as an antipasto for an Italian party.

SPICED, LAYERED VEGETABLES

MAKES 1 LARGE BOWL OF
VEGETABLES. SERVES 20.

1 head of cauliflower, trimmed into flowerets

3 large carrots, scraped, cut into thick diagonal "Chinese" slices, parboiled to a bright orange

2 large red bell peppers, seeded, cut into strips

2 large yellow bell peppers, seeded, cut into strips

½ pound snow pea pods, parboiled

6 small zucchini, cut into chunky slices

195

For the Brine:

1½ tablespoons salt

4½ cups water

1 cup white wine vinegar

1 tablespoon dill seeds

2 teaspoons mustard seeds

¼ teaspoon ground turmeric

1 tablespoon black peppercorns

4 cloves garlic, peeled

While you arrange the vegetables, bring all the brine ingredients to a boil.

Layer the vegetables into a clean hot glass jar (jars) or bowl. I like to start with white on the bottom, then build thorugh the spectrum of yellow, orange, red, and shades of green. (You can, if you wish, insert a decorative spray of chives or a fan of pea pods on one side of the glass to make a pattern.)

Take the brine off the heat. Let it cool briefly, then pour slowly over the vegetables until they are covered. Cool to room temperature, cover, then store in the refrigerator for at least 3 to 4 days. These will keep easily for 2 weeks.

To serve, place the whole container on the table with a ladle on the side, or drain the vegetables, arrange them on a serving dish, and serve with olives, feta cheese, and bread sticks.

— ❧ —

APPLES

If you are choosing apples that have two colors, look at the background color, not the red, to determine sweetness. The brighter and darker the green, or the deeper the yellow behind the red, the more the apples are ripe.

—Illinois farmer Joseph Naber

If you have not experimented with tamarind yet, here is a recipe that makes excellent use of this exotic ingredient. Sold in paste form or as a pressed block of sticky, seedless, dried fruit pods, its slight acidity is wonderful in chutneys and preserves.

APPLE-TAMARIND CHUTNEY

MAKES 3 PINTS OF CHUTNEY

6 Granny Smith apples (or other tart apples)
2 cups currants or dark raisins
1 cup minced onions
3 tablespoons tamarind paste
1 packed cup light brown sugar
½ cup honey
1½ cups apple cider vinegar

¼ teaspoon ground ginger
1 large pinch of cayenne
1 large pinch of ground allspice
1 large clove garlic, minced
Zest and juice of 1 lemon

3 pint mason jars with lids, sterilized

Peel, core, and chop the apples.

Place all the ingredients in a large, heavy, nonaluminum pot. Stir until mixed. Bring to a boil, lower the heat to simmer, and cover. Cook for 30 minutes, stirring every 10 minutes.

Uncover the pot and continue cooking for another 30 minutes. Stir more frequently as the cooking time nears an end. Turn up the heat if necessary to cook off any excess liquid if the mixture is at all watery. The chutney should have reached a thick, jamlike consistency in around an hour's time.

Ladle it into the sterilized pint jars, seal, and store.

This makes an excellent gift. You can eat it with curries, use it to accompany roast lamb, or spread it on slices of grilled eggplant.

I've not had great success making this jam with store-bought berries, but the deep red, just picked, still-smelling-of-the-sun strawberries you find in farmers' markets work perfectly. You also need the weather on your side for this recipe. Three days of hot sun need to be arranged. And lastly, you'll need to figure the logistics of this endeavor. I use two large glass bowls as domes that fit into round quiche dishes. You might use a piece of glass or clear plastic, but whatever the cover, it should fight tightly so no insects can get at the berries. Children are fascinated by this process.

SUNSHINE AND STRAWBERRY JAM

MAKES AROUND 3 PINTS OF JAM

2 quarts impeccable strawberries
4 pounds sugar

3 pint mason jars with lids, sterilized

Make the jam on a hot, sunny morning.

Gently rinse the berries so as not to bruise them, then remove the hulls.

Place the berries in a large nonaluminum pan and sprinkle the sugar over them. Let stand for 45 minutes.

Turn the heat to medium-low and bring the berries to a simmer. Shake the pot if necessary and give a gentle turn of the spoon, but refrain from stirring so as to leave the berries as whole as possible. Simmer for 20 minutes.

Pour the berries out into shallow containers such as quiche dishes or platters with high rims. Cover with glass and leave upon a table and out in the sun or in a sun room. Turn the berries very gently (a child's job) twice a day. (You may wish to bring the berries in from the outside each night.)

At the end of 3 sunny days, the juices should have congealed. Place the jam into hot sterilized jars and seal. This makes a good freezer preserve.

I've a standing order to bring my sweet neighbor the first pints of small, soft home-grown figs to appear at my local market. I bring the figs, she makes and shares these preserves from a recipe handed down from her grandmother, and we are both happy.

EVA KIRKLAND'S OLD-FASHIONED FIG PRESERVES

MAKES 5 PINTS OF PRESERVES

3 cups water
6 cups sugar
4 pounds figs, rinsed and left whole

5 slices lemon, approximately ⅓ inch thick, seeded
5 pint mason jars with lids, sterilized

Combine the water and sugar in a large nonaluminum pot. Bring to a good agitated rolling boil. Add the figs, cover the pan, and cook slowly for 45 minutes. Be sure to regulate the heat so that the fruit is at a bare simmer.

After 45 minutes, remove the lid and add the lemon slices. Continue to simmer uncovered for another 45 minutes.

Remove from the heat, cover the pot, and let stand overnight so the figs can soak up the syrup.

The next day, bring the figs back to a brief simmer, then ladle them into sterile jars. Slip a slice of lemon down the side of each jar so it shows decoratively. Seal the jars. Mrs. Kirkland stores hers in the freezer.

Eastern Farmers' Market
Detroit

After Lansing, I traveled to Detroit. Evocations again of childhood driving east on Interstate 96. When I was young, my parents would sometimes let me stay out of school for a surprise trip to Detroit. We had a round of activities—eat at Stouffers (when it used to be a large restaurant); get a ginger ale at Vernors; shop at Hudson's (my mother); ride the escalators; see the newsreel, attend a Tigers baseball game . . . then ride home through the night, me always asleep by the time we got back.

I already knew that something was awry in Michigan. I had read about the hardships of my home state from a distance and over time, but my memory retained a bucolic vision of a bright and vibrant life. You can, indeed, go home again, but not with the same young eyes. What I saw now was a state washed with a tint of gray, perhaps a fallout from industrial dreams. Lansing hadn't grown the way I thought it would; nothing looked quite prosperous. It was like a plant that had been cramped in its growth by the confines of a container too small . . . tenacious life in soil too poor to sustain it . . . people existing but in an economy bereft.

Detroit, however, was downright startling. Those streets I remembered were there, the stores the same height and size, but everything was boarded, chained, iron-gated. Hudson's sat forlorn, cracked, deserted. The whole inner city was discarded as if some terrible discriminating disaster had been visited upon it. We stayed at the venerable old Pontchartrain Hotel, which clung to the riverside where life still seemed healthy, though the Renaissance Center nearby was close to empty and when you walked in the place, the void resounded. A brave little elevated tourist train sped around the top of a metro circle. Not many people on it, a not-pretty view beneath of shuttered stores, high-noon-empty streets.

I'd come for the Saturday Eastern Farmers' Market. During the week, the market sold mainly wholesale. Semis drove up and took away loads of produce for supermarket consumption, but on Saturday, 60 percent of the sellers were true truck farmers. Some of them would drive 250 miles from the west side of the state to sell each week. Saturday was also a "distress" day. Produce that wouldn't hold over the weekend was sold to less affluent buyers at lower prices.

The Eastern market grows at the edge of the downtown business district. It's a ten-acre site at the hub of a wholesale market district that has been in place since 1889. It reminded me a bit of the old Les Halles district in Paris—lots of specialty stores along the side streets that spun off from the market sheds, the beginning of a set of restaurants open long hours that served good, solid food. One in particular, the Russell Street Deli, had just opened to gastronomic acclaim. You could get a good meatless Reuben sandwich there, fine pancakes and soups.

Chuck Pierce, the jovial market manager, leads me around the five large sheds that compose the market and points out market old-timers. There's a whole string of interrelated families, lots of marriages created from the market. A farmer brings his daughter to help sell on Saturday, she meets the nephew of a neighboring farmer at the next stall, and after a year of Saturday courtship, they marry.

Lots of vendors here whose families came to farming during the Depression. With jobs scarce, they turned to the soil to support themselves, and the earth responded.

Toward the end of the afternoon, I talked to Russell Rist about his honey. Mr. Rist is of middle years, with sandy-red hair moving toward white. He sits me down on a crate behind his pickup and grumbles at me. Turns out he doesn't like bees all that well, but his recounting of the bee world reminds me of a microcosmic society—its politics, and personalities, and economy neatly intact.

RUSSELL RIST ON BEES

"Can't imagine why you're interested in them. They're the doggonedest creatures. Well, I got into this business with my father in 1935. Times were hard then. Never did like bees, never did know how to make friends with them like some people do. I respect 'um, but they sure do take lots of looking after.

"In the winter those old bees hibernate and eat honey. You want them to build up and get strong, so when you extract honey in autumn you leave enough for the bees to live on over the winter, but it sure is a monotonous kind of diet, don't you think?

"In winter they eat so they can stand low temperatures. They cluster . . . the colder it is the tighter they cluster.

"When the temperature gets around 55° in spring, they start flying. They void themselves of all they ate in winter. The queen will start laying eggs. She'll lay more eggs than her own weight, maybe 100,000 eggs. If too many eggs are laid, they hatch, and the prime population becomes too large. If bees get crowded, they decide they have to swarm. The old lady queen stops laying and she raises queen cells all over the place. Scout bees go out and decide where the new real estate is, and the queen goes out with the swarm and takes half the bees with her. You can't let that happen, but if it does, then virgin queens left will start beeping. They'll sting each other until only one is alive and she has to be accepted by the society as the new queen. She can't be too nervous. Different hives have different personalities, all due to the queen. If she's ugly, she passes it on to the rest of her colony and you better get rid of her.

"So the new queen needs to mate. She'll fly higher and higher, the drones will go up after her till they fall off, then one drone is left and he mates with her and dies. You think you do a woman a good deed and . . . well, never mind.

"The queen will outlive a regular bee five or six years. It's all due to royal jelly. Used to be a fad for that in the fifties where you could get twenty-five dollars a pound, now once in a while someone from Europe asks. People want to buy pollen for energy, too, lots of vitamins in it. Around July 15 you want the honey to start coming in. Scout bees, all immature females, will go out and find fields. They'll come back on the sides of the hive and start dancing, pointing their tails and indicating an area maybe two miles away. Bees usually only forage one kind of plant at a time. We get clover in summer, buckwheat in fall, dandelion and fruit bloom in spring. Buckwheat is good on pancakes and I put clover in my coffee, but if they get honey from thyme, it smells like old socks and all you can sell it for is baker's honey.

"As the honey comes in, we put more boxes on top of each other. Sometimes we move hives toward fields from clover to buckwheat—chug on over washboard roads moving them hives and the bees get mad because they want to be foraging. You better duck when you free them.

"In the hottest of summer, the fanner bees keep cooling the air. It will be 100° outside, and only 90° inside their own air cooling system. They're good housekeepers. When you want to extract the honey, you give them a little smoke from a bellows, blow it over the top of the frame to keep them groggy. Right now we're taking honey off.

"The amount of honey bees produce is down now. Used to be 200 pounds in a hive, now its more like 50 pounds. There's less foraging areas so the bees can't find so many clover blooms. I used to manage 3,000 hives. I've got 200 hives now, average 40 pounds per hive. You're lucky if you get 40 cents a pound for it. You need about 500 colonies to make a living. I reckon I make half my living from those old bees. Shouldn't be so hard on them, but if I never got stung again in my life can't say it would matter."

–❦–

By late afternoon, the entire spectrum of urban life had passed through the market walkways. Whites come in the morning bringing their children. They sought the best produce, paid the price, bought the children a hot dog at the central food stand, glanced briefly at the blind blues singer tapping out rhythms with his cane.

Midday, Indians and Arabs appeared and bartered most seriously. They bought large bags of cucumbers, eggplant, and squash. Their children helped carry the produce away. At noon, too, an altercation arose in the parking lot. Somebody pulled a gun, police were called, there were heated arguments in tongues unknown to me.

Early afternoon, blacks came. There were bargains to be had by this time. On Sunday the market would be closed and anything not sold was money lost to the seller. The mothers bought cabbages and greens and melons and the children spent time listening to the blues singer and helping him sound out his rhythms.

By late day, a scent of high fruit perfumes the market. Peaches, plums, melons, and tomatoes fill the air. They've lost their tempers under the day-long sun, grown petulant, and burst. The wasps and bees have swarmed in for long drinks of nectar. I hope they fly back to Mr. Rist's hives and make a honey fit for kings.

Even later, the gleaners come, mixed shades and colors. They carry away cabbage leaves, cracked carrots, tomatoes fallen splat from crates, overripe fruit. A good market can feed everyone.

FIG AND HONEY ICE CREAM

MAKES 1 GOOD QUART OF ICE CREAM

2 cups milk

1 cup honey

Pinch of salt

2 eggs plus 1 egg yolk

½ cup stemmed, soft dried figs cut into small dice

1½ cups heavy cream, very chilled

Place the milk in a medium-sized saucepan and bring to a scald. Remove from the heat, add the honey and salt, and stir until dissolved.

Whisk the eggs in a bowl until blended, then whisk in the hot milk slowly so as not to cook the eggs.

Return the mixture to the saucepan and cook, stirring constantly, over medium-low heat until it thickens and coats a spoon. Do not allow it to approach a boil. (Coating a spoon means that when you run your finger down the back of the spoon there should be a clean, neat path and the liquid should not be so thin that it runs back into the path.)

Add the figs to the custard. Cool to room temperature, then refrigerate until chilled. Whip the cream until it is just lightly thickened. Fold the cream into the custard mixture. Freeze in an ice cream maker.

Good honey is wonderful in this quick "preserve." I will give you the procedure. The number of bottles you want to make will determine how much dried fruit you buy. To make really spectacular presents, buy some of the pale, watery blue glass bottles made in Italy that are available at most import stores these days. Fill and top with honey, then tie strands of raffia around the bottle's neck for a gift of handsome, umbered fruit.

ITALIAN HONEYED FRUIT

Dried pears
Dried apricots
Dried peaches
Dried prunes
Small dried figs

Hazelnuts
Whole almonds with skins
1 cinnamon stick per jar
Honey

Choose an assortment of dried fruits in a quantity that will fill your chosen jars. For every 4 cups of fruit, have 1 cup of nuts. You will need 1 good cup of honey for every pint container.

Rinse the jars in steaming water and place them upside down on clean toweling to dry.

Bring the honey to a simmer. Add the dried fruits and return to a simmer.

Remove the fruit from the heat and ladle it into the prepared jars. Slide a cinnamon stick down the front of the prettiest side of the jar so that it can be clearly seen.

You will need to top up each jar with honey, so, if necessary, bring more honey to boil, then pour it into the jars. Lid or cork the jars.

This is delicious ladled over vanilla ice cream.

Here is a long-cooking but basically easy conserve that you can use as a jam or an ice cream topping. The following recipe cooks down to 1 pint, but you might consider doubling it and giving the second pint as a gift.

PEAR HONEY

MAKES 1 PINT OF PEAR HONEY

6 slightly ripe but not soft d'Anjou or
    Bartlett pears (around 3–3½ pounds)
1 cup sugar
2 tablespoons honey

Juice of ½ lemon

1 pint or 2 half-pint mason jars with lids,
    sterilized

Peel, quarter, and core the pears. Cut them in rough chunks and put them and the sugar in a food processor or blender. Blend until smooth.

Place the ground pears in a nonaluminum pan. Add the honey and lemon juice and cook over low heat at a slow simmer for 1½ to 1¾ hours. Stir from time to time so that the mixture doesn't stick.

Pear honey is done when it falls away from the spoon in a thick sheet. You can further test doneness by placing a spoonful on a plate. Let it sit for 1 minute, then look to see if any clear liquid has been expressed around the rim of the jam. As long as you can see that excess water, you need to keep simmering.

When the jam is very thick, almost like an apple butter, place it in the sterile jar or jars. Seal, cool, and store in the refrigerator. It is also possible to freeze this preserve.

This is a "meaty" vegetarian sandwich. The filling functions as a two-week preserve if you wish to keep it on hand in your refrigerator.

RUSSELL STREET DELI-STYLE MEATLESS "REUBEN" SANDWICH

MAKES 8 SANDWICHES

For the Filling:

2 large red onions
½ small cabbage
1 cup water
⅓ cup honey
2 tablespoons salt
2 tablespoons vinegar

16 slices rye or pumpernickel bread
Softened butter
Russian dressing or a mix of ketchup
*   and mayonnaise*
16 thin slices Swiss cheese
Mustard on the side

To make the filling, peel, core, and halve the onions. Slice the halves very thin. Slice the cabbage into the very thinnest shred possible. There should be around 2 cups of each vegetable. Combine them in a bowl.

Bring the water, honey, salt, and vinegar to a boil. Cook for 2 minutes, then pour over the vegetables. Cover the vegetables with a small saucer and place a weight on it (a can will do) to press them down. When cool, refrigerate overnight.

To make the sandwiches, drain the vegetables and press them well by handfuls to expel all water.

Generously butter one side of each bread slice. Spread the other sides with abundant Russian dressing. Put a piece of cheese over the Russian dressing on each slice. Put ½ cup of vegetables on half of the slices.

Place 3 tablespoons of butter in a large frying pan. When it sizzles, place 1 slice with vegetables

207

and 1 without, buttered side down, in the pan. Fry until the cheese becomes transparent, then press the sandwich together. Weight the sandwich down with a heavy object (use the can again) for about 15 seconds. Turn it over and press is again for another minute.

Slice the sandwich through on the diagonal and serve.

PENNSYLVANIA DUTCH COUNTRY

Central Market

Lancaster

IF YOU WANTED, YOU COULD SPEND COUNTLESS days and weeks each fall around Lancaster, Pennsylvania, visiting farm markets, flea markets, and country fairs. The small towns, nestled in some of the most exquisitely evocative landscape in America, have their markets on staggered weekdays and always on Saturday. They take their markets seriously. There are usually covered buildings, a sense of permanence about these places. A larger market, such as the Green Dragon in Ephrata, will rapidly show you that the conventional produce-oriented markets of most towns become entirely different creatures in the Amish country. There's every flea market item you can think of—clothing, hardware, crafts—plus every industrious housewife seems to be represented with baked goods or quilted objects.

The large influx of tourists into the area threatens to turn some of these markets into circuses when buses unload at the entrance and Mammom runs amok. It is all the more impressive, then, that Lancaster's Central market, the nation's oldest publicly owned, continuously operating farmers' market, remains as pure as it does. Oh, there is a smattering of "foreign" stalls—a German deli, a small section of Greek ingredients—but basically what you find is all those extraordinary regional foods for which the area is famous. There's the Shenk's stand where you get old-fashioned cup cheese in mild, medium, and sharp. Sometimes called "Brie without the bother," it does indeed look like the thick runny innards of a classic Brie. You can buy Schmierkäse, a type of cottage cheese that you eat with apple butter, or ball cheese, like a dense round Swiss.

As "putting up" is a major concern of most Mennonite and Amish women, the stalls are a mosaic of jars—bright kraut-stuffed peppers, pumpkin butters, and spiced vegetables. There are potpie squares, dried apple slices (schnitz) in packages, shellbark hickory nuts, and black walnut kernels. One man grinds fresh horseradish root; Willow Valley Bakery outdoes all the other bakeries with its huge, cream-filled dewy buns. There are beautiful tables of produce carefully arranged. And it's here that I saw sweet potato tails for the first time—skinny, immature New Jersey sweets you can peel and eat raw if you choose, so tender are they. There are cases of housewifely dishes—potato balls and baked lima beans; cracker puddings and Jell-Os, all those staples of good Mennonite home cooking. (If you wanted to avoid the large markets, you could tour the county just visiting farms where the wives have established small kitchens behind the house. When the children are grown and gone, the women keep cooking commercially for their neighbors.)

Among the surprising sights in Central market are the vendors who sell nothing but celery. You'll not see these small sprigged heads, each with five or six stalks, anywhere but here. The celery is laid with care on tablecloths; it is blanched to the palest lunar green. When you eat it, it is cold, sweet, seemingly without strings. Ray Kreider, a slim, dark-haired young man who chews on his thoughts before he spits them out, is a second-generation celery farmer.

RAY KREIDER

"I'd probably like to grow soybeans, corn, anything better than celery. It would be less labor, but it won't pay as good. This celery is Penn Crisp celery developed by Penn State. This is not a keeping celery, it has a shelf life of a week. We raise it for local market sale. The reason it is expensive is that each stalk probably gets handled ten or eleven times during its life. That is labor intensive.

"In late winter we steam the ground in the middle of the morning with a high-pressure cooker. We sow seed in 'tobacco bed' forms, then cover the beds first with straw, then muslin sheeting. The straw helps to keep the cloth off the ground. When the seedlings are high, we transplant them out to the fields—fill ten acres altogether between June and July. To bleach it in the summer, we roll plastic over it. If it's hot, it bleaches in a week. In colder weather, we dig a trench a foot deep and put six rows of celery in it. We put paper over the top, and when it freezes mid-November, we shred straw, then roll plastic over it, and plow dirt over the edge to hold it. In winter, we can slit the plastic, reach down, and pull out really white celery in January and February.

"My father started the business in 1944. I guess I could do most any other job, but I learn a lot on the farm. You can teach children to work with you and the father's always home. We're almost self-sufficient. When my children grow, if they want this life I hope they can get it. I hope farm land is affordable and the price of crops stable. You can't put more expenses in than you get out.

"Here, you eat a piece of this celery. You won't get anything like this down where you come from. You can cook it or slice it into dressing, but mostly people just start gnawing on it like you're doing now."

At a farmhouse market you might see great scoops of this mixture ready to take home and bake. It's absolutely delicious, and particularly handy around holiday season, as both potatoes and dressing combine in the mixture and it can be made up a day ahead. You can also freeze the balls in a plastic bag and later defrost, butter, and bake them.

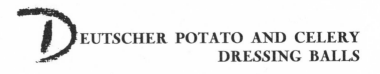

DEUTSCHER POTATO AND CELERY DRESSING BALLS

SERVES 6

3–4 cups soft bread crumbs

2 cups mashed potatoes

3 stalks celery, finely diced

1½ tablespoons rubbed sage, or 1 tablespoon
   dried sage or fresh chopped

2 teaspoons salt

Plenty of freshly ground pepper

2 tablespoons grated onion

2 tablespoons minced fresh parsley

1 egg

⅓–½ cup milk or cream

1 stick unsalted butter, melted

Mix all the ingredients except the butter in a large bowl. You will be scooping the mixture with an ice cream scoop, so add just enough milk or cream to moisten but not loosen it too much. Let the mixture sit for 15 minutes so that the bread can absorb the milk. (This can also be refrigerated overnight.)

Preheat the oven to 350°F. Butter a 9-x-13-inch baking pan or a 10-inch quiche dish. Using an ice cream scoop (or your hands) scoop out generous balls of the mixture and place them rounded side up, in the baking dish. Drizzle the melted butter over the scoops.

Bake for around 45 minutes, or until the dressing balls have expanded and crisped to a golden brown on top.

In the Lancaster market you can see pint boxes of New Jersey White sweet potato tails—the slender tubers that are dug up when only three to four inches long and less than an inch around. I brought some back home with me and played with them. They are so tender and sugary in taste they steam up in no time. Get a farmer who grows sweet potatoes to save you some from an early crop if possible. If you purchase large potatoes for this dish, choose slender, narrow, pale skinned varieties and cut them in long quarters.

SWEET POTATO TAILS WITH HONEY MUSTARD

SERVES 4–5

*1 heaped pint sweet potato tails, or 3–4
  long, thin, white-skinned sweet potatoes
  sliced in quarters lengthwise*
3 tablespoons butter
2 tablespoons honey mustard

⅓ cup heavy cream
½ teaspoon salt
Freshly ground pepper to taste
¼ cup toasted pecan halves

Place the potato tails or quarters in a steamer and steam until tender, 5 to 8 minutes for tails, more like 12 to 15 minutes for quartered sections.

Melt the butter in a large frying pan and add the potatoes. Let them brown on one side.

Whisk together the honey mustard, cream, and salt. When the potatoes have browned, add the cream, shake the pan to loosen the potatoes, and continue cooking for about 1 minute more. The cream should disappear and caramelize down to a nice sugary-looking glaze that just coats the potatoes.

Place in a serving dish, grind on fresh pepper, and sprinkle with the toasted pecans. Serve at once.

In any Amish country market, there are sweet baked lima beans—an interesting textural change from the traditional navy bean. Note that the cooking process is easy, but the cooking time is long. You can also use the soak-overnight method of softening dry beans if you wish.

BARBECUE BEANS WITH RUM

SERVES 10–12 PEOPLE;
LEFTOVERS REHEAT NICELY

1 pound large dried lima beans

7 cups water

1½ cups finely chopped onion (1 large onion)

½ cup brown sugar

1 cup ketchup

⅓ cup maple syrup

⅓ cup corn syrup

1 tablespoon salt

1 tablespoon Liquid Smoke

¼ teaspoon Tabasco sauce

1 tablespoon Worcestershire sauce

1 tablespoon white vinegar (wine or distilled)

¼ cup dark rum

Rinse the beans and pick out any foreign matter. Place the beans in a large pot and cover with the water. Cover and bring to a boil. Boil for 4 minutes, then turn off the heat and let sit for 1 hour.

Preheat the oven to 325°F.

Place all the remaining ingredients in a large bowl. When the beans have softened, drain them, reserving the cooking liquid. Add the beans to the seasoning ingredients. Measure 3⅓ cups of cooking liquid and add it to the beans.

Pour the beans into a large baking dish, cover with foil, and bake for around 6 hours. At the end of 5 hours, it is possible to control the baking time a bit by removing the foil, turning the heat up to 350°F., and watching until the top is browned and caramelized and the juices are at an acceptable point.

This is a standard dish found in Moravian homes and most Pennsylvania Dutch farm markets. Reminiscent of English nursery foods, cracker pudding may be something of an acquired taste, but if you like it, you *really* like it. The traditional recipe uses white sugar and doesn't have the toasted topping.

PENNSYLVANIA DUTCH CRACKER PUDDING

SERVES 6–8

4 cups milk

35 saltine crackers

2 eggs

1/2 packed cup light brown sugar

1/4 cup cornstarch

1/2 cup shredded or flaked coconut

1 teaspoon vanilla extract

For the Optional Topping:

1/3 cup toasted coconut mixed with 1/3 cup
  toasted quartered, pecans

Place the milk in a saucepan and bring to a scald over medium heat. The milk will steam, turn frothy-looking on top, begin to agitate. Remove from the heat immediately and set it aside.

Crush the crackers by hand or with a rolling pin until they are like a gravelly sand.

In a medium saucepan, whisk together the eggs, sugar, and cornstarch. Add the cracker crumbs and mix thoroughly. Slowly pour 1 cup of scalded milk into the cracker mixture, stirring constantly. Pour in the remaining milk and the coconut. Place the pan over medium-low heat and stir constantly until the mixture comes to a boil. This will take around 8 minutes, and you must not neglect your stirring or the mixture will stick.

Remove from the heat and cool for 5 minutes before adding the vanilla.

Place the pudding in a serving bowl—or spoon it into 6 to 8 individual serving dishes. Scatter on the topping if desired, and refrigerate.

–⁕–

This may be close to my favorite recipe in this book. It's inspired by an at-home Pennsylvania Dutch recipe given to me by my friend Naomi Sphar, of Sphar's Century Farm Bed and Breakfast near Lititz, where I always stay when I'm in Pennsylvania Dutch country. In Moravian homes, Egg Cheese is heavily sugared and eaten with molasses poured over—you can try it that way if you wish, but when it is plain, it almost resembles the fresh, delicate, made-that-day Brousse cheese of Provence. Set the "cheese" out plain on a summer's day and eat it spread on fresh buttered bread. Grind on salt and pepper, and have a bowl of just-picked radishes on the side. You will also like the garlic-herb variation.

EGG CHEESE

SERVES 6–8

1 cup milk
1 cup heavy cream
5–6 granules of sugar—count them
2 teaspoons flour

2 eggs
1 cup buttermilk
Radishes

Place the milk, cream, and sugar in a medium-sized saucepan and bring just to a scald—the liquid will steam, have small bubbles at the edge of the pan, begin to look like it is going to heave into a boil. Remove from the heat.

Place the flour and eggs in a bowl and whisk together. Whisk in the buttermilk. Slowly whisk the hot milk into the eggs. Pour back into the saucepan and whisk over medium heat until the mixture starts a slow boil. Stop stirring, regulate the heat to a simmer, and cook for 15 minutes. The contents of the pot should be at a slow blub, blub.

To mold the cheese, you can do any of the following: use a 1-pint cheese mold or a *coeur à la crème* dish; line a small sieve or colander with damp cheesecloth; or just use a small sieve if the mesh is fine enough.

When the cooking time is up, the mixture will show a soft, fine, cream-colored curd on the top. Gently pour the cheese into the selected mold. Drain over a bowl until the cheese cools to room temperature. Cover and refrigerate the cheese, still in its mold and over the draining bowl, for at least 8 hours. Unmold and serve slightly cool but not chilled along with radishes.

—❧—

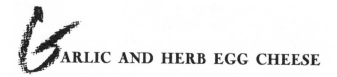

GARLIC AND HERB EGG CHEESE

Add 2 pressed cloves of garlic and ½ teaspoon salt to the buttermilk. Just before pouring the cheese into the mold, add ¼ cup mixed minced fresh parsley and chives.

RADISH SEEDS

"With slow sprouters like carrots, parsley and sprouts, mix ⅓ weight of radish seed so that when it germinates, it will break soil crust and make it easier for the main crop to get up and growing vigorously."

—the "Cook's Garden" catalogue

— ✀ —

If you spend the night with Naomi sometime, get her talking about her life on the farm. She's a real activist.

"We were dairy farmers. Had thirty cows and sold a ton of milk every two days to Hershey chocolate. The problem with farming these days is they force you to get big or to get out. If you can't expand enough to hire help, it gets to be too much as you get older. We had to sell our herd three years ago. My husband and I just couldn't do it all any more, and if you're a dairy farmer, you never get a day off. Of course, a produce farmer is at the mercy of the weather, but at least he has his Sundays.

"Now I attend a lot of farmers' meetings. What I'm concerned about is the chemical companies. We just don't stop them, and it doesn't seem fair to me. We may have banned certain dangerous chemicals in the States, but people don't realize that they're getting all those chemicals right back. They go down to Mexico, South America, get sprayed over the vegetables that are shipped back to our stores. We've got to get this stopped. . . ."

Just down the Lititz pike from the Sphar farm, on the way back to Lancaster, I found the Thomas Farm Market Store, which is yet another variation on Amish country farm markets. It combines a produce market on one side with a bake shop on the other, and most everything there comes from nearby farmers and their wives . . . dried bunches of flowers, varieties of apples—lots of them this time of year—apple butter with handwritten labels, nuts, squash, pumpkins. . . .

The bake shop is run by Karen Harnish and her husband (an elderly aunt helps sell). She is an extraordinarily hard-working young woman from a conservative Moravian family. With her long hair in a bun, her square face and sharp nose, she has an almost classic Germanic look. We sat halfway between the shop and the ovens so she could "smell" when the cakes were done:

"We lived in a four-generation household, so I learned baking from my great-grand-mother. I remember making cookies with her. We'd make fifteen kinds. She had big china platters and we spread the cookies out on them and put them down in the basement around the holidays. When neighbors came by or the men came in from the field, my mother would say, 'Now you go down and make a nice assortment,' and I'd arrange them on a plate for a present.

"I started working for the Thomas family when I was ten. Every Saturday when I was ten to fifteen, I went to the Central market in Lancaster and sold their produce. I loved it. I'd work from 6 A.M. to 6 P.M. It seemed like the big city to me. During lunchtime I'd walk around the market all by myself and feel so grown up. I earned twenty dollars a day. That was a lot of money and I saved it all.

"When I was in the twelfth grade, I met my husband and we got engaged. About that time the Thomases asked if I wanted to run a bakery in their farm market. I took my saved money, got a loan from my grandmother for the rest, and taught my fiancé to bake while we were engaged for two years. He was a farmer but we thought we'd try baking for ten years.

"We started the shop six months before we were married. A man we didn't know came in and ordered rolls for eighty people and said the customer was fussy. Well, since we had just started, we worried about it all night. We got up and started baking at 2 A.M. We wanted it to be perfect, so we threw away two batches that didn't look right. The next night I went to church to help paint a mural of the *Mayflower* with a Bible verse on it for a Thanksgiving party. Walked into the church and everyone jumped out and said, 'Surprise! Surprise!' Moravian bridal showers are supposed to be surprises. Here it was Thanksgiving and we weren't getting married till March. I usually have a good nose for hearing everything going on, but I had no idea. Then they brought out the food and there were the rolls and I thought, Oh no, we went and baked our own rolls and we're so tired we aren't going to live through this. But we did, of course, and it was a good party.

"Well, we're into our fourteenth year now. We work seventy hours a week and I sell at Root's Market on Tuesday. We have three kids. The first I'd bring to work in a playpen. When I had the second, it came. Three was too much. Now Andy who's eleven is starting to help mix batters. I tell them if you want to have clothes on your back you have to help. Doing this we can all work together. Our thirteenth anniversary we spent the whole night baking. No phone, no customers, a nice time for family discussions. It's a good life as long as you get sleep sometimes.

"I like my decorated cakes, and my shoofly pie is better than other people's because the recipe came from out of family rather than a cookbook. It's a lot of steps—you have to make the crumbs, make the goo, make the crust, pour it in just so. The secret is in the molasses. Use old-fashioned barrel molasses, the kind you put on the table to serve with egg cheese or eat on fresh bread. You can make a good shoofly cake, too, if you want!"

If you like molasses flavor but find, as do I, that the stickiness of the pie is a bit too much of a good thing, try this less-sweet cake version.

OLD-FASHIONED SHOOFLY CAKE

MAKES 16 SERVINGS

3½ cups all-purpose flour
1 teaspoon ground ginger
1½ teaspoons ground cinnamon
Heads of 8 cloves, crushed
1 teaspoon salt
1 cup brown sugar

1 cup white sugar
1 cup vegetable shortening, or ½ cup
   shortening plus ½ cup butter
1¾ cups boiling water
¾ cup molasses
1 tablespoon baking soda

Grease and flour a 9-x-13-inch baking pan. Preheat the oven to 350°F.

Blend the flour, spices, salt, sugars, and shortening to fine crumbs. Reserve 1 cup of the mixture for topping and set aside.

Pour the boiling water over the molasses and stir until dissolved. Stir in the baking soda. When the bubbling chemical reaction subsides, stir the liquid smoothly into the dry ingredients. Pour the batter into the prepared pan. Give the pan a good thunk to settle the contents, and cut a knife down 2 to 3 times through the center of the batter to help the cake rise evenly. Sprinkle with the reserved cup of crumbs.

Bake for around 50 minutes, or until a toothpick inserted into the cake comes out clean.

This is a delicious icebox cookie that is nice to keep on hand in the freezer. You can make homemade ice cream sandwiches, using these cookies as large crisp bases for either vanilla or black walnut ice cream. Or you can make them with a handsome sugar crust—children like to get involved with this process.

BLACK WALNUT COOKIES WITH A BROILED SUGAR CRUST

MAKES AROUND 3½ DOZEN COOKIES

1 cup black walnuts
2 eggs
⅓ cup raisins
⅔ cup granulated sugar
⅔ cup light brown sugar
2 sticks butter, melted
½ teaspoon salt

1½ teaspoons baking soda
½ teaspoon ground cinnamon
3 cups all-purpose flour
1 egg white beaten with 2 teaspoons water
  for glaze
Granulated sugar for glaze

Pulverize the walnuts in a food processor and set aside.

Place the eggs and raisins in the processor and blend. Scrape the egg mixture into a mixing bowl and stir in both sugars and the melted butter. Add the salt, baking soda, cinnamon, flour, and nuts.

Place a double thickness of wax paper on the counter, divide the mixture in two, and form each half into double-wrapped cylinders approximately 4 inches long. Refrigerate until firm. (The dough may also be freezer-wrapped at this point.)

To bake, preheat the oven to 350°F. and grease a cookie sheet. Cut ½-inch slices of dough and press them down on the cookie sheet until they are thin rounds approximately 3 inches in diameter. Bake for 6 to 8 minutes. Watch carefully as the cookies are thin and can overbrown easily.

Cool the cookies on racks. When cool, they can be eaten as is or topped with an appealing sugar crust. To make the crust, barely dampen the top of each cookie with a thin layer of egg glaze. Place 1 teaspoon sugar on each cookie and spread it to the edges with your fingers.

Heat the broiler until hot, then place the cookies under the unit until the sugar starts to bubble, crackle, and turn to a golden glaze. Do not let it burn. Remove immediately and cool.

A classic cookie with lots of extra chips and a healthy, sophisticated taste.

ORANGE CHOCOLATE CHIP COOKIES

MAKES AROUND TWENTY
4- TO 5-INCH COOKIES

Juice from 2 oranges
1½ sticks unsalted butter, softened
1 packed cup light brown sugar
1 large egg plus 1 egg white
1 teaspoon vanilla extract, or 2 teaspoons
Grand Marnier

1¾ cups flour
Scant ½ teaspoon baking soda
½ teaspoon salt
Zest from 1 orange
12 ounces chocolate chips

Place the orange juice in a small pan and start it reducing over high heat to 2 tablespoons. Refrigerate briefly to cool.

While it reduces, cream the butter and sugar. Add the eggs and vanilla or Grand Marnier.

In a separate bowl, mix the flour, baking soda, salt, and orange zest.

Stir the cooled reduced juice into the butter-sugar mixture. Stir in the flour and then the chocolate chips. The dough will be damper than most chocolate chip cookie doughs. Refrigerate it for at least 30 minutes before baking the cookies.

Preheat the oven to 350°F. Grease a cookie sheet. Place 2 heaping tablespoons of dough on the tray for each cookie. Press the dough down with water-dampened fingers. The cookies will spread, so bake only 6 per standard baking sheet.

Bake for around 7 minutes. Cool briefly before removing to a cooling rack.

Scrape the pan clean, regrease, then continue until all the cookies are baked.

These pretty tartlets are a specialty of The Goodie Shoppe in Lancaster. Lemon curd tarts are a common dessert in the area, and Moravian housewives pride themselves on making the thickest, densest, most flavorful lemon filling.

LEMON CURD TARTLETS

MAKES AROUND 16 SMALL TARTLETS
OR 1 LARGE TART

For the Lemon Curd:

¾ cup strained fresh lemon juice

6 tablespoons (¾ stick) unsalted butter

¾ cup sugar

6 egg yolks

1 tablespoon finely grated lemon zest (make sure to get only the yellow surface)

Around 16 small baked tartlet shells, or 1 9-inch pie shell

Confectioners' sugar

Small candied violets or violet-colored candies

In a heavy, medium-small saucepan and over very low heat, whisk together the lemon juice, butter, sugar, and egg yolks. Stir constantly until the egg mixture thickens, around 15 minutes. Be very careful not to curdle the yolks, and do not allow the mixture to come anywhere near a boil. The final mixture will be about as thick as a medium fudge sauce, and it should thicken further as it chills.

Stir in the zest, scrape the mixture into a small bowl, and cover tightly with plastic wrap. Chill completely.

Fill the tart shells generously. Sift a bit of confectioners' sugar over their tops. Place a candy flower in the center of each. Serve cold.

You see these chocolate-black sandwich cookies in every Pennsylvania Dutch market. They are plump and irresistible-looking but the traditional Crisco filling makes them disappointing to eat. Filled with a rich pecan buttercream, they delight both adults and children. Be aware that one cookie feeds two people. This is a good bake-sale item.

WHOOPIE PIE COOKIES WITH PECAN BUTTER FROSTING

MAKES 12 LARGE FILLED COOKIES:
EACH COOKIE SERVES 2

For the Cookie:

1 cup butter, at room temperature

2 cups sugar

2 eggs

1 cup buttermilk

1 teaspoon vanilla extract

1 teaspoon salt

1 cup cocoa powder

4 cups all-purpose flour

2 teaspoons baking soda

1 cup hot tap water

For the Frosting:

1 cup butter, at room temperature

2 teaspoons vanilla extract

¼ cup milk

3 tablespoons flour

4 cups confectioners' sugar, sifted after measuring

2 egg whites

Pinch of salt

1½ cups pecans broken into large pieces

Preheat the oven to 375°F.

For these cookies, it helps to use a mixer of some sort. Cream the butter and sugar together until smooth and fluffy. Add the eggs and beat until smooth. Stir in the buttermilk and vanilla.

Add the salt and cocoa and beat until evenly colored. Add the flour in 2 batches (you will have to scrape down the sides of the bowl once or twice). Dissolve the baking soda in the hot tap water and stir the water into the dough by hand.

Grease a heavy baking sheet. Spoon out 6 cookies onto the sheet. Use a good 3 tablespoons of batter for each cookie, and let them spread to about 2½ inches in diameter with a thickness of ⅓ inch.

Bake for around 9 minutes, or until the top springs back at a light touch. Cool slightly before removing to a cooling rack. Scrape the baking sheet, regrease, and continue baking. You should aim for 24 cookie halves.

To make the frosting, whisk or beat the butter until very soft. Add the vanilla and milk, then the flour. Add 3 cups only of the confectioners' sugar.

In another bowl, beat the egg whites until very frothy. Add a pinch of salt. Continue beating and slowly adding the last cup of confectioners' sugar. Beat until the eggs are shiny and smooth. They should look like meringue and form a ribbon when allowed to drip from the beater. Fold the egg whites into the butter mixture. Fold in the pecans.

To assemble, place twelve of the cookies flat side up on a counter. Divide the frosting evenly over the cookies. Top with the remaining cookies. To store, wrap each cookie in plastic wrap. Refrigerate before serving.

A MENNONITE FARM WOMAN'S DAY

"**Y**ou are interested in this?

"We get up at 6 A.M. and have breakfast. This morning cereal, peaches, eggs, toast, juice, coffee, chocolate chip cookies—not large. At 7, we start five of us out picking 'loupes. We picked eight rows and finished at 9. Then we picked 150 heads cauliflower; 25 boxes broccoli. We got to market late—around 11. Today we got $1.85 for our large melons, 85 cents for mediums, 55 cents for small. I wrote it here on the inside of my hand with a pen. Now I'm waiting for my husband. He went to the bank with the money. We'll go home and take a break for an hour.

"My daughters are doing the washing and cooking the meal. We'll have a casserole for lunch of meat, potatoes, and peas left over from last night. Then maybe the children will go swimming in our big stock tank. Around 3 or 4 P.M., when the heat is off the day, we'll go out and pick melons. We'll have supper then—steak, mashed potatoes, succotash, muffins made with homemade apple butter, then 'loupe and ice cream for dessert. At 9:30 we're usually in bed. You see, nothing out the ordinary."

—Anna, Leola Farm Market

IDDEN APPLE BUTTER MUFFINS

MAKES 12 LARGE (3-INCH) OR
16–18 SMALLER MUFFINS

1½ cups all-purpose flour

1 cup light brown sugar

1 stick butter

1 teaspoon ground cinnamon

2 teaspoons baking powder

2 eggs, separated

1 tablespoon distilled white or
apple cider vinegar

1 teaspoon baking soda

⅓ cup milk

⅔ cup apple butter

Preheat the oven to 400°F. Grease a muffin tin or tins.

In a large bowl, mix the flour, sugar, butter, and cinnamon to a coarse meal or streusel-like crumb —use your fingertips, it's easiest and quickest. Measure out 1 cup of the crumbs and set it aside for the topping.

Stir the baking powder into the remaining mixture.

Beat the egg whites until they are stiff but still glossy.

Combine the vinegar and baking soda. When the bubbles settle down, stir in the egg yolks and milk. Pour this liquid and the beaten egg whites over the dry ingredients and immediately combine the batter with a 15-second stirring and folding. Do not expect a smooth, thoroughly moistened dough—there will be lumps of flour, slicks of egg white showing.

Quickly spoon the mixture into the tins. Place a tablespoon of apple butter in the center of each muffin, then divide and sprinkle the reserved streusel crumbs over the top.

Put to bake at once for 20 minutes. Cool for 5 minutes before turning out of the tins.

These raspberry-filled cookie-tarts are particularly delightful when cut into heart shapes, a traditional Pennsylvania Dutch motif.

RASPBERRY "PENNYPIES"

MAKES AROUND 12 TARTS

For the Pastry:

1 stick unsalted butter, at room temperature
1/2 cup confectioners' sugar, sifted
1 large egg

1 teaspoon lemon juice
1 teaspoon vanilla extract
1 1/2–1 3/4 cups flour

For the Filling:

Around 1 3/4 cups thick raspberry jam
  with seeds
1/2 teaspoon ground cinnamon

1 egg, separated
1 tablespoon plus 2 teaspoons water
Confectioners' sugar

To make the pastry, cream the butter and sugar together until smooth . . . a machine makes short work of this. Add the egg, lemon juice, and vanilla. If you are using a machine, the mixture soon comes smooth. By hand, it tends to look a bit like scrambled eggs for a while. Whisk hard and it will amalgamate. Stir in 1 cup of the flour, then continue adding flour until you can scrape out the dough into a ball on a floured surface. Try not to overwork the dough. It will be softer than piecrust. Roll the dough into a ball and flatten it to a 1-inch-thick pancake. Wrap it in plastic or foil and refrigerate for at least 1 hour.

Preheat the oven to 350°F. and lightly grease a baking sheet. Flour a surface, roll out part of the dough to a 1/4-inch thickness (scatter more flour lightly on top as necessary), and cut out 3-inch hearts or circles. Place the shapes on the baking sheet.

Mix the jam with the cinnamon. Spoon mounded tablespoons into the center of half the cookies.

(Choose thinner cookies for the bottoms, thick cookies for the tops.) Beat the egg white with the tablespoon of water. Moisten a finger with the egg white and run it around the exposed edge of the cookies. Place the remaining cookies on top and gently press around the edges so that the tarts are firmly sealed. Mix the egg yolk with the 2 teaspoons of water and brush over the tarts. Make a tiny slit through the top layer of each tart with the tip of a knife.

Bake the pennypies for 12 to 15 minutes, or until golden. Remove from the oven and cool completely on a rack. Give a light sifting of the confectioners' sugar to finish the pastry.

BLUEBERRIES AND HUCKLEBERRIES

"In Colonial days, blueberries were known as Hurtleberries. Blueberries and huckleberries are not the same. Huckleberries have 10 large seeds; blueberries have many more smaller ones."

—Tennessee Department of Agriculture blueberry brochure

HOME-STYLE BREAD AND BUTTER BLUEBERRIES

SERVES 8

1 cup sugar
Finely grated zest and juice
   of 1 small lemon
¼ teaspoon ground ginger
8 slices firm bread (such as Pepperidge
   Farm Classic)

4 tablespoons (½ stick) unsalted butter,
   softened or melted
1 quart washed blueberries

Preheat the oven to 350°F. Lightly butter a nonaluminum baking or gratin dish approximately 8 x 10 inches.

Mix the sugar with the lemon zest and ginger.

Cut the crusts from the bread. Butter one side of the slices, then cut them in half diagonally.

Arrange half the bread, butter side up, in the dish. Top with half of the berries. Sprinkle on half the sugar. Top with the remaining bread, the remaining blueberries, and top with a scattering of the remaining ½ cup of sugar. Sprinkle on the lemon juice.

With the flat side of a spatula, press down firmly on the berries to settle the contents and start the juices flowing.

Bake for 30 minutes. Remove from the oven and press the berries down again to compact them. Return to the oven and bake for another 30 minutes.

Cool for at least 30 minutes before serving. This is at its best when just warm. Serve with thick, unsweetened whipped cream or crème fraîche, if so desired.

—✂—

You could try this with any of the old-fashioned apples that small farmers cherish.

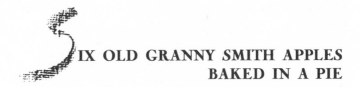

SIX OLD GRANNY SMITH APPLES BAKED IN A PIE

SERVES 6

For the Piecrust:

1 generous cup all-purpose flour
1 teaspoon sugar
Pinch of salt

1 stick unsalted butter, well chilled
Ice water

For the Filling:

1 cup sugar
¼ cup water
1½ teaspoons ground cinnamon
2 tablespoons butter
6 Granny Smith apples

2 tablespoons Calvados or light rum
6 cinnamon sticks
1 egg yolk beaten with 2 teaspoons water
for glaze
⅔ cup heavy cream, chilled

Make the piecrust by combining the flour, sugar, and salt in a bowl. Cut the butter into cubes and work it into the flour until the flour is the texture of fine meal. Add ice water by the tablespoon just until you are able to gather the dough into a neat, smooth ball. Press the ball into the flour, then flatten it to a 1-inch-thick round. Cover with plastic wrap or foil and refrigerate for at least 30 minutes.

Make a cinnamon syrup by combining the sugar, water, cinnamon, and butter in a saucepan. Heat to a boil, then turn the heat down and simmer for 5 minutes. Remove from the heat.

Preheat the oven to 350°F.

Peel the apples, leaving them whole. Cut a neat round core down through the center. Place the apples in a buttered gratin or soufflé dish that holds them as snugly as possible.

Stir the Calvados into the cinnamon syrup. Using a good half of the liquid, spoon the syrup down the center of each apple.

Roll out the pie dough on a floured surface until it is ¼ inch thick. Drape the dough loosely over the apples. Gently press the dough so that it drapes into the spaces between the apples. Tuck it in around the edge of the dish, then let it hang over the rim. Cut off a ½-inch overhang and crimp the dough around the edge of the dish in a nice pattern.

Make a slit through the dough into the cored center of each apple and insert a cinnamon stick. Brush the dough with the egg yolk glaze. Bake the "pie" for around 45 minutes (if the top seems to be overbrowning, cover it with foil).

To serve, whip the cream until it starts to thicken. Whip in the remainder of the cinnamon syrup. Dish out an apple per person with some of the crust, and pour the cinnamon cream over the top.

— ⚬ —

It is the small farmers and apple growers who are cherishing and preserving "antique" strains of apple varietals that are near extinction. Why limit yourself to boring Red Delicious when you can go to farmers' markets and find . . .

REAL APPLES

"And pluck til time and times are done" . . .
   (Black Gilliflower,
      Hubertson's Non-Such Pippin,
         Ox Hart Pippin,
            Wolf River,
               Sheep Nose,
                  Tolman Sweets,
                     Spitzenberg,
                        Winter Banana)
"The silver apples of the moon" . . .
   (Opalescent,
      Lady Apple,
         Duchess of Oldenburg,
            Roxbury Russet,
               Sops of Wine,
                  Maiden Blush,
                     Westfield See-No-Further)
"The golden apples of the sun."
   (Golden Russets,
      Cox's Orange Pippin,
         Pit Maston Pineapple,
            Jona Gold,
               Spy Gold,
                  Northern Spys,
                     York Imperials,
                        Matzu's Japanese Golden,
                           King Luscious)

—quotation from William Butler Yeats, "The Song of Wandering Aengus"

—Apples from Dane County Market, Wisconsin;
Sonoma Antique Apple Nursery, California;
Breezy Hill Orchard, at Union Square, New York

The Leola Produce Market

I would almost like to keep Leola to myself, so endearing is it in its unheralded state. Slip past the town of Leola, turn left on Brethren Church Road, and you will come to the Leola Produce Market. All around is neat farmland, a vista built with such precision that it looks like it has been laid out with a child's blocks: large green-gold squares and rectangles of fields, small white squares of houses, and silver cylinders of barns, meticulous and tidy. What strikes one is the look of well-managed, manageable farms. Nowhere in America is the farmer-as-fine-craftsman so evident as in the Amish country.

The Leola Produce Market was founded several years ago by a dozen Mennonite businessmen/farmers who wanted to wholesale their produce. It opens early in the morning several days each week. The sellers come from around the neighborhood—bearded husbands bringing loads of vegetables in on carts hauled by sure, heavy Clydesdales; the wives in faded flower prints and neat snoods hurrying over with the children in carriages drawn by fine-boned trotting horses. The horses are hitched on one side of the building, where they stand patiently all morning, stamping and tail switching in their traces, large digested meals piled behind them. The buyers park their trucks on the other side of the long cement wharf of a building so as not to frighten the horses.

All this chill autumn morning, until the lots are sold, workhorses draw carts down a channeled path and over a scale so the men can see eye to eye with the goods and judge them fairly. Paul Horst, the auctioneer, sings, "One a he, one a hay, sold today a dollar and a quarter [that's the extent, anyway, of what I make out of the swift current of his chant]," and a mountain load of cabbage moves out of the viewing block to a waiting truck bound for New Jersey. When all the big loads are sold, the small items are auctioned. A bushel of gourds, three crates of eggplant; two dozen corn husk dolls, a single bowl of wild ground cherries—small ripe fruits that look like yellow tomatillos in their paper husks. "Psst," says a voice, "You there—I haint been seeing you here before."

A cane hooks around my arm and pulls me back. Sitting flat atop a metal weighing table, his legs straight out in front, with a stubbled face like a half-mown wheat field, is Clyde R. Pfautz. Clyde sits in court by the scales because everyone passes by there sooner or later. It's one of the privileges of the old men of the market ("market rats," he calls them). He and Walter Ecenrode will spend the morning here until the auction's done, then go to the Ephrata market and play checkers until the auction starts there in the late afternoon.

Right now he is after me to go and filch a handful of ground cherries when no one is looking.

"Got to have me some of those ground cherries, sweet as honey they are. 'Yude-kosshe,' we call them. My wife, she used to bake ground cherry pies, them great big square ones. Maybe I'll buy those, then some evening when it's slack I'll peel off the papers and she can add sugar and make dough and I'll have me a yudekosshe pie.

"Where you be coming from?" he asks.

"North Carolina," I say.

"How long you be taking to get there from here? That South is far. I'll tell you a story now if you won't go getting upset. There's these tourists from South who stop at an Amish man's farm market. They see a big hubbard squash and don't know what it is. The farmer he tells them it's a mule egg, so they buy it to take home.

"They's riding along and stop to have a picnic. The old squash rolls out of the car and down the road back into the bushes. A rabbit jumps out of the bushes and they think the egg's hatched. The man starts yelling at his wife and she say, 'Oh, Jed, calm down. It wasn't big enough to hitch a wagon to anyway.' You like that, hey?

"I started when I was twenty years old. I sold eggs, apples, and apple butter. I ran an old '28 Chevy truck 'til 1936. I'd be out in that huckster truck til nine or ten each night. I was just a dumb sixth grader in school, but I knew you don't sell nothing if you don't have nothing. Well, I saved a little money, not much, but enough to buy me a little piece of land. Beamus Gerber, he helped me with a loan. One day I went around the bend by Cal Beglar's house and he said from the sounds of your vehicle you need another truck. So I went to an auction and saw the truck I needed, but it was $900 and I only had $650. Pappy Fry, my old teacher in school, was outside the lot helping the auctioneer. When I bid the whole $900 to get the truck, he said, 'If you make a false bid I'll kill you. I could shake you in school and I can shake you yet.' Well, to top it off, I went around to Adam Gill—he had silver you know—money. He had $100 bills wrapped up in a trunk and lots of farms. He sat on that money, maybe did a little jockeying from time to time. Now I'm not too well booked in money but I know you have to have money to invest. I talked Adam Gill into making up my $250 and I went and bought that truck right in front of Pappy Fry, and within six months that truck was paid off I worked so hard. Now I'm resting pretty good, but then, oh, I huckstered the streets of Shillington and went down to Philly without thinking.

"I grew tomatoes, peppers, corn, beets, agriculture beans—those purple ones that look like a bird's egg when you shell them. I really flew. I had eight youngsters to tend to. My wife and I both worked hard. I remember my wife in bed one time waiting for a baby to be born and there she was shelling lima beans.

"Now I go fishing a lot. My wife she makes quilts. I can't stand seeing her quilt and she tells me she'll quit when I stop bringing home so many damn fish. If you want a recipe now, I'll give you one."

CLYDE R. PFAUTZ'S RECIPE

1 cup water
1 teaspoon salt
1 large tablespoon sugar
1 cup yellow cornmeal

"You take your water and your salt and your sugar and bring it to a boil, then stir in the yellow cornmeal. Stir until it's tacky. Let it cool down, then put it in a plastic bag and knead the thing like butter. You take little balls of it and make pointy ends like a diamond on each side so it doesn't fall off. Fix it good and tight on the hook and fish from the bottom will come straight up. Best damn carp bait you ever did have.

"Sometimes when I'm fishing I dream I go back down to Philly with a truck and a load. Can't do it any more, but I sure can dream about it. Yah, that was a good life.

"Go steal us some more yudekosshe. You're leaving then? Well, take your time and hurry back."

— ❦ —

"Farmers have more time to think than city people do. And that's why I've always thought and said that farmers are the smartest people in the world."

—Harry S Truman

The Leola market was perfumed with pears on my late fall trip.

Here is one of the nicest, gentlest desserts I know. It makes an elegant entertaining dish because most of the work can be done in advance. Choose pears that are still firm but just beginning to give.

GRATIN OF PEARS WITH MASCARPONE

SERVES 4–5

5 Bartlett or d'Anjou pears
Juice of 1 lemon
3 tablespoons Poire liqueur or light rum
Ground cinnamon

3½ ounces Mascarpone (failing that, soft
    whipped cream cheese)
1 egg
⅓ cup sugar

Lightly butter a baking dish, preferably a 10-inch round quiche pan (an oval will do, but round is better). Preheat the oven to 350°F.

Cut the pears in half lengthwise. Peel them, cut out the seeds and core, and rub lightly with lemon juice as you finish each half.

Place a pear half, cavity down, on a cutting surface and cut across into thin slices. Hold the pear together as you slice so it remains a compact unit. Slide a spatula under the pear and transfer it to the baking dish. Press the pear down gently with the flat of your hand and it will fan out flat, with its short point to the center, its large rounded end to the edge of the dish. Sprinkle with more lemon juice. Continue cutting and fanning all the halves but 1. The round dish should hold 9 halves. Cut the tenth, but leave it nicely rounded in the center of the dish.

Sprinkle the pears with Poire and a light dusting of cinnamon. Cover with foil and put to bake for 30 minutes.

Remove from the oven and, with a bulb baster, draw off all the juices that have been rendered. Bring the juices to a boil in a small pan and reduce to 2 tablespoons.

Whisk the reduced juices, the Mascarpone, and the egg together.

(The dish can be assembled to this point and continued several hours later.)

Preheat the broiler as hot as it will go. Drizzle the Mascarpone 'round and 'round over the top of the pears and scatter on the sugar. Place the dish under the broiler and watch carefully. Within a minute or so the top should be speckled brown and gold, and the sugar should have formed a most delicate crust. Serve at once.

A farm market is the only place in America you'll find a persimmon pudding for sale. Late in the season, after the first frost, the fruit puckers and wizzens on the trees and finds its sweetness only after frost kills all else around and brings the persimmon to a sort of tropical intensity. These pudding are mostly in the markets of the South and mid-Atlantic states. They sit, squat, almost black pies, wrapped in plastic bags, a sure autumnal sign that all the living earth has gone to rest.

END-OF-THE-SEASON PERSIMMON PUDDING

SERVES 8–10

2 cups wild persimmon puree (rub the soft flesh through a sieve)

1 cup light brown sugar

1 stick unsalted butter, very soft

½ cup flour

2 tablespoons cornstarch

¼ teaspoon salt

A few gratings of nutmeg

¼ teaspoon ground cinnamon

¼ teaspoon ground allspice

½ cup Carnation evaporated milk

½ cup whole milk

4 eggs, beaten

1 cup buttermilk

½ teaspoon baking soda

Preheat the oven to 325°F. Butter a 9-x-13-inch Pyrex baking dish or quiche pan.

Mix the persimmon puree, sugar, and butter and beat until well blended.

In another bowl, stir the flour, cornstarch, salt, and spices together.

Stir the dry ingredients and the evaporated and whole milk alternately into the persimmon puree. Stir in the eggs. Add ½ cup of the buttermilk.

Stir the baking soda into the remaining ½ cup of buttermilk. When it has finished bubbling, stir immediately into the pudding batter and pour into the baking dish.

Bake for 20 minutes. Reduce the heat to 300°F. and continue cooking for another 1¼ hours, or until the pudding is well browned and starts to pull away from the sides of the pan.

Cool completely in the baking dish. Serve chilled, with optional whipped cream or a hard sauce if you so choose.

EPILOGUE,
ONE YEAR
LATER

—IN LYNCHBURG, VIRGINIA, DENCIA HUNTER HAS had her ninth child, a baby girl. After a brief hiatus she's back at the market making biscuits. The baby's there, too, in a small open cooler unit that everyone has blanketed and pillowed just for her.

⚘—In Lynchburg, John Covington graduated valedictorian of his class and is attending Hampton-Sydney College, fifteen miles from home, so he can be near the market.

⚘—At Fantome Farm in Wisconsin, Anne and Judy's goats bore a new crop last spring —lady politicians:

Winnie (Mandela)

Shirley (Chisholm)

Barbara (Jordan)

⚘—In Dallas, all of 1991 celebrates the market's fiftieth year. The Dallas City Council gave a $20 million birthday present, a vote of confidence to guarantee the market's future.

⚘—In California, Lynn Bagley reports that by the end of 1990 there was a yearly 25 percent increase in the number of California Certified Public Markets.

⚘—In Pennsylvania, Clyde R. Pfautz is back for another season by the Leola Produce auction scales and will challenge all comers to a game of checkers.

⚘—According to Hilary Baum of the Public Market Collaborative, there are over two thousand farmers' markets in America at the start of this new decade.

SOME CIRCULAR THINKING

IO GOOD THINGS TO DO TO RESET OUR MINDS ABOUT FOOD

1. Demand and get the best for our bodies.
   We may not be able to stop the cumulative blight around us, but we can refuse to ingest it. Search out the best in prime food, therefore . . .

2. Shop farmers' markets.
   Buy just-picked produce from real farmers. To encourage them to go organic . . .

3. Accept less-than-perfect-looking product.
   Organic sometimes has a less-than-haughty hybrid look. To find out why . . .

4. Ask farmers questions.
   Find out how they grow things. Be willing to spend a bit more for organic as the farmers absorb the extra expenses of transition to organic. If you don't have a farmers' market available to you . . .

5. Start a farmers' market.
   Send for the booklet, "Greenmarket, the Rebirth of Farmers' Markets in New York City," Greenmarket, 24 West 40th Street, New York, NY 10018. It will tell you how. If you can't start a farm market . . .

6. Start a community garden.
   Send $3.00 to: Minnesota Green, Attn.: Rick Bonlender, Minnesota Horticul-
   tural Society, 1970 Folwell—161 Alderman Hall, Saint Paul, MN 55108 . . .
   for a copy of "Creating a Community Garden." If you can't do that, at
   least . . .

7. Make demands at your grocery store.
   Ask them to have an organic section. Request that it carries produce in season
   from local farmers. If you rarely cook in . . .

8. Make demands at your favorite restaurants.
   Ask where they get their produce. Support restaurants who shop at farm
   markets. Further . . .

9. Make demands on agribusiness.
   Keep abreast of chemical use and abuse. Boycott when necessary. Don't be
   afraid to . . .

10. Make demands on government.
    There should be "no detectable residues" in our food supply legislation. Only
    then can we . . .

1. Demand and get the best for our bodies . . .

etc.

 MARKET FINDS

I WISH I COULD GATHER ALL YOU READERS UP IN A bus and drive peacefully around the country on an all-farm-market itinerary. It would take three months of Saturdays, but what wonderful foods we would find. Failing such a dream trip, I've collected a listing of shops and people who have agreed to send items through the mail. You will have to write or speak to them personally to negotiate prices and mailing costs, and not all items may be available at all times, but here's a good way to taste some of the bounty of our land.

HONEY-ORANGE ALMONDS

Don and Rodney, the Stackhouse brothers, turn the almonds from their orchard into succulent, barbecue, hickory smoke, garlic-onion, soy roast, and, my favorite, honey-orange flavors. You can find their stands in eight different farm markets in the San Francisco area and in Pike Place market, or you can write for price lists to:

Stackhouse Brothers' Orchards
13501 Cogswell Road
Hickman, CA 95323
(209) 883-2663

They have sampling packages, and, of course, you can buy plain almonds.

ANTIQUE APPLES

Breezy Hill Orchard in New York State's Hudson Valley produces a variety of heirloom apples. Their mail order "Codlins & Pippins" price list will tell you of rare and unusual apples that can be shipped from late August through Christmas.

Breezy Hill Orchard
Centre Road
Staatsburg, NY 12580
(914) 266-5967

APPLE SYRUP, JAZZLE JAM, CIDER APPLESAUCE

At the Woodring Orchard stand in Pike Place Market, you can taste chunky cider applesauce made from Golden Delicious apples, and apple cider syrup, a good alternative to pancake syrup. Jazzle jam tastes and feels like strawberry jam but is made from French prunes. Write or call:

Woodring Orchards
5420 Woodring Canyon Road
Cashmere, WA 98815
1-800-548-5740

CHUKAR CHERRIES

These pitted Bing cherries sold at Pike Place market are carefully dried, with no sugar or preservatives, to make a chewy, delicious snack. The cherries are wonderful in the kitchen —use them in desserts, to accompany duck, in fruit salads, and in sauces. They'll send along some recipes when you order from:

Chukar Cherry Company
P.O. Box 510
306 Wine Country Road
Prosser, WA 99350
(509) 786-2055

CULTURED BUTTER, WISCONSIN FARMERS' MARKET CHEESES

Willi Lehner, the award-winning Forgotten Valley Cheese Company, and Fantome Farm combine their offerings in the Blue Mont Dairy Company catalogue. You can order traditional cultured butter; plain, black pepper, or garlic goat cheeses; Brick, white Cheddar, farmer's cheese, and several others from this Wisconsin source. Note that the dairy discontinues shipping cheese and butter by mail between May 15 and October 1 (during these months you can find them at the Madison or Evanston, Illinois, farmers' markets). Write for a free brochure:

> Blue Mont Dairy
> 10930 Cty F
> Blue Mounds, WI 53517

For a guide to other Wisconsin Cheese Factory outlets and tours, write:

> Marketing Division
> 801 W. Badger Road
> P.O. Box 8911
> Madison, WI 53708

FAVA BEANS, CHIOGGIA BEETS, SPACE AGE BROCCOLI

Martin's Farm gets many of its seeds from Johnny's Selected Seeds. For candy-striped chioggia beets, fava bean seeds (be sure to get the nitrogen inoculant for greater bean production), and Minaret "space age" broccoli, write or call:

> Johnny's Selected Seeds
> Foss Hill Road
> Albion, ME 04910
> (207) 437-9294

The catalogue is free and they accept Mastercard and Visa orders.

For a good seed source on the West Coast, write for the catalogue of:

> Nichol's Gardens
> 1190 N. Pacific Highway
> Albany, OR 97321
> (503) 923-9280

EDIBLE FLOWERS, FLOWER SYRUPS, AND CRYSTALLIZED BLOSSOMS

If you need assorted edible flowers for a special occasion, or would like to purchase crystallized blossoms not available on gourmet grocers' shelves, write or call Maxine Sessoms, the owner/grower of:

> Maxi Flowers a la Carte
> 1015 Martin Lane
> Sebastopol, CA 95472
> (707) 829-0592 (FAX number the same)

She can arrange for UPS, overnight delivery of stock, pansies, primroses, Johnny-jump-ups, violas, bachelor's buttons, dianthus, wild violets, roses, nasturtiums, marigolds, miniature gladiolus, poppies, pelargoniums, borage, and mixed floral petals—not all at one time, of course, but according to the season.

FLOWER-DECORATED GARLIC BRAIDS

Pretty, flower-entwined dried garlic braids can be ordered from:

> Bill Reynolds
> Eel River Produce
> 56 Shively Flat Road
> Scotia, CA 95565
> (707) 722-4309

Bill suggests you call for prices, as he can make up short or long braids to your specifications. He also sells plain braids and bulk garlic in twenty-five pound cases.

PEARL SUGAR

Order Pearl Sugar (*Parl Socker*) for Currant Bars from:

> Fredrickson and Johannesen
> 7719 5th Avenue
> Brooklyn, NY 11209
> Telephone (800) 445-1357

Will fill phone orders. Free catalogue of Scandinavian products.

PENNSYLVANIA DUTCH SPECIALTY FOODS

To order cup cheese, ball cheese, apple and pumpkin butters, pickled watermelon rind, chow-chow, and cabbage-stuffed peppers, send for the mail order price list from:

Shenk's
Zimmerman Foods Corp.
1980 New Danville Pike
Lancaster, PA 17603
(717) 393-4240

They will UPS most of the best-known items found in the Lancaster market.

READING TERMINAL MARKET ITEMS

Though you can't have hot homemade pretzels unless you actually visit Reading Terminal, you can purchase Uncle Jerry's Pretzels—big, handmade, hard "beer" pretzels that are one and a half inches thick. They come in whole wheat, oat bran, and sesame seed—all made in a Mennonite bakery and mail ordered only by:

Pennsylvania General Store
Reading Terminal Market
12th and Arch Streets
Philadelphia, PA 19107
1-800-545-4891

Owner Mike Holahan will tell you also about scrapple and Lebanon bologna and will send you a brochure about other market items.

RURAL ENTERPRISE MAGAZINE

To learn more about farm markets, farm market tours, specialty foods, and how to become a direct marketer, subscribe to:

Rural Enterprise
P.O. Box 878
Menomonee Falls, WI 53051

A one-year subscription costs $8.95.

SEEDS FOR MARKET GARDENERS

For the "world's largest selection of salad greens" plus a wondrous assortment of vegetable, herb, and edible flower seeds, get your name on the mailing list of:

The Cook's Garden
P.O. Box 65
Londonderry, VT 05148

Many growers have mentioned to me the special knowledge and help that Ellen and Shepherd Ogden provide for the professional market gardener. There is a bulk price list available and they accept phone orders.

SEED PRESERVATION

Information on all aspects of saving seeds can be obtained by joining:

Seed Savers Exchange
Rural Route 3, Box 239
Decorah, IA 52101

Membership costs $15 per year and includes three publications. You will learn about preserving our vegetables' heritage by maintaining and distributing the seeds of rare and endangered vegetable varieties.

For seeds especially suited to the West Coast, join:

The Seed Saving Project
Dept. LAWR
139 Hoagland Hall
Davis, CA 95616

For a $3 membership fee, you will receive newsletters and a chance to request seeds for scores of plants that are not available in most commercial catalogues.

SHIITAKE AND OYSTER MUSHROOM TREES

Follow the directions (and funny they are), and within two weeks you can be raising generous amounts of expensive mushrooms in your dank basement. To order a mushroom tree (actually it looks more like a Brie-crusted log), write:

H-S Farming Company
Mushroom Kits
P.O. Box 724
Healdsburg, Ca 95448
(707) 838-4570

The company will air-freight east of the Rockies.

SORGHUM

Pure "honey drip" sorghum, with no corn syrup added, is made from cane on the farm of James and Annie Mathews. Their sorghum is clear, amber-colored, and much milder than blackstrap molasses. You'll want some to make Odessa Piper's Hickory Nut Sorghum Pie (page 43). Write or phone for prices and shipping:

James and Annie Mathews
Route 2, Box 254A
Bethany, MO 64424
(816) 425-3594

They'll include their own recipe brochure with each order.

FRENCH MARKET STRING BAGS

The French carry small string *filets* to market to do their shopping. The filets wad easily into small spaces when not filled, and they are a good alternative to paper and plastic shopping bags. For $8.95, you can get two grocery-sized bags. Write to:

Seventh Generation
10 Farrell Street
Burlington, VT 05403
(802) 655-6777

Seventh Generation is also a good source for nontoxic bug sprays and other environmentally sound items.

A TASTE OF TEXAS

For sampling boxes of Texas products, pecans, sweet onions, dried chile pepper ristras (strings), and a tin bucket of fajita marinades and seasonings, write or call:

> The Mirth Food Company
> Travis County Farmers' Market
> P.O. Box 402171
> Austin, TX 78704
> 1-800-950-8632

Michael Lacky or Ruth Anne George can help you with price lists, gift ideas, and farmer's baskets.

HONEST WILD RICE

. . . not paddy grown and processed, but gathered in the traditional canoe-harvested way. Call or write Greg Isaaksen:

> W9935 CTH CS
> Poynette, WI 53955
> (608) 635-2705

He will tell you about prices (shipping is expensive, but the rice is cheap, so you will always come out ahead of retail store prices). He's out at the lake harvesting in August and September, and at the Dane County market every Saturday, but you can catch him most other times at his home. (That address is the fire number that all rural Wisconsin homes sport. CTH stands for County Truck Highway.)

WREATHS AND PORTAL PIECES

Issie Sime lives on Washon Island in Puget Sound. There she gathers larkspur, quaking grass, ferns, and woodland moss to make her handsome twenty-four and twelve-inch curved portal wreaths, which flex gracefully over doors. She will make custom-designed pieces in sizes and colors of your choosing and send them UPS, or you can visit her in Pike Place market on weekends. Write or call:

Issie Sime
The Wreath Connection
P.O. Box 239
Washon, WA 98070
(206) 567-4000

She also sells a by-product of wreath-making, "Grapewood Smoke"—dried cured grapevine chips that are good for smoking salmon.

FARM MARKETS ACROSS AMERICA

THIS IS BY NO MEANS A COMPLETE LISTING OF markets. What follows is a selection of established produce and city markets that are worth searching out on travels and certainly worth knowing within each state.

ALABAMA

Montgomery

Montgomery State Farmers' Market
1655 Federal Drive, on the corner of
Coliseum Blvd.
Daily, 24 hours, year-round
Wholesale and retail
Pecan-cracking and peanut-roasting services

ALASKA

Anchorage

Anchorage Farmers' Market
Corner 5th and C Streets
Saturday 9 A.M.–2 P.M., in season (short!)
Cold crops and lingonberries

ARKANSAS

Pine Bluff

Pine Bluff Farmers' Market
Ford and Walnut Streets
Tuesday, Thursday, Saturday,
7 A.M.–3 P.M., year-round

CALIFORNIA

For a listing of Certified Farmers' Markets
write:
California Dept. of Food and Agriculture
Direct Marketing Program
P.O. Box 942871
Sacramento, CA 94271-0001

Berkeley

Berkeley Farmers' Market
Derby Street, between Milvia and Martin
Luther King Jr. Way
Tuesday, 2 P.M.–7 P.M.; 2 P.M.–dusk, in
winter, year-round

Davis

Davis Farm Market
4th and C Streets
Wednesday, 2 P.M.–6 P.M.; Saturday,
8 A.M.–noon, year-round

Los Angeles

Grand Central Market
317 South Broadway, downtown Los Angeles
Daily, 8 A.M.–4 P.M., year-round
*Meat, produce, baked goods, Mexican food
stands, operating tortilla factory. A fascinating
place.*

San Diego

Chino Najo, The Vegetable Shop
6123 Calzada del Bosque
Rancho Santa Fe
Tuesday–Friday 10:00 A.M.–3:30 P.M.;
Saturday and Sunday, 10 A.M.–noon,
year-round
*Though not a farmers' market, this produce
stand is nationally known. The outlet to a
family-run farm, its offerings include state-of-the-
art varietals. Alice Waters and Wolfgang Puck
are clients.*

San Francisco

Alemany
100 Alemany Blvd.
Tuesday–Friday 8:30 A.M.–5:00 P.M.;
Saturday 6:00 A.M.–6:00 P.M., year-round
*A very old established market. Lots of good
oriental produce.*

San Luis Obispo

"Downtown"
Hiquera Street at Chorro
Thursday, 6:30 A.M.–9:00 P.M., year-round
*The "flagship" nighttime community market/
festival that other California cities study when
they want to revive public spirit and dying
downtown main streets.*

Santa Barbara

Santa Barbara Market
Costa and Santa Barbara
Saturday, 8:30 A.M.–noon, year-round
Spectacular flowers; glimpses of Julia Child

Santa Monica

Santa Monica Market
Arizona Avenue and 2nd Street
Wednesday, 10 A.M.–3 P.M., year-round

San Rafael

Marin County Certified Farmers' Market
Marin County Civic Center Fairgrounds
Sunday, 9 A.M.–2 P.M.; Thursday, 8 A.M.–
1 P.M., year-round
*The largest organic farmers' market in the
nation*

Santa Rosa

Santa Rosa Market
4th and B Streets, Veterans Memorial
Building
Thursday, 5:30 P.M.–8:30 P.M.; Wednesday,
Saturday, 9 A.M.–noon, June–September

COLORADO

Boulder

Boulder Farmers' Market
Central Park
Saturday mornings, end of May–October

CONNECTICUT

Hartford

Hartford Downtown Farmers' Market
Old State House Square
Market Street
Monday, Wednesday, Friday, 10 A.M.–2 P.M.,
July–October 31

DELAWARE

Wilmington

Wilmington Farmers' Market
Wednesday, Thursday, Friday in season
*A precarious market that needs to
find a home. Get after local officials. Call
Delaware Department of Agriculture
for latest location.*

DISTRICT OF COLUMBIA

Eastern Market

Historic Market Building
D Street
Real farmers on Saturdays, in season

FLORIDA

Pompano Beach

Pompano Beach Farmers' Market
1255 Atlantic Blvd.
Monday–Friday, 8 A.M.–5 P.M., year-round

GEORGIA

Atlanta

Atlanta Farmers' Market
16 Forest Parkway
Forest Park
Daily, 24 hours, year-round
Wholesale, retail

HAWAII

Honolulu, Oahu

Alamaana Farmers' Market
1020 Auahi Street
Daily, 7 A.M.–6 P.M., year-round
Tropical fish, Kona oranges, guavas

IDAHO

Boise

Boise Farmers' Market
Corner 8th and Bannock, downtown
Friday, 5:30–9:30 P.M., May–September

ILLINOIS

Evanston

Farmers' Market
Maple Avenue, between Clark and
Church Streets
Saturday 8 A.M.–3 P.M., mid-June–October
*For a good farm market guide and listing of
pick-your-own farms, write:*

Illinois Dept. of Agriculture
Division of Marketing
P.O. Box 19281
Springfield, IL 62794-9281

INDIANA

Bloomington
Bloomington Community Farmers' Market
East 6th Street parking lot, 2 blocks east of
Court House Square
Saturday mornings, mid-May–October

Indianapolis
Indianapolis City Market
Market and Alabama Streets, across from
Market Square Arena
Monday–Saturday, 6:00 A.M.–3:30 P.M.,
year-round
A classic city market in an 1800s Gothic arcade
that started as a haymarket

IOWA

Dubuque
Dubuque Farmers' Market
13th and Central
Saturday 6 A.M.–noon, May 6–October 21
For more information and directory write:
Iowa Dept. of Agriculture and Land Stewardship
Henry A. Wallace Building
Des Moines, IA 50319

KANSAS

Kansas City
City Market
Fifth and Walnut Streets
Monday–Friday, 6 A.M.–5 P.M.; Saturday,
5 A.M.–5 P.M., year-round
Music, produce, restaurants, musicians

LOUISIANA

Bastrop
Morehouse Parish Farmers' Market
307 E. Madison Avenue
Monday–Saturday, 7:30 A.M.–4:00 P.M.,
year-round

Lafayette
Acadiana Farmers' Market
801 Foreunan Drive
Tuesday, Thursday, Saturday, 5:30 A.M.–
11:00 A.M., year-round
Hot peppers, mirliton squash

New Orleans
French Market
1008 North Peters Street
24 hours, year-round
Newly refurbished and celebrating its 200-year
anniversary in 1991

MAINE

Brunswick
Brunswick Mall at the Center of Town
Tuesday, Friday, 9 A.M.–5 P.M., mid-May–
Thanksgiving
Maine wild blueberries

MARYLAND

Baltimore
Lexington Market
400 West Lexington Street
Monday–Saturday, 8:30 A.M.–6:00 P.M.,
year-round
One hundred thirty merchants sell in this old
historic market—lots of ethnic eateries. Don't
miss crab cakes at John W. Faidley's restaurant.

Bethesda
Montgomery Farm Women's Cooperative
Market
7155 Wisconsin Avenue
Wednesday, Saturday, 7 A.M.–4 P.M.,
year-round

MASSACHUSETTS

Amherst
Amherst Commons Farmers' Market
Saturday mornings, in season

Boston
Copley Square Farmers' Market (in park)
St. James Street, front of Trinity Church
Thursday–Friday, 11 A.M.–5 P.M., July–
November

Newton
Newton Farmers' Market
Cold Spring Park
70 Crescent Street
Tuesday, 2–6 P.M., July 10–October 30
*Organic growers, locally dried
apple chips*

Springfield
Springfield Farmers' Market
Civic Center
E. Court and Main
Wednesday, Friday, 11 A.M.–3 P.M.,
in season

MICHIGAN

Detroit
Eastern Farmers' Market
2934 Russell

Monday–Friday, 5 A.M.–noon; Saturday,
5 A.M.–6 P.M., year-round

Lansing
Lansing City Market
Tuesday, Thursday, Saturday, year-round

MINNESOTA

St. Paul
St. Paul Farmers' Market
290 E. Fifth Street
Saturday, 6 A.M.–1 P.M.; Sunday, 8 A.M.–
1 P.M., May–October
*Buffalo meat, fresh trout, oriental produce
grown by Hmong settlers from Laos*

MISSISSIPPI

Jackson
Jackson Farmers' Market
352 E. Woodrow Wilson
Monday–Saturday, 7 A.M.–6 P.M.; Sunday,
1–6 P.M., May–October
*Parched and boiled peanuts, sugarcane in fall,
pickled squash*

MISSOURI

St. Louis
Soulard Market
730 Carroll Street
Monday–Friday, 8 A.M.–5 P.M. (till 5:30 on
Wednesday), year-round
Live poultry

MONTANA

Helena
Helena Farmers' Market
Memorial Park, Main Street

Tuesday, 5–7 P.M., June 26–September 25;
Saturday, 11 A.M.–2 P.M., May, June, and
August—no market in July
*Wild huckleberries, chokecherries, organic
produce*

Missoula
Missoula Farmers' Market
Next to Burlington Northern Train Depot,
downtown
First Saturday in June through first Saturday
in October, 9 A.M.–past noon; Tuesday
evening market, July–September

NEBRASKA
Lincoln
Haymarket Farmers' Market
In front of Lincoln Station
7th Street, between P & Q
Saturday, 8:00 A.M.–12:30 P.M., June 2–
October 20
*Ethnic baked goods, poppy seed and prune
kolacky, entertainment, demonstrations*

NEVADA
Fallon
Workman's Market
Reno Highway
Daily, 10 A.M.–6 P.M., year-round
Heart of Gold melons

NEW HAMPSHIRE
Concord
Concord Farmers' Market
New Hampshire Savings Bank parking lot
N. State Street
Saturday, 9 A.M.–noon, mid-May–October
Organic growers, wool and sheep skins

NEW JERSEY
Elizabeth
Peterstown Market
Elizabeth Avenue (Peterstown section)
Tuesday, Thursday, Saturday, 7 A.M.–3 P.M.,
May–October

NEW MEXICO
Albuquerque
Farmers' Market
7605 Central Avenue, N.E.
Parking lot of Country and Western Club
Caravan East
Tuesday, Saturday, 6 A.M.–noon, in season

Santa Fe
Sanbusto Center
Montezuma and Guatelupe
Tuesday, Saturday, 7 A.M.–1:00 P.M., June–
October
Unusual chilis, blue corn, baked goods

NEW YORK
Ithaca
Ithaca Farmers' Market
Dewitt Park, Buffalo and Cayuga Streets
Tuesday, 9 A.M.–1 P.M.; Saturday, on
Taughannock Road, in season

Manhattan
Union Square Greenmarket
14th Street and Union Square
Wednesday, Friday, Saturday, 8 A.M.–6 P.M.,
year-round

Queens County
Farmers' Market Jamaica
153rd Street and Jamaica Avenue
Jamaica, Queens
Friday, Saturday, 8 A.M.–6 P.M., April–
December

NORTH CAROLINA

Carrboro
Carrboro Farmers' Market
Behind fire station off Main Street
Saturday, 7 A.M.–noon, in season

NORTH DAKOTA

Bismarck
Bismarck Farmers' Market
North Brook Mall
Tuesday, 2–6 P.M.; Saturday, 8 A.M.–noon,
July–October
Wild grapes, wheat for wheat weaving

OHIO

Cleveland
West Side Market
West 25th and Lorain Avenue
Monday, Wednesday, 7 A.M.–4 P.M.; Friday,
Saturday, 7 A.M.–6 P.M., year-round
*A dramatic market hall; many Eastern
European vendors*

Columbus
The North Market
Spruce Street
Tuesday–Saturday, 9 A.M.–6 P.M., year-round.

Cincinnati
Findlay Market
100 W. Elder
Wednesday, 7 A.M.–1:30 P.M.; Friday,
7:00 A.M.–6:00 P.M.; Saturday, 6:00 A.M.–
6:00 P.M., year-round

OKLAHOMA

Norman
Norman Farm Market
615 E. Robinson
Wednesday, Saturday, 8 A.M.–2 P.M., in
season
Organic produce

OREGON

Gresham
Gresham Farmers' Market
City Hall parking lot
Saturday, 8 A.M.–2 P.M., mid-May–October

PENNSYLVANIA

Lancaster
Lancaster Central Market
Market Street and Penn Square
Tuesday, Friday, 6 A.M.–4 P.M.; Saturday,
6 A.M.–1 P.M., year-round

Leola
Leola Produce Market
Brethren Church Road, just past downtown
Monday–Saturday, early mornings, in season

Philadelphia
Reading Terminal Market
12th and Arch Streets

Monday–Saturday, 9 A.M.–6 P.M., year-round
Wonderful historic city market

SOUTH CAROLINA
Columbia
Columbia State Farmers' Market
1001 Bluff Road
Monday–Saturday, 24 hours, year-round
Wholesale and retail

Greenville
Greenville State Market
1354 Rutherford Road
8 A.M.–6 P.M., daily year-round
Wholesale and retail

SOUTH DAKOTA
Sioux Falls
Downtown Farmers' Market
Phillips Avenue and 10th Street
Wednesday, Saturday, 7:30 A.M.–1:00 P.M.,
June 1–October 31

TENNESSEE
Chattanooga
Eleventh Street Farmers' Market
734 E. 11th Street
Daily, year-round
Wholesale and retail

Memphis
Farmers' Market at Agricenter
7777 Walnut Grove Road
Monday–Saturday, 7 A.M.–6 P.M.,
March 1–November 30

*For a guide to pick-your-own farms and markets,
write for a consumer's directory to:
Tennessee Dept. of Agriculture
Division of Marketing
Box 40627, Melrose Station
Nashville, TN 37204*

TEXAS
Austin
Travis County Farm Market
6701 Burnnett Road
Monday–Saturday, 8 A.M.–6 P.M.; Sunday,
10 A.M.–4 P.M., year-round

Dallas
Dallas Farmers' Market
Pearl Street at Freeway
Monday–Saturday 8 A.M.–5 P.M., year-round
Wholesale and retail

UTAH
Salt Lake City
Utah Farmers' Market
5300 S. 360, West, next to Farm Bureau
Building
Friday, Saturday, noon to dusk, August–
October

VERMONT
Brattleboro
Brattleboro Farmers' Market
At Brattleboro Commons
Wednesday, Saturday mornings, in season

VIRGINIA

For a complete listing write to:
Virginia Retail Farmers' Market
Virginia Dept. of Agriculture Guide
P.O. Box 1163, Room 702
Richmond, VA 23209

Lynchburg
Bateau Landing
Main at 12th Street
Most farmers Friday, Saturday, in season,
early morning to midday
Lots of activities and festivals

Richmond
Seventeenth Street Farmers' Market
100 17th Street
6 A.M.–9 P.M., daily, year-round

WASHINGTON

Seattle
Pike Place Market
1st Avenue and Pike
Monday–Saturday, 9 A.M.–5 P.M.; Sunday,
2–5 P.M., year-round

WEST VIRGINIA

Charleston
Charleston Farmers' Market
Capital Street Exit (off of I77)
April 1–January 1
8 A.M.–6 P.M.
Closed Sunday

WISCONSIN

Madison
Dane County Farmers' Market
Capital Square
Saturday 6 A.M.–2 P.M.
April–November

CANADA

Most Canadian markets combine fresh
farmers' produce with retail outlet stores

Kitchener, Ontario
Kitchener Farmers' Market
Corner Duke and Frederick Streets
Year-round
Saturday 5 A.M.–2 P.M.
Mid-May–October, Wednesday 7 A.M.–
2 P.M.
German specialties; Koch cheese

Montreal, Quebec
Atwater Market
138 Atwater Avenue
South of Notre Dame
Year-round
Monday–Wednesday 7 A.M.–6 P.M.;
Thursday and Friday 7 A.M.–9 P.M.; Saturday
and Sunday 7 A.M.–5 P.M.
*Home-cured smoking leaf tobacco; unusual
berries*

Jean-Talon Market
Jean-Talon Street, between Cas Grain and
Henri Julien
Year-round
Daily 8 A.M. on
Surrounded by Little Italy

Ottawa, Ontario

The By Ward Market
55 By Ward Market Square
Year-round
Daily 8 A.M. on
Canada's oldest outdoor market. Taste beaver tails, a fried pastry.

St. John, New Brunswick

St. John City Market
47 Charlotte Street
Year-round
Monday–Thursday 8:30 A.M.–5:30 P.M.;
Friday 8:30 A.M.–9 P.M.; Saturday 8:30 A.M.–
5:30 P.M.; closed Sunday
Fish-and-chips and fresh seafood

Toronto, Ontario

St. Lawrence Market
92 Front Street E
Year-round
Retail market daily except Sunday; Farmer's market in North Building
Saturday 5 A.M.–5 P.M.
Fresh Nova Scotia salmon; Argentinian sausage; gooseberries

Vancouver, British Columbia

Granville Island Public Market
Open year-round
Real farmers late June to late September
Wednesday, 9 A.M.–4 P.M.

GENERAL INDEX

INDEX OF FOOD AND RECIPES

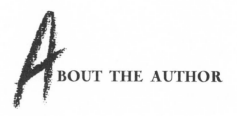

ABOUT THE AUTHOR

Judith Olney has been an international consultant to Time-Life's Good Cook series, and has taught cooking classes and appeared as a media spokesperson throughout the United States. In addition to writing for *Cuisine, Gourmet, Food & Wine, HG,* and other national magazines, she is the author of five cookbooks, including *Summer Food, The Joy of Chocolate,* and *Judith Olney on Bread.*

Childhood trips to the Lansing, Michigan, farm market and a rural life on a working farm sparked Judith Olney's love for farmers' markets. She has lived, cooked, and visited markets in Europe and Africa as well as America. Ms. Olney now lives in Durham, North Carolina.